D0528679

THE MEASUREMENT OF MODERNISM

A Study of Values in Brazil and Mexico

LATIN AMERICAN MONOGRAPHS, No. 12
Institute of Latin American Studies
The University of Texas

THE MEASUREMENT OF MODERNISM

A Study of Values in Brazil and Mexico

By JOSEPH A. KAHL

NORTHWEST MISSOURI
STATE COLLEGE LIBRARY
MARYVILLE, MISSOURI

PUBLISHED FOR THE *Institute of Latin American Studies* BY

THE UNIVERSITY OF TEXAS PRESS, AUSTIN AND LONDON

112543

Library of Congress Catalog Card No. 68–63239
Copyright © Joseph A. Kahl, 1968

Type set by G&S Typesetters, Austin
Printed by The Steck Company, Austin
Bound by Universal Bookbindery, Inc., San Antonio

309.18
K12m

To the Memory of

SAMUEL A. STOUFFER

PREFACE

In 1960, Professor L. A. Costa Pinto, director of the Latin American Center for Research in the Social Sciences, Rio de Janeiro, kindly invited me to spend a year in Brazil as Visiting Sociologist, with the financial support of UNESCO and the Social Science Research Council of New York. This monograph is the result of his invitation.

I had long been interested in the process of transformation from traditional to industrial society, and had begun some studies of it in Mexico. The year in Brazil provided an opportunity for a more ambitious field research. I decided to concentrate on one particular aspect of the process, namely, the contrast in values about work and career that would differentiate a "traditional" from a "modern" orientation. I was curious about how the changing division of labor, so easily seen from census statistics, affects the lives of men: How does a peasant learn to think and act like a factory worker, or the son of a small-town storekeeper become a big-city accountant? Do they change their ideas about life in a way that is proportionate to the change in jobs?

I realized that I could not get completely satisfactory answers to the questions raised above without actually following men who were moving from the farm to the factory and watching them change their values. Yet I decided not to do so, and instead chose to make static contrasts between diverse types of men. There were several reasons for this decision not to take a longitudinal approach: I had only one year available, and part of it had to be used to switch from Spanish to Portuguese; I could not hope in so short a time to understand the richness of Brazilian culture as well as could local sociologists, like Juarez Rubens Brandão Lopes, for instance, who were already engaged in qualitative studies of new factory workers; I had hopes of developing some measuring instruments that later could be used in other countries. So instead of doing a longitudinal and qualitative study, I developed a questionnaire and generated some statistics, thereby satisfying the expectations of my colleagues at the Center that I could behave like a typical North American sociologist.

The Center supplied me with two excellent young sociologists as research assistants, Edgard Dutra Neves and Jeanne M. Mauro. We began with a short series of preliminary, qualitative interviews, recorded on tape. The purpose was to seek the sense of problem about career, and the style of speech, typical of various categories of men. We interviewed in Rio de Janeiro, and included both factory workers and white-collar employees. Then we spent some time in a small town in the interior in order to see how similar and different would be the perspectives of provincial men. Our professional colleagues at the Center—Professors J. Roberto Moreira, Thomaz Pompeu Accioly Borges, and Waldemiro Bazzanella—were of inestimable help in finding field sites for us, and in guiding our evolving formulation of the research problem. I am indebted to them and to Professor Costa Pinto for advice and counsel, and for friendship that turned a task into a pleasure.

After we had collected and analyzed more than twenty-five interviews for background, we began to construct a questionnaire. About this time I became acquainted with a Brazilian sociologist who was thoroughly familiar with survey research, Professor Gláucio Ary Dillon Soares, and he became technical consultant par excellence.

We developed the questionnaire, trained university students as interviewers, and collected more than six hundred interviews in Rio de Janeiro and in the provinces, covering both manual and nonmanual workers. As the questionnaires were precoded, it was simple to convert the data to IBM cards. Then all of a sudden, the year was over; with data cards in my suitcase, I returned to St. Louis.

Various duties and distractions at Washington University kept the data analysis from proceeding at a brisk pace, but enough work was accomplished to suggest that the questionnaire was a good tool, and that the material would take on deeper meaning if another country could be studied for comparative purposes. The United States National Science Foundation provided funds through grant G24222, and in the summer of 1963 a slightly revised questionnaire was administered to more than seven hundred men in Mexico, and additional qualitative interviews were gathered there. Once again, I had the collaboration of Professor Soares, but this time he was field director; his assistants were Concepción Luna Clara and Cesar Moreno Pérez. Our consultant and strong right arm was Professor Raúl Benítez Zenteno, of the National University of Mexico.

All the data analysis was done at Washington University and with the unending help of its Social Science Institute, directed by Professors N. J. Demerath, Gilbert Shapiro, and David J. Pittman. Research assistants included Gláucio Soares, Daniel Abbott, Stanley M. Davis, John E. Lyman, Mrs. Marilyn Merritt, and Ted Goertzel. Our cordial secretary was Mrs. Dorothy Altheimer. The University's Computer Center (aided by NSF grant G22296), under Richard A. Dammkoehler, was always cooperative. The University's Committee on Latin American Studies, with Ford Foundation financing, was also helpful.

Several colleagues served as statistical advisors through the mazes of factor analysis: Robert L. Hamblin, Dorothy L. Meier, L. Keith Miller, and Gilbert Shapiro. Three friends read the manuscript and offered line-by-line suggestions for its revision and improvement: N. J. Demerath, Robert L. Hamblin, and Alex Inkeles. Other helpful comments on the manuscript were given by: Raúl Benítez Zenteno, Otis Dudley Duncan, Munro S. Edmonson, Peter Heintz, Edgar Schein, and Lee Rainwater.

And of course I am indebted to the many men who answered our questions, and to the managers who allowed us into their firms.

To all who participated in this research I offer my gratitude for its strengths and my absolution from responsibility for its weaknesses.

In preparing this report, I faced a dilemma: whether to write a terse, technical monograph for a specialized audience, or a book for a wider group of readers. The first choice would put me in communication with a limited number of men, primarily sociologists who were themselves studying aspects of socio-economic development—and perhaps also with their students. Speaking to them, I could use professional shorthand (jargon, if you prefer) and could stress the tricks of measurement and the findings that seemed novel in terms of an understood tradition of accumulating research. The second choice would place me in contact with a much larger body of persons concerned with development: social scientists of various disciplines, and practitioners in government and business. But to communicate properly with them would require a much larger book, with full explanation of the sociological tradition, and many comparisons of my approach and my results with those of other researchers.

I have opted for the technical monograph. Thus the reader should expect brevity rather than comprehensiveness; I offer here a report that is on the order of a long journal article. Yet, I do not completely forget the reader who is not a sociologist of development. By using a minimum of jargon, and by giving selected references to the most important relevant literature, I try to make the results accessible to serious readers of various backgrounds.

Decks of IBM cards with the original data, plus the most important scale scores, are on deposit with International Data Library, Survey Research Center, University of California, Berkeley. Readers who wish to make additional calculations may obtain data cards and code books from it.

A word concerning the dedication of this volume to Professor Samuel A. Stouffer is in order. He was chairman of the faculty committee that guided my doctoral dissertation fifteen years ago. One of the findings of that research was an unexpected strength in what we came to call the "pressure" exerted by parents on sons with respect to their careers: various satisfactions and frustrations of the parents could be seen as guidelines which they used to shape the ambitions of their sons toward the world of work. My contribution was through qualitative interviews; later, Stouffer wanted to test the phenomenon with a simple attitude scale that could be administered to large groups of boys to measure their perception of their parents' desires. I helped him develop a "pressure barometer," but unfortunately he died before it was fully refined. In fact, the news of his premature death came to me while I was in Brazil. Readers who knew him will see in this monograph a continuation of our common interest, and will note, I trust, places where the style of thought and investigation of Stouffer has left a lingering trace on his student. He emphasized simplicity of technique in research and clarity of exposition in writing, insisting always that they be applied to problems of major import. Although he sought middle-range theories of social process, he never depreciated careful description of social reality, for he realized that much academic theory and many prescriptions for practical reforms were based on supposed "facts" that were not true. He was uncommonly gifted: more versatile as theorist, more powerful as teacher, and more inspiring as a man than he himself realized. A phrase of dedication is small return for what he taught me, but if it reminds those of us who knew him of his lasting influence upon us, it will serve a purpose.

JOSEPH A. KAHL

Washington University
St. Louis, Missouri
May 1966

TABLE OF CONTENTS

LIST OF TABLES

Table		Page

LIST OF FIGURES

Figure		Page

THE MEASUREMENT OF MODERNISM

A Study of Values in Brazil and Mexico

SAMPLE

CHAPTER I

The Modernization of Values

The world transforms itself as more and more countries seek to
enter the mainstream of contemporary civilization. From a past which
encouraged, through isolation, the proliferation of a great variety of
cultural forms, we enter a future which tends to unify all nations
through similar themes: the pursuit of a high standard of living
through industrial modes of production utilizing advanced technology; the organization of large-scale social units for efficient production and distribution, and for execution of public tasks—in other
words, private and public bureaucracies; a population educated beyond the minimum criterion of literacy. True, there appear to be two
somewhat different paths toward this same goal: welfare capitalism,
and socialism. But seen from the long view, in comparison to traditional societies, they are structurally more similar than different.
True, too, there are variations in approach that reflect national cultures, for the Japanese and the Americans and the French and the
Russians do not do everything the same way. But the extent of their
differences appears to be declining; they do more things the same
way every year as they react to the standardized demands of industrial life.

One of the most interesting questions that we can raise about the
contemporary world is this: To what degree does industrialism create
a common culture for all peoples? This broad question has implications for all the social sciences; each has techniques of study which
can contribute to its answer. This monograph does not pretend to be
a general discussion of the entire problem. Rather, it focuses on a
single aspect, and applies certain techniques of measurement that
promise to contribute some useful data which will lead us a step
forward in our understanding. It is a specific technical exercise in
sociology which takes on meaning when seen in the context of other

112543

such exercises in adjoining disciplines of social research. It reports
on a study of those value orientations that are the principles used by
men to organize their occupational careers. It seeks to delineate and to
measure a set of values that represents a "modern" view of work and
life. The laboratory is provided by two Latin American countries that
are undergoing a rapid process of industrialization: Brazil and Mexico.

Traditional Society versus Modern Society

Most social scientists dealing with Latin America have used as a
tool of analysis some aspect of the dichotomy between "traditional"
and "modern" society, and have analyzed the processes of transition
from one to the other. For example, Redfield wrote of the contrast
between "folk" society and "urban" society; Lambert used "The Two
Brazils" as the title of his book; and Germani has as his subtitle the
phrase "From Traditional Society to Mass Society."[1] The dichotomy
is used in several ways. It refers to a classification of societies which
would make Haiti traditional, Argentina modern, and Peru some-
where in between. But these authors also recognize that *within* any
one of these societies, some geographical regions and some social
strata are more modern than others. And they even state that within
a given individual there may exist tensions resulting from the conflict
between traditional and modern values.

"Traditional society" and "modern society" are abstractions, mental constructs that create simplified models in order to help us understand the central factors that explain the complexities of historical
reality. They are "ideal types," in which a limited number of characteristics in "pure" form are used to develop the theoretical model.[2]

What are the characteristics that are usually used to contrast traditional with modern society? The ones which follow seem most
common:[3]

1. *The division of labor.* The most simple index of this characteristic is the proportion of the labor force engaged in agriculture; tradi-

---

[1] Robert Redfield, *The Folk Culture of Yucatán*; Jacques Lambert, *Os dois Brasis*;
Gino Germani, *Política y sociedad en una época de transición: de la sociedad tradicional a la sociedad de masas*. Of course, the thinking of these men was influenced
by earlier analysts of the modernization of Europe, such as Marx, Tönnies, Weber,
and Durkheim.

[2] At this point, I use the ideal type for purposes of theory-building; later, I shall
indicate its limitations in empirical operations, and suggest a way to move from
types to variables.

[3] For a sophisticated version of the contrast between traditional and modern
society in Latin America that develops the model beyond my summary statement,

tional societies may have 70 to 80 per cent of the workers tilling the soil; modern societies can get by with less than 10 per cent on the farm. More subtle indices divide the nonagricultural labor force into traditional sectors, such as artisans, priests, and lawyers, and into modern sectors, such as industrial workers, clerks in bureaucracies, and engineers.[4]

2. *The state of technology.* A traditional society uses customary techniques of production, handed down from father to son. A modern society uses sophisticated engineering based upon the latest fruits of world-wide scientific research.

3. *The degree of urbanization.* Since modern agricultural technology permits a small proportion of the labor force to feed the remainder of the population, using a low ratio of men to land, most of the society becomes urban.

4. *The economy.* Traditional society is based on localized markets, where much of the production is for a meagre level of subsistence, although a plantation type of crop or minerals may enter world markets. Modern society is based on complex commercial markets unifying all parts of the nation; per capita production and consumption are high.

5. *The system of social stratification.* Traditional society is deeply divided between landlords and peasants. Modern society has a range of statuses that reflects the range of positions in the division of labor: there are many, and the distinctions between them are not so sharp. The distribution of prestige, of income, and of power becomes more equalitarian, and the rate of mobility between strata increases.

6. *Education and communications.* Traditional society is in the main illiterate, although the tiny elite may have a high level of humanistic and legal scholarship. Modern society is literate, there is widespread secondary education that blurs the distinction between elite and mass, and the entire system of education moves toward the technical and the pragmatic. The mass media cater to the bulk of the

---

see Germani, *Política y sociedad en una época de transición*, especially Chaps. III, V, and VI. Germani relies heavily on the theoretical work of Talcott Parsons. For comprehensive statements, see Bert F. Hoselitz and Wilbert E. Moore (eds.), *Industrialization and Society*; and E. de Vries and J. M. Echavarría (eds.), *Social Aspects of Economic Development in Latin America*.

[4] See A. J. Jaffe, *People, Jobs and Economic Development,* especially Appendix D. The theory Jaffe uses is a general one, but the statistics concern Puerto Rico and Mexico.

population, cognizant of its primary and secondary education, and they shape thought in new images that replace customary symbols.

7. *Values.* Traditional values are compulsory in their force, sacred in their tone, and stable in their timelessness. They call for fatalistic acceptance of the world as it is, respect for those in authority, and submergence of the individual in the collectivity. Modern values are rational and secular, permit choice and experiment, glorify efficiency and change, and stress individual responsibility.

Causes and Effects

Like all ideal types, this one carries the implication that the central characteristics used to develop the model are causally interrelated. Modern technology, complex division of labor, widespread education, predominance of cities, secular values stressing change, an "open" class system—all these reinforce one another. And in combination, they can be used to deduce additional probable characteristics of a modern society, such as a stress on the nuclear family, relative equality between the sexes, high prestige for youth in contrast to old age, a low birth rate, and so on.[5]

Since this monograph is a report on a study of traditional and modern values, a few words are in order concerning the role of values in the total model of societies in transition. Some authors, following a Marxist bent, stress that values are results and not causes. They hold that the basic structure of the technology and economy puts people in social roles that define their interests, and that the expression of those interests gets "rationalized" (in the Freudian sense) and eventually "institutionalized" (in the Weberian sense) in values.

Other theorists note that values, once established in the minds of men, take on an independent force. Traditional values can stem the tide of technological and economic development when people prefer to keep on doing things in the old and customary ways, as shown in any of a hundred studies by applied anthropologists who tried to introduce change into a small and static community.[6] And for an illustration of the power of values to remake the world, let it be recalled that a group of men committed to modern ideas can seize political power

[5]Some of the data supporting such interrelations are given in Germani's Chap. VI (see note 3, above), in my "Some Social Concomitants of Industrialization and Urbanization" (*Human Organization*, XVIII [Summer, 1959], 53–74), and in William J. Goode, *World Revolution and Family Patterns.*

[6] See George M. Foster, *Traditional Cultures: The Impact of Technological Change.* On a larger scale, see L. A. Costa Pinto (ed.), *Resistências a mudança.*

and introduce social changes to transform the economy, as the Japanese demonstrated in the late nineteenth century, and the Russians a few decades later. The Japanese case is especially interesting, for the elite turned to modern technology in order to preserve certain traditional cultural forms and guarantee national independence, and they learned to blend the old and new in ways that may require some modification of the generalizations we gain from the Euro-American experience.[7]

Depending upon the perspective chosen, values can be treated as either causes or effects. In the very long run, they can usually be recognized as the institutionalization of objective conditions and interests. Otherwise, one could not explain the striking similarities observed in the values of men separated by time and space but unified by circumstance, such as bureaucrats in Moscow and Washington, or slum-dwellers in Paris and Buenos Aires. Yet in the short run, values determine circumstance; most men behave the way their culture has taught them to behave, for they perceive through cultural lenses the alternatives available to them.

The study of values has importance for two different types of problems:

1. *The transformation of society*. Economists and sociologists often seek some strategic characteristics that either promote or inhibit the social and economic development of a nation as a whole. Since Max Weber wrote *The Protestant Ethic and the Spirit of Capitalism* in the early part of this century, scholars have been interested in the drive of entrepreneurship that leads a few men to behave differently from most by attempting to develop new enterprises that eventually lead the whole society toward development.[8] Others seek the conservative values that inhibit development even when the objective circumstances seem promising; Latin Americans have long wondered why their part of the world has lagged behind Europe and North America, despite abundant natural resources.

2. *The mobility of individuals*. It is recognized that persons born in the middle class are given many advantages that make it easy for them to stay there, among which the commitment to appropriate values is of significance. But it is also known that certain men in the

[7]See John W. Bennett and Iwao Ishino, *Paternalism in the Japanese Economy*.

[8]Recent versions of this type of research are reported in two books: David C. McClelland, *The Achieving Society*, and Everett E. Hagen, *On the Theory of Social Change*.

working class somehow learn middle-class values, and thus behave in ways that aid them (or their sons) in climbing into the middle class.

Obviously these two problems are connected, for ambitious and mobile men, if produced in sufficient quantity, can transform society. The same measuring tools for values might well suffice for both approaches. However, it should not be forgotten that the first problem concerns long-run historical change, and the second concerns short-run biographies. Thus, in historical analysis the variable of values will be linked to many others of a predominantly economic nature, whereas in biographical analysis, the variable of values will be linked to others in the theory of social stratification which measure sociological and psychological factors.

The samples on which our field work was based were not panels of men who were reinterviewed over long periods of time, but groups who were interviewed simultaneously. Hence the only implications for historical change we can develop are those which follow from contrasts between the values of men in the modern cities of Rio de Janeiro and Mexico City, and men in small and old-fashioned towns in the interior of Brazil and Mexico. Such implications are suggestive, but they are scarcely adequate as tests of propositions about the sweep of history.

The purpose of this study is primarily methodological: to make an advance in the description and measurement of values. Since values are subjective inclinations in the minds of men, they are impossible to see and hard to measure, and we lack national statistics such as those used in indices of the division of labor or the degree of urbanization. Consequently, theorists of social development have usually speculated about values and included them in their models of societies in transition, but have been unable to be very precise about them. They have been used as implied intervening variables. The present report is a step forward in the technique of direct measurement.

Values and Norms

What are values? They are general orientations toward basic aspects of life: abstract principles that guide behavior.[9] ". . . faith, hope,

[9]See Clyde Kluckhohn, "Values and Value-Orientations in the Theory of Action," in Talcott Parsons and Edward A. Shils (eds.), *Toward a General Theory of Action;* M. Brewster Smith, "Personal Values in the Study of Lives," in Robert W. White (ed.), *The Study of Lives;* and Judith Blake and Kingsley Davis, "Norms,

and charity, these three: but the greatest of these is charity." This phrase comes close to predicating the core values of the Christian tradition.

There is both a prescriptive and an existentialist component to values, for they not only tell a man how he *ought* to behave, but they also contain an implication of how the world actually *is* (or is perceived to be). The good Christian should have faith in the Lord and hope in the afterlife, but these prescriptions are based on beliefs that God and Heaven exist.

When values are applied to specific situations to generate precise rules of conduct, sociologists call those rules "norms." The abstract value "charity" comes to be defined in terms that carry references to certain roles that we play in society, so as to tell the incumbent of one role how to behave toward the fellow in the reciprocal role. Thus we are told to love our neighbors, to honor our fathers and mothers, to forgive our enemies.

It is a common value-system that holds a society together; through it, the members are taught to perceive the world in similar ways, and to act toward one another in a predictable fashion. Occasionally, the press of circumstance leads a man to violate the rules, but public opinion finds this threatening and demands punishment through law or other sanctions. A society without strong common values is unable to reach collective decisions and create viable institutions. And a man without belief in the values of his group is a man who is confused and distraught.[10]

Since values are abstract principles, they cannot be touched or seen in the physical world. Indeed, the men in whose minds they exist are not always fully conscious of them. How, then, can we study them scientifically? The observer must listen to what people say, and watch how they behave. From this information, he then distills out the central rules that explain the consistency of words and actions displayed by the people under observation. When these rules are reached in tentative form, the observer can express them to his subjects and ask them to comment. The more philosophically minded among them will be able to refine and correct the first impressions of the social scientist.

Values and Sanctions," in Robert E. L. Faris (ed.), *Handbook of Modern Sociology*, and the empirical works cited in those review articles.

[10] See Emile Durkheim, *The Division of Labor in Society*, passim.

In this way we tentatively approach an understanding of the value system of a group, always recognizing that it is a distillation from many observations, an abstract set of principles, and that we cannot expect to gain with it 100 per cent accuracy of prediction of what a given man will do in a given situation. But, through its useful simplification, we can indeed predict what most men will do in most situations. We achieve scientific parsimony through a limited set of values describing the core of a culture, rather than a long list of hundreds of specific norms.

When the observer already has a fairly good idea about the value system of a given group, he can test his impressions not only by conversations with the members, but also by a more formal means of interviewing: a questionnaire which asks a large number of subjects to agree or disagree with a list of attitude statements that express the hypothesized values. In this way, the scientist can not only get at the average consensus, but also see how certain strata within the society differ in their values from other strata, even if only as a matter of degree or relative emphasis.

Career Values

Some values are more closely related to work and career than others. They range from specific norms about how a worker should treat his boss or approach his tasks, through more general ideas about the relation between education and profession, to even more abstract principles about predictability and orderliness in life which indicate something about how a man's career can be seen as a series of steps in a known sequence. Those values which have implications for a man's current work behavior, or for his long-range career planning, are of special interest to the present research.

Once again using the ideal type as a mode of theory-building, we can posit that traditional society has one set of work values, and modern society another. The former could be described as follows:[11]

Work is merged into life in a way that does not distinguish it as a separate activity with its own norms. Work is part of one's general status, and thus is to be accepted without deliberate plans for change. Son follows father as peasant, artisan, or merchant, and learns the techniques of work by watching his father. Life is personalized through ties to relatives, and

[11] For a good ethnographic account of this perspective, see Marvin Harris, *Town and Country in Brazil*. Also, George M. Foster, "Peasant Society and the Image of Limited Good," *American Anthropologist*, 67 (April 1965), 293-315.

their claims take precedence over the impersonal and abstract demands of career. Work and life are stable, and the individual takes a fatalistic view of his position.

That description of values in traditional society can be usefully contrasted with this synthetic view of work in urban-industrial society:[12]

Work in the city is separate from the rest of life in the sense that a man works in a place apart from his family, and his work takes on a momentum of social relationships unrelated to the extended family. A job is seen as part of a long career, which is a sequence of related activities starting with formal education specifically designed to prepare for work, leading through some type of apprenticeship or learning experience, toward full mastery of the job, and ending in formal retirement. Deliberate decisions are made to further a career which are based on values of impersonality, efficiency, and ambition to get ahead. New ideas and techniques are highly regarded, and general values of active control over self and environment are prized.

Three Men

As illustrations of real men who approach (but do not, of course, exactly match) these abstract models, let us listen to the words of three Brazilians who were interviewed, using a tape recorder, during the early stages of the research.

The first man was a farm laborer who expressed in almost classic form the old-fashioned view of life and work, though even he was beginning to sense the winds of change:

"Here we have no minimum wage, but we don't get hungry. We have everything, plenty of water, and we don't have to buy anything; we can grow what we need; in the city, the best a man can do is be a worker who pays rent and buys things.

"I didn't like it and had to walk a long way to school. Real education is upbringing; the education of the cradle, of father and mother, is more important than schooling. My brothers and I, we didn't have free time for school; the work in the fields to help my father was heavy. Nobody spoke to me about continuing [after second grade], and besides, that way there was more time to work in the fields.

"Today there is less obedience by children to parents, but in my time, there was blind obedience; I had to finish my chores before I could go to school.

"To fool the boss is the same as to fool God. The poor man has to help

[12] For syntheses of the literature on the transition to a modern work culture, see Wilbert E. Moore, *Industrialization and Labor*, and W. E. Moore and A. S. Feldman (eds.), *Labor Commitment and Social Change in Developing Areas*.

the boss or he's the one who will suffer; my job is to plant; I know when things ought to be done, taking advantage of the weather that God sends. "The world of today seems another world; obedience has gone. The son is no longer interested in the father; the employee does not stick with the boss; the daughters go out without telling where they are going."[13]

His daughter was indeed of a different generation with a different world view; she said: "I want to leave the countryside because in the country the farmworker and his family are slaves of the landowner; the time for slavery has already gone, but anyone who stays here stays as a slave."[14]

Let us contrast the work values of that farm laborer with those of an office manager for a small firm in a town in the interior of Brazil. The man was thirty-three years old when we interviewed him; his father had also been an office worker in a nearby town. The father had hoped to start a business of his own, but the coffee crash of 1930 wiped out his savings, his hopes, and most of his friends. The father was a man with a primary-school education, and felt handicapped by the lack of further training. His son reported:

"The ideal of my father was that I should have some university special-ization, depending upon my talents, but it was impossible because of his financial situation. This ideal was a result of the lack of education that he felt in himself, and he wanted to provide better for his children. As he always said: 'A man without education, without culture, is worth nothing. I have my worth, but it is a relative one, and I want my children tomor-

---

[13] "Nós aqui, não temos salário mínimo, mas não passamos fome. Aqui há de tudo, água com fartura e nós não precisamos comprar nada, pode-se criar o que quizer; na cidade, o máximo para a gente chegar é a operário, que pode pagar aluguel e com-prar coisas . . . Eu não gostava e tinha que caminhar muito para ir à escola. A leitura serve para muita coisa, mas o que vale mais é a educação do berço, do pai e da mãe, é mais importante que a leitura (instrução). Eu e meus irmãos, não nos sobrava tempo para a escola, e o trabalho na roça para ajudar meu pai era muito. Ninguém me falou como continuar os estudos [depois do segundo ano] e além disso me sobrava mais tempo para trabalhar na roça. Hoje em dia, há menos obediência dos filhos para os pais, porque no meu tempo, havia obediência sega, eu tinha que terminar a tarefa para poder ir à escola . . .
"Enganar ao patrão é o mesmo que enganar a Deus. O pobre tem que ajudar o pa-trão senão êle é que perde. O meu ofício é o plantio, sei quando se deve fazer certas coisas, aproveitando o tempo que Deus dá. O mundo de hoje parece outro mundo, não há mais obediência; o filho não se interessa pelo pai; o empregado não liga o patrão; as filhas quando saem não dizem onde vão."
[14] "Eu quero sair da roça, porque no campo e lavrador o família dêle são escravos de fazendeiros. Êsse tempo de escravidão já passou, mas quem fica aqui é como escravo."

row to have a more complete value.' I think the same way; I want to give my children much more."[15]

The office manager had completed the course in a private secondary school in the nearby town where his father worked and where he grew up. He wanted to study engineering because he was good in mathematics and science in school, but his father did not have the money to send him to the university and suggested that he take a short course that would give him an immediate skill that he could use to earn his living while studying. He accepted his father's advice, and studied accounting while he worked for a three-year period in Rio de Janeiro. He then returned to the interior, and soon obtained his position as office manager. But he was unsatisfied:

"One of my goals—now that we are in the epoch of goals[16]—is to evolve professionally. I am sorry not to be further along, to have contact with people of better education, more advanced, in order to make progress in my profession. For, in addition to being a worker with the need to earn a living for my family, I have the desire to be a real accountant. Unhappily, in the interior people don't have much room for that, for in general there are only small firms which don't offer a chance to progress technically in one's work, so sooner or later I'm going to move to a big city. The truth is that I prefer to live here, in the interior, where life is more calm and peaceful, but I have an ideal and I want to fulfill it."[17]

Contrasting his own ambitions with the attitude of his wife's brothers, who are medium-scale farmers, he said:

[15] "O ideal de meu pai era que eu fizesse um curso superior, dependendo da minha inclinação, mas a impossibilidade surgiu em decorrência da situação financeira dêle. Êsse ideal decorreu da falta que sentiu da educação, a qual quís dar aos filhos. Como êle sempre falava que o homem sem educação, sem cultura, nada vale—'Eu tenho meu valor, mas é um valor relativo, portanto, eu quero que os senhores venham ter amanhã, um valor integral.' Penso da mesma forma, quero dar aos meus filhos muito mais."

[16] He was referring to the practice of the then President of Brazil, Juscelino Kubitschek, to publicize a set of detailed *metas*, or goals, for his administration.

[17] "Uma das minhas metas, já que estamos na época das metas, é evoluir profissionalmente. Sinto não estar mais elevado ainda, ter contacto com pessoas de mais cultura, mais atualizadas para desenvolver mais ainda minha profissão, porque além de eu ser um profissional com o fito de arranjar sustento para minha família, eu tenho vontade de fato de ser contabilista. Infelizmente no interior a gente não tem muito campo para isso, porque em geral são firmas mas pequenas, não oferecem um campo cem por cento para se desenvolver técnicamente, tanto que mais cêdo ou mais tarde eu procuro um centro grande, não vejo campo no interior para desenvolver. A verdade é essa, prefiro viver aqui, no interior a vida é mais pacata, mais calma, mas tenho um ideal e quero cumprir êsse ideal."

"They are typical of farmers hereabouts, they don't educate themselves; secondary school is a lot for them, and they return to the farm. They don't give much value to study, even about agricultural matters; a farm that provides a living is what they want; they don't even learn modern methods of agriculture. Yes, they would like more income, but they are so fixed in the traditions of their fathers and grandfathers that they don't want to try innovations. Today it is getting a little better, because the farmer vaccinates his cattle and bathes them, but even so, it is still very primitive."[18]

Finally, let me quote the words of a print-shop foreman in Rio de Janeiro. He is a man of primary-school education, the son of a manual worker who had never been to school. The foreman is utterly devoted to his work; he finds it interesting and challenging, and reads technical books to learn about new types of printing presses. He enjoys the responsibility of leadership, although he recognizes that it sets him somewhat apart from the men. He said:

"I believe that the principal factor in my success was my professional skill as a printer and, above all, my honesty, since I was always 100 per cent honest, even when the advantages were not on my side. I always put my work above everything else. I believe that my spirit and my character allowed me to get the confidence of the owners of the firm.

"A worker has the right to suggest ways to simplify the work and improve production, and that will be to his benefit as well as the firm's, because where there is more production there will be higher salaries.

"My closest friends are outside of my work, for on the job I never had close friends, because I have a dynamic spirit about work and that's contrary to the views of the majority. I have this spirit because I'm looking out for my own good and not that of the group; I think that everybody has to go by his own opinion and not by the opinion of the group, and I follow my own opinion and it always works well for me. I don't have enemies on the job; on the contrary, I can count on everybody's collaboration, but I know that some are envious because they haven't gotten as far as I have."[19]

[18] "Isso também, é uma coisa típica no fazendeiro desta região. Não se educam, fazem ginásio quando muito, mas voltam para a fazenda. Êles não dão muito valor ao estudo, mesmo no meio ambiente dêles. A fazenda dando resultado é o que serve; nem os métodos modernos de agricultura aprendem. Isso é uma concepção tôda especial, êles querem mais renda, mas são tão arraigados nessas tradições de seus pais, seus avós, que não querem inovações. Hoje já melhoraram um pouco, porque o fazendeiro já vacina o gado, dá banho, mas mesmo assim está ainda muito primitivo."

[19] "Creio que o fator principal de haver galgado esta posição foi a minha habilidade profissional como impressor, e acima de tudo a minha honestidade, pois sempre fui honesto cem por cento, mesmo quando as vantagens não me eram favoráveis. Sempre prezei muito a parte profissional acima de qualquer outra coisa. Acredito

The foreman feels that he has had to struggle hard in life, since he started with a limited education, but believes that he has achieved considerable success, about to the level he had originally dreamed of. He has no specific achievements in mind for his future, except to keep learning and progressing, for he says: "I'm too young to stop, don't you think?" He was, in fact, thirty-one years old. He has two children, does not want more because of the high cost of educating them, and plans to send them to a university to learn a liberal profession.

Contrasting the three men, we note that one is "traditional" in values, the other two "modern." One of the modern men lives in a small town in the interior, and thus cannot be said to have first learned his values from the bustling metropolitan environment of Rio de Janeiro; in fact, he learned them from a father of lower-middle-class background, and had them reinforced in the secondary school where he mixed with the tiny elite of the town. The foreman came from a working-class background and had only a primary education, but he seems to have absorbed a version of modern work perspectives from his experiences on the job itself. Interestingly enough, he glories in his manual and technical skills, and earns from them a very comfortable income (he lives in a modern apartment house); yet for his children he dreams of the traditional liberal professions.

Thus, we begin to notice that "modernity" is related to social-class background as well as to place of residence, that it can be shaped by experiences in school and also on the job, that a man can concurrently hold values that stress a somewhat old-fashioned view of professional elitism and a more contemporary view of technical skill and prestige at an intermediate level. We note that personal ambitions, interpersonal relations, formal education, technical skill—all are intertwined

---

que foi com meu espírito e meu caráter que consegui a adquirir esta confiança dos donos da firma.

"O profissional tem o direito de sugerir meios para simplificar o trabalho e melhorar a produção, o que virá em seu benefício próprio e da firma onde trabalha, porque havendo, haverá maior salário.

"Amizades mesmo, tenho fora do ambiente de trabalho, porque dentro dêle nunca me dei a muita amizade, pois tenho um espírito dinâmico de trabalho e isto contraria a maioria. Eu tenho êste espírito porque miro o meu benefício e não o da coletividade. Eu acho que cada um deve marchar por sua opinião própria e não pela opinião de uma coletividade e eu marcho pela minha opinião a tenho me dado bem. Não tenho inimigos declarados dentro de recinto de trabalho, pelo contrário, conto com a colaboração de todos, mas sei que alguns têm inveja porque não fazem por onde para chegar até onde cheguei."

aspects of work and career values. And there is a clear line of influence from fathers to sons.

From Ideal Types to Variables

Most social scientists have used the "ideal type" as a device for constructing their classifications of societies or of value systems. The ideal type is an abstraction from reality that emphasizes the extremes of key attributes in order to suggest causation. For instance, Robert Redfield considered a culture that is sacred, collective, and organized to be "folk," and one that is secular, individualistic, and disorganized to be urban. He believed that the attributes at each pole are mutually dependent and reinforce one another. He also believed that they are determined by certain other characteristics of an ecological nature; thus folk society is associated with small size, isolation, and homogeneity, and urban society with their opposites.

The intellectual recognition of such types out of the complexity of historical process is a useful step in theory-building. It simplifies and organizes our thoughts, indicates the attributes that are important, and suggests some of their interrelations. But once the model is constructed, everyone has trouble using it. Immediately one thinks of intermediate types that approximate neither pole. Then he begins to puzzle over "mixed" types, or situations in which an attribute that is usually associated with the folk pole coexists with an attribute from the urban pole.

The theorist begins to move from a model of the ideal type (in which the key attributes combine in a fixed way, so that in pure form one gets only two approximations to social reality—one at each end of the polar extreme), to a set of profiles (in which each attribute can vary independently of the others, and all sorts of combinations are possible). Profiles are more flexible, and one can apply them with less strain to the observed variations of the real world.[20] However, they contain a fatal flaw, based on the rules of combinations and permutations: if one has, for example, five attributes and each is conceived of as a dichotomy, as in the case with Talcott Parsons' pattern variables, there are 32 possible types defined by various combinations. And if one is daring enough to trichotomize each attribute, as does Florence Kluckhohn, the number of possible types jumps to 243

[20] See Talcott Parsons, *The Social System*, Chap. II; and Florence Kluckhohn and Fred L. Strodtbeck, *Variations in Value Orientations*. Parsons' more recent views can be found in his *Structure and Process in Modern Societies*.

(three to the fifth power). In order to become more realistic, we have sacrificed parsimony.

There is a way out of our dilemma, one that involves a switch from either-or *attributes,* which are then cross-classified, to continuous *variables,* which can then be intercorrelated. We can use the ideal type or profile methods to suggest to us the values that are most important to study in detail. But we can treat them as variables instead of attributes.

A useful procedure is to try to define each variable in as "pure" form as possible, uncontaminated by others. In this way, each variable will represent a single dimension that can range from low to high, with several intermediate gradations. Then we can construct a series of very specific attitude questions, each of which is a test of a man's commitment to the value under consideration. If we combine several such questions, or items, into a single scale, his idiosyncratic reactions to the wording of each item will tend to cancel out, and his score on the scale will represent an index of his position on the underlying value which is reflected in all the items.

Once we have constructed several scales measuring the several values considered important, we can collect field data from a large sample of respondents. They all can be assigned a score for each scale, and the patterns of interrelationship between those scores can be studied. In this way, we discover *empirical* types through induction from the data, and need not burden the mind with all the possible *theoretical* types that can be deduced from cross-classifications of attributes.

The field data can readily be reduced to simple patterns with the standard techniques of multivariate statistics, which are now easy to use as a result of the blessings that come from electronic computers. We can identify the most usual combinations of values, those that fit comfortably together to form a pattern or type whose components tend to reinforce one another. In this way, we can empirically define a general syndrome of modernism in values. But we can also spot interesting deviations: subtypes of individuals who are modern on most values, but traditional on some. Next, we can attempt to explain both the tendency toward consistency in modernism, and the deviations from it, by seeking intercorrelations with background variables that give clues about the causes of modernism. And finally, we can predict certain attitudes or behaviors that appear as a result of modernism.

The Components of Modernism

Following such a methodological aim, we subdivided into its components the ideal type of work and career values which contrasts the traditional with the modern. *Each component was conceived of as a separate variable that ranged from the traditional pole to the modern pole—with the possibility of a number of intermediate points.* We attempted to construct an attitude scale that would measure each variable separately from the others—thus we sought "pure" or "unidimensional" scales. We chose those perceptions and values that have been important in earlier researches, as well as those which were prominent in the conversations of some twenty-five Brazilians whom we interviewed (with a tape recorder) at the very beginning of our field work.[21]

Our first variable was *activism* (its opposite: fatalism). Almost all observers have stressed this component as central to the contrast between the rural and the industrial value-systems. The whole structure of a peasant's experience tends to make him (and often, but perhaps not quite so consistently, his landlord) a fatalist. Lacking sophisticated technology, he is dependent upon the existing ecological offerings: the weather, the soil, the seeds. He is subjected to the power of those in higher status, and has little recourse when he is exploited and plundered. He learns to take life as it comes, to adjust to it and accept it, rather than try constantly to change it. He often ends up consoling himself with a religious belief that things will be better in the afterlife.

By contrast, the modern man uses technology to shape the world to his own desires. He comes to feel that control and change are not only desirable, but possible.[22] He becomes an activist. The item which

---

[21] The formulation of the variables was much influenced by the schemes of Talcott Parsons and Florence Kluckhohn, cited in note 20. For instance, activism can be seen as a combination of Kluckhohn's "future time" and "mastery over nature." Several other investigators, mostly former students of Parsons and Kluckhohn, have been developing measuring instruments of this type in a series of researches conducted in the United States since the early fifties: see my "Some Measurements of Achievement Orientation," *American Journal of Sociology*, LXX (May 1965), 669–681. And Kluckhohn herself has devised some ingenious instruments which are described in her book. See also Samuel A. Stouffer, *Social Research to Test Ideas*, Chap. III.

[22] I am speaking of the modern man who is fully participant in his society; marginal men at the very bottom of the status hierarchy, even in big cities, often behave like peasants, for they too are subject to manipulation beyond their control. As

most clearly measures this value dimension is as follows; agreement with it denotes a fatalist, and disagreement an activist:[23]

Making plans only brings unhappiness, because the plans are hard to fulfill.

Connected with activism is a belief that the social system is open to individual advancement, that a man can, if he wishes and tries and has some luck, change his status. In sociological jargon, he sees status as achieved rather than ascribed. We call this a perception of *low stratification of life chances*, as indicated by disagreement with items such as this one:

A person needs good connections to get ahead in the occupational world.

Very closely associated with the view of career life-chances is a perception of the local community. Traditionalists see the community as dominated by a small elite that pays little attention to the opinion of the mass. Modernists are more inclined to see it in democratic terms, hence to see themselves as able to influence public policy.[24] We call this scale *low community stratification;* a key item measuring it is disagreement with the statement:

The control of this city is in the hands of a small group of people, and an ordinary citizen has not got much to say about things.

We believed that a modern man would put great stress upon success in his career, even to the point of sacrificing other rewards, such as time for recreation. We thus devised a scale of *occupational primacy*, with the following as a key item:

The most important qualities of a real man are determination and driving ambition.

Traditional society usually involves deep ties with relatives; one lives closely with his kinfolk, he shares his successes and failures with them, and indeed he often works and shares property with them. By those who value it highly, it is called "family responsibility"; those who find it a block to freedom and individual initiative call it "nepotism." We devised a scale for the modern view of extended family re-

---

will be shown later on, low status makes a man traditional—in our terms—even more than does provincial location.

[23] The full list of items for each scale will be found in Chapter II, along with the sources of those which were borrowed from other researches.

[24] For a full discussion of this point of view, published after our field work had been completed, see Gabriel A. Almond and Sidney Verba, *The Civic Culture*.

lationships called *low integration with relatives.* One of the items was (disagree):

When looking for a job, a person ought to find a position in a place located near his parents, even if that means losing a good opportunity elsewhere.

In a similar vein, we constructed a scale of *individualism,* tapping a desire for independence from close ties with workmates, giving freedom to push forward in one's own career, like the print-shop foreman quoted earlier.

Ordinarily, those who live in a small, closed society, with a sense of powerlessness toward nature or men in high status, will cling to relatives for security and, as a correlate, have a high distrust of outsiders. Following suggestions from Alvin W. Gouldner, and also from the earlier "Cornell Values Study," we included a scale of *trust,* with items such as (disagree):

It is not good to let your friends know everything about your life, for they might take advantage of you.

Taking a lead from Daniel Lerner, we developed a scale measuring participation in the *mass media.* We assumed that the traditionalists would depend upon local gossip, whereas the modernists would be avid readers of newspapers, devotees of radio (and television), and followers of national and international events. One question was:

Are you interested in following national news in the newspapers and on the radio?

We believed that those who were "integrated" in the modern world of work would accept the advantages of bureaucratic organization, and thus be in favor of *big companies,* and that they would also accept the desirability of *manual work,* in contrast to the traditional elitist disdain for any activity that involves the use of tools. We provided scales to test these hypotheses.

We devised a scale to measure *preference for urban life* in contrast to enthusiasm for the atmosphere of the provinces.

Finally, we added three scales to the questionnaire in Mexico that had not been used in Brazil. Two were suggested by Alex Inkeles: the first concerned attitudes toward roles in the nuclear family—called *family modernism*—and the second concerned the degree of *religiosity.* Another scale, *risk-taking,* was borrowed from Lawrence K. Williams, and measures the propensity of an individual to reach out for success on the job even at the price of possible failure.

Empirical Syndrome of Modernism

At this point, let me briefly anticipate results that will be given in full detail in later chapters, and summarize the central findings of the research. The general value syndrome of modernism, which has been discussed in most theories of transition from traditional to modern society, was supported by the field data in both Brazil and Mexico. Its core consists of seven scales that are closely interrelated; on the average, a man who is high on some will also be high on the others, although there is room for variation. They are:

> Activism
> Low Integration with Relatives
> Preference for Urban Life
> Individualism
> Low Community Stratification
> Mass-Media Participation
> Low Stratification of Life Chances

There are some additional values associated with modernism, but to a lesser degree: trust in people, an attitude in favor of manual work, and a distaste for large companies (the last is contrary to our expectations). And to judge from the Mexican sample alone, a propensity to take risks in one's career and an attitude in favor of modern roles within the nuclear family are also associated with modernism. Occupational primacy and low religiosity are not, despite our expectations.

Generally speaking, persons in Rio de Janeiro and Mexico City were modernists, and people in small towns in the interior of Brazil and Mexico were traditionalists. But social status predicted modernism much more than did geographical residence: the higher the status, the more modern the response.

The similarities between Brazil and Mexico (and indeed, the United States) were striking, once social status and metropolitan-provincial residence were controlled. It seems that position in the social structure determines the degree of modernism, and nationality differences are not important.[25]

---

[25] After this manuscript had been completed, the preliminary results of parallel research by Alex Inkeles and his colleagues were published. See David Horton Smith and Alex Inkeles, "The OM Scale: A Comparative Socio-Psychological Measure of Individual Modernity," *Sociometry*, 29 (December 1966), 353-377.

Conclusions

This chapter began with a description of the model of transition from traditional to modern society which is used by most sociologists studying Latin America. Then the ideal type of traditional versus modern values relevant to occupational life was developed, and illustrated by quotations from three qualitative interviews. It was shown that this model could be used as a guide to empirical research using a survey instrument if the components of the ideal type were taken one at a time and treated as variables. A set of scales was constructed, so that each variable could be measured separately from the others. The scales were developed first in research in Brazil, then replicated in Mexico. Once the separate scales were determined, their interrelations were studied in order to identify the underlying syndrome of modernism.

The most important results of the research, to be explained in later chapters, were these: (1) "modernism" in values can be measured, and the basic empirical pattern closely matches the theoretical predictions; (2) although the components of modernism are interrelated in the minds of most men, it is possible for some men to be modern on a few values and traditional on others; (3) social status predicts modernism much better than does provincial versus metropolitan residence; (4) there are no important differences in attitudes between Brazil and Mexico (and probably the United States), once position in the social structure is controlled; (5) modernism in values can be used as a predictor of educational aspirations and accomplishments, and also of ideas about the number of children considered ideal, in a way that goes beyond predictions based solely on position in the social structure.

CHAPTER II

The Operational Definition of Modernism

In this chapter the details of scale construction are given, along with the statistical methods used to identify the syndrome of modernism. Also, the sample of respondents is described.

The research began in 1960 with a series of qualitative interviews in Brazil. I asked some friends to introduce me to the owners or managers of a few business firms in Rio de Janeiro, and then requested the latter to allow me and my assistants to talk to some of their employees. We chose adult men at the peak of their careers: neither young beginners, nor men about to retire. We sought factory workers at various levels of skill and income, office clerks, and low-level managers. We decided to omit casual laborers (such as unskilled men in construction work), and also university-trained professionals or executives, as we suspected that such persons, at the very bottom and the very top of the occupational hierarchy, might have lives sufficiently unlike the rest to demand an entirely different approach.

We used a tape recorder, and conducted a "focused" interview: we had picked out certain themes, but allowed the conversation to range freely anywhere among those themes. There were no fixed questions. The themes included: early life and relations to parents (particularly their advice concerning school and work); school memories; decisions about the amount of schooling to be sought; first and subsequent jobs; opinions about present job—the tasks, the fellow-employees, the boss; satisfactions with the present and desires for the future; married life, including educational and occupational ambitions for children. We made written summaries of the interviews, using as an outline the sequence of themes just presented, and including many verbatim quotations.

After a few weeks in Rio de Janeiro, we went to a small town of about 10,000 persons in the state of Minas Gerais (which I will not identify here in order to protect the anonymity of our respondents). It is more than four hours by road from Rio, and until the road was completed in recent years, the journey took two days by train. It is a trade center, which gathers milk (in the old days, coffee) for shipment to the coast. There is a small textile mill, and a couple of other minor enterprises. We stayed there two weeks and collected interviews similar to those previously gathered in the capital city.

Altogether, we obtained some thirty-five life histories. From them, we learned a lot about varying views of life and work, and got some feel for the actual words and phrases used by different sorts of men to describe themselves.

The Questionnaire

In constructing the questionnaire, we followed the central theoretical constructs that were common in the literature (as described in the previous chapter), but shaped and focused them with the aid of the interview material. We attempted to get a set of attitude items to form a scale for each value which seemed important, and which could be defined separately from the others. We sought to define and measure the most important value orientations that guided thought about education, work, and career. In addition, of course, we included the usual questions about each respondent's socio-economic background.

We pretested the questionnaire on a few dozen men of various levels in the occupational hierarchy, and improved the wording of the items. Then we trained about twenty university students as interviewers. They read the questionnaire to the respondents (however, the men were encouraged to peek over the shoulders of the interviewers so that they could both see and hear the questions). On the average, the interviews lasted about forty minutes. All the answers were precoded, and fit onto two standard IBM cards.

Three years later, the research was repeated in Mexico. The order, however, was reversed: we gave the questionnaire first, and then from our sample selected twenty-four men of various types for qualitative interviews designed to illuminate in depth the meaning of their responses to the questionnaire. The Mexican questionnaire was in the main a direct translation into Spanish of the same instrument used in Brazil; however, some items that had not worked well in Brazil were eliminated, and some new ones added.

The Samples

In designing the samples for our study, we decided against samples that would be "representative" of any given geographic community. For one reason, we could not afford it. But more importantly, it would not suit our purpose, since our aim was to compare various subgroups within the population, not to describe the distribution of some characteristics among the population. Thus we needed fairly large numbers of men within each of our major subgroups. We wanted to know something about the values of white-collar workers and factory workers in the metropolis, versus those of white-collar workers and factory workers in small, provincial towns.

We decided, therefore, to interview among workers in the capital city of each country, and also in some small towns. The towns were chosen to range from 5,000 to 10,000 people, to be distant from a large city, to be commercialized enough to have wage and salary workers, but to be as traditional as possible in general outlook.

Now, it must be admitted that small towns of the sort just described are not fully traditional—they do not reach the extreme pole of the traditionalism-modernism axis. Yet we wanted to use a standardized questionnaire, one that asked about attitudes toward school, job, and career. We thus needed people who had been exposed to schools and who held jobs that paid wages. Peasants would not have served; although they could be assumed to be more traditional in values, the routine of their daily lives is such that an entirely different questionnaire would have been necessary to interview them. So, we chose towns that had a commercialized economy—often a few small factories—but were set in rural zones. Most of the inhabitants maintained close ties to rural ways of living; indeed, a substantial number had started life as peasants.

Our sampling method might be called "quota samples of convenience." First we defined the types of communities desired—the capital cities of Brazil[1] and of Mexico, and small provincial towns. For the latter, we could not depend upon a single town in each country, for it was difficult to find enough wage and salary workers in just one small town, especially in white-collar jobs. In Brazil, we picked the towns through a lucky accident: each of the two chief research assistants originally lived in a suitable community, one in Minas Gerais, the

---

[1] Rio de Janeiro in early 1960, just before Brasilia was inaugurated.

other in Rio Grande do Sul. After they had gained experience with the questionnaire in Rio de Janeiro, each went to his home town, hired one or two assistants, and conducted interviews in his own community and in adjacent ones. One of the towns had a relatively new cement plant; the others were dependent on trade and minor processing of agricultural products. In Mexico, we used several communities in the state of Hidalgo; some had small textile mills, others were agricultural trade centers.

We picked firms to enter by seeking a variety of types: some large and modern enterprises like automobile manufacturing; some smaller ones like print shops and automobile-repair establishments, some large office firms like insurance companies, some small office establishments like banks or post offices. Usually we went into a firm because we knew someone who would introduce us to the manager and help us gain entry—a task which was not always easy. Our experience was that managers were suspicious of social research, and hard to convince, but workers were cooperative and easy to interview.

Once inside the doors of a firm, we tried to get men of most grades of skill and income, and from both office and shop. We confined ourselves to men between the ages of twenty-five and forty-nine years, in order to concentrate on the peak years of occupational career. And, as mentioned earlier, we eliminated illiterate casual laborers at the bottom of the hierarchy, and all men with university degrees at the top.

The samples can be described by two distributions: place of residence, and occupational level. For the former, we defined three groups: *provincials* (those interviewed in the small towns); *migrants* (those who had lived in towns of fewer than 20,000 at the age of ten, but were living in the capital cities at the time of the interview);

RESIDENCE	BRAZIL	MEXICO	OCCUPATIONAL LEVEL[2]	BRAZIL	MEXICO
			Unskilled or		
Provincials	184	270	semiskilled manual	164	154
Migrants	132	126	Skilled manual	152	238
Metropolitans	311	344	Foremen	37	60
Total	627	740	Low white-collar	202	188
			High white-collar	72	100
			Total	627	740

[2] Skilled manual work was defined as that which required at least three months of training. Low white-collar workers included routine office workers, sales clerks

metropolitans (men living in Rio de Janeiro or Mexico City who had been living in large cities at the age of ten).

The Scales

The basic results of our attempts to construct attitude scales to match the theoretical variables discussed in the first chapter are shown in Table 1. In each instance, the questions of items that belong within a given scale were factor-analyzed *as a separate group*, and the principal axis loadings are given in the table.[3]

---

in stores, and supervisors with fewer than five subordinates. High white-collar workers included supervisors with five or more subordinates, and highly qualified technicians (like accountants)—but not with university degrees (many had some university training).

[3] Factor analysis, as is well known, is the process which uses as its basic data the matrix of intercorrelations between items, and extracts from it a common denominator—the single, underlying dimension or factor which explains that part of the variance which is common to all the items. Developed many years ago by psychologists studying intelligence, it was used to extract a common dimension of intelligence, an IQ score, which was taken from the answers to a large number of separate questions. Each question had some variation unique to itself, but also some which reflected the general intelligence-level of the respondent. Thus a man of high intelligence was expected to answer most of the questions correctly, even though their content ranged from arithmetic to vocabulary.

More sophisticated versions of factor analysis seek to identify more than one dimension out of a set of items. Consequently, it is possible to use the technique to measure separately skills in arithmetic from skills in vocabulary, even though the two tend to be correlated. We can, therefore, get an over-all score for intelligence, or break that score into component parts, such as a score for arithmetic and another for vocabulary. When we extract more than one factor, we classify not only individuals, but also items in the test, indicating which ones primarily reflect arithmetic and which ones primarily reflect vocabulary. If the statistical results match our intuitive understanding of the content of the items, we are satisfied.

The mathematical details of factor analysis are complex, but the results are quite simple and neat. If, for example, we start with seven items which were made up to test a man's degree of "activism," we can take the results from a large sample of respondents and arrange them as they appear at the beginning of Table 1. Each item is assigned a "loading"—the correlation coefficient between the item and the underlying dimension common to all the items. We use as an arbitrary cut-off point a loading of .35. If a given item fails to reach that point we reject it as a part of the scale on the basis that it is not sufficiently saturated with the common dimension to be a useful indicator of it. In this way we empirically "purify" each scale, testing by field operations whether or not our intuitive judgment was sound when we invented the items in the first place. The item with the highest loading in each scale is the most powerful indicator of the common dimension—the best single definition of what the scale measures.

For a brief description of factor analysis, see Hubert M. Blalock, Jr., *Social Statistics*, Chap. XXI. For a full technical treatment, see Harry H. Harman, *Modern Factor Analysis*.

During the first stage of field work in Brazil, we included more items than are shown in the scales in Table 1. Those which had loadings below .35 on a given scale were eliminated as being unsuitable; they added up to about 15 per cent of the items we started with. In a few instances, two scales that were designed as separate ones turned out to have such a close relation as to be readily combinable into one; or a scale that was built as one turned out to be dividable into two (as shown by the extraction of a second factor plus rotation). Therefore the apparent neatness of fit between the theoretical discussion above, and the empirical results in Table 1, is somewhat artificial, for the actual field operations clarified our thinking about the definition of the variables. Yet to report each step in the scale construction would be tedious, so I give here the final stage without every intermediate decision.

When we began field work in Mexico, our basic purpose was replication, so all the useful items from Brazil were translated into Spanish and used over again. But we did add a little more: we introduced some items phrased in a negative direction from the majority (to deal with the problem of "acquiescence set," described below), and we added a few new scales. Unless otherwise noted, all items paralleled the Likert format: the respondent could choose between "Agree very much," "Agree a little," "Disagree a little," or "Disagree very much."[4]

The comparability of results in the two countries is most gratifying. Using as our definition of an item that "works" or fits into a given scale—a principal axis factor loading of .35 or more—we see that of the thirty-six items that were used in both countries, and had a satisfactory loading in one of them, only one item (No. 27) failed to reach a satisfactory loading in the other. (If no loading is indicated in Table 1, it means that the item was not used in that country.) Furthermore, a number of the scales had been previously used in research in the United States, as indicated in the footnotes to Table 1. Consequently, we can have considerable confidence in the stability of the instruments. (See Appendices C and D for Portuguese and Spanish versions of the items.)

There is one limitation to be noted. Unfortunately, the bulk of the

---

[4] We deliberately omitted a neutral-response category in order to encourage a choice, but if the respondent insisted he could not answer, the interviewer wrote down "Don't know." If the sum of such responses on a given item reached ten or more, a neutral category was added during the recoding process. Otherwise, the few "Don't know's" were thrown into the modal-response category.

items are phrased in a direction in which agreement would indicate "traditionalism," and we found that persons of low socio-economic status tended to be traditionalist in their replies. But we also noticed that persons of low status tended to be very polite to their status superiors (such as the university students who interviewed them). Therefore some of the traditionalism expressed in their answers may reflect the tendency to agree to any question, regardless of the content of the item. We believe this "acquiescence set" inflates somewhat the correlations between traditionalism and low status, and may inflate somewhat the loadings in those scales where all the items are phrased in the same direction. However, two items are phrased in the opposite direction (Nos. 6 and 27), and quite a few are not in the Likert format of agree versus disagree, but require a forced-choice answer that depends upon the content of the item (Nos. 7, 23, 33–35, 41, and 44–58). Therefore, though "acquiescence set" is a disturbing element, it is not sufficient to make the results spurious.[5] (*Table 1 begins on p. 30.*)

Modernism I

Once the items that belonged within a given scale were definitely decided upon, we then constructed a scale score for each man in the sample, combining his responses to all the items in that scale. This procedure reduced the effects of a man's idiosyncratic response to the wording of any given item and thereby increased reliability of measurement. The procedure was done for each country separately: a sum was computed in which a response of "Disagree very much" received a score of 1, and the other answers received higher scores through "Agree very much," which got 4.[6] These numbers were weighted by the loading the item had in the factor analysis for that particular scale, which meant that the "best" items—those most closely related to the underlying dimension—received the most weight (this procedure for weighted sums was automatically done by the computer program which calculated the loadings in the first place; unweighted scales

[5] For studies of acquiescence set as a personality variable, see Arthur Couch and Kenneth Kenniston, "Yeasayers and Naysayers," *Journal of Abnormal and Social Psychology*, 60 (March 1960), 151–174. Actually, we had trouble composing Likert format items phrased in the direction of modernism that would reach satisfactory loadings. It may be that forced-choice items work better than Likert items, especially with persons of low status, since they have a general tendency to agree.

[6] Some of the scales were then reversed in scoring, so that all of them came out with higher scores indicating the "modern" direction.

TABLE 1

Fourteen Value Scales

	LOADING, BRAZIL	LOADING, MEXICO
I. Activism		
1) Making plans only brings unhappiness, because the plans are hard to fulfill.	−.74	−.63
2) It doesn't make much difference if the people elect one or another candidate, for nothing will change.	−.65	−.58
3) With things as they are today, an intelligent person ought to think only about the present, without worrying about what is going to happen tomorrow.	−.63	−.67
4) We Brazilians [Mexicans] dream big dreams, but in reality we are inefficient with modern industry.	−.57	−.54
5) The secret of happiness is not expecting too much out of life, and being content with what comes your way.	−.47	−.61
6) It is important to make plans for one's life and not just accept what comes.	. . .	+.46
7) How important is it for you to know clearly in advance your plans for the future? (very important)	. . .	+.41
II. Low stratification of life chances		
8) A person needs good connections to get ahead in the occupational world.	−.71	−.75
9) The son of a laboring man does not have a very good chance of rising into the liberal professions.	−.70	−.54

NOTES:

Unless otherwise indicated, all questions are in Likert format, with four possible answers:

> a) Agree very much   c) Disagree a little
> b) Agree a little   d) Disagree very much.

A positive loading indicates agreement; a negative loading indicates disagreement. No loading indicates that the item was not used in that country. Each scale was factor-analyzed separately from the others, and the loadings are those of the first principal axis.

Item sources: to improve comparability with other researches, many items were borrowed with permission. A summary of many of these other researches will be found in my "Some Measurements of Achievement Orientation," *American Journal of Sociology*, LXX (May 1965), 669-681.

	Loading, Brazil	Loading, Mexico
10) Businessmen have good connections that make it easy for their sons to become successful.	−.70	−.71
III. Low community stratification		
11) The control of this city is in the hands of a small group of people, and an ordinary citizen has not got much to say about things.	−.84	−.74
12) People do not like to admit it, but this city is actually made up of many tight cliques or groups.	−.73	−.69
13) This city is not too friendly a place; you can only make friends with people who are pretty much of the same sort as yourself.	−.67	−.77
IV. Low occupational primacy		
14) The job should come first, even if it means sacrificing time from recreation.	−.68	−.58
15) The best way to judge a man is by his success in his occupation.	−.61	−.67
16) The most important qualities of a real man are determination and driving ambition.	−.64	−.80
17) The most important thing for a parent to do is to help his children get further ahead in the world than he did.	−.45	...
V. Low integration with relatives		
18) When looking for a job, a person ought to find a position in a place located near his parents, even if that means losing a good opportunity elsewhere.	−.76	−.73
19) When you are in trouble, only a relative can be depended on to help you out.	−.75	−.78
20) If you have the chance to hire an assistant in your work, it is always better to hire a relative instead of a stranger.	−.64	−.65
VI. Individualism		
21) In order to be happy, one must behave in ways that other people desire, even if one has to suppress his own ideas sometimes.	−.75	−.73
22) I prefer the kind of job where one is part of a group, and where everyone participates equally in the credit for good work.	−.62	...

	LOADING, BRAZIL	LOADING, MEXICO
23) When you are in a group, do you prefer to make the decisions yourself or do you prefer to have others make them? (self)	...	+.73
VII. Trust		
24) It is not good to let your relatives know everything about your life, for they might take advantage of you.	−.78	−.66
25) It is not good to let your friends know everything about your life, for they might take advantage of you.	−.74	−.71
26) Most people will repay your kindness with ingratitude.	−.55	−.67
27) Most people are fair and do not try to get away with something.	(+.32)	+.38
28) People help persons who have helped them not so much because it is right but because it is good business.	...	−.62
29) You can trust only people whom you know well.	...	−.40
VIII. Mass-media participation		
30) Are you interested in following national news in the newspapers and on the radio? (very much)	+.85	+.78
31) Are you interested in following international news in the newspapers and on the radio?	+.79	+.75
32) Are you interested in following local news in the newspapers and on the radio?	+.76	+.65
33) Can you tell me the name of the President of the United States? (correct answer)	+.41	+.49
34) Do you often discuss political problems with your friends? (often)	+.48	+.52
35) Can you tell me the name of the President of Mexico [for Brazilians], the President of Brazil [for Mexicans]? (correct answer)	+.36	+.49
IX. Anti big companies		
36) In general, big companies are more honest and efficient than small ones.	−.77	−.71
37) Big companies are usually fair with their employees, and give each man an equal chance to get ahead.	−.74	−.75
38) Young people have a better chance to get ahead		

	Loading, Brazil	Loading, Mexico
in a big company than by working on their own account.	−.73	−.66
X. Pro manual work		
39) To work with tools is not as good as to work with papers.	−.78	−.72
40) Jobs that make you dirty your hands are bad jobs.	−.67	−.79
41) Would you prefer an office job with a smaller salary, or a factory job with a larger salary? (prefers factory)	+.57	+.40
XI. Preference for urban life		
42) In general, life is better in small cities where you know everybody.	−.85	−.85
43) People in a big city are cold and impersonal; it is hard to make new friends.	−.85	−.85

XII. Family modernism. In this scale and in Scales XIII and XIV, the first statement is the positive one; agreement with it leads to a plus sign in the loading.

Which statement do you prefer?

44) If husband and wife are unhappy, they should be allowed to divorce, *or* (Marriage is a sacrament, and should never be ended by divorce).	...	+.52
45) When families are large, the parents should limit the number of children, *or* (Parents should never in any way limit the number of children).	...	+.36
46) A wife should make her own decisions even if she disagrees with her husband, *or* (A good wife is one who always obeys her husband).	...	+.69
47) On occasion, children should be allowed to disagree with their parents, *or* (Obedience and respect for authority are the most important things for children to learn).	...	+.64
48) There's no reason why married women shouldn't work if they want to, *or* (Married women ought to stay at home and not work for money).	...	+.62

	LOADING, BRAZIL	LOADING, MEXICO

XIII. Low religiosity

Which is most important for the future of Mexico?

49) Hard work by the people themselves, *or* (Help from God).   . . .   +.54

50) Do you consider yourself more religious or less religious than your father? (less)   . . .   +.64

51) Do you consider yourself to be religious? (very)   . . .   −.75

52) How often did you go to church in the last two months? (never or seldom)   . . .   +.75

XIV. Risk-taking

The kind of job I would most prefer would be:

53) A job where I am almost always on my own, *or* (A job where there is nearly always someone available to help me on problems that I don't know how to handle).   . . .   +.48

54) A job where I have to make decisions by myself, *or* (A job where I have to make few decisions by myself).   . . .   +.58

55) A job where I am the final authority on my work, *or* (A job where there is nearly always a person or a procedure that will catch my mistakes).   . . .   +.52

56) A job where I could be either highly successful or a complete failure, *or* (A job where I could never be too successful but neither could I be a complete failure).   . . .   +.65

57) A job that is constantly changing, *or* (A job that is changing very little).   . . .   +.47

58) An exciting job but one which might be done away with in a short time, *or* (A less exciting job but one which would undoubtedly exist in the company for a long time).   . . .   +.41

The specific sources of the items were:

1. Items 1, 3, 18, and 22 from the "V-scale" of Fred L. Strodtbeck and Bernard C. Rosen. See Strodtbeck, "Family Interaction, Values and Achievement," in *Talent and Society*, ed. D. C. McClelland; and Rosen, "The Achievement Syndrome, A Psychocultural Dimension of Social Stratification," *American Sociological Review*, 21 (April 1956), 203-211. The items were used in Brazil by Carolina Martuscelli

would not change the rank order of respondents by much).[7] Some scales were then reversed in direction, so that high scores would always indicate "modern" answers.

The rank order of men in each country was then divided into four approximately equal parts—and these quartile scores were then taken as the index of each man's position on the given value scale. They in turn were punched onto IBM cards, and used for the cross-classifications, the mean scores, and the regression analyses which appear below and in later chapters. Obviously, we have "standardized" the scales within each country by using quartile scores.

It was our original hypothesis that the fourteen variables were all aspects of the central syndrome of traditionalism versus modernism, but that they were not so tightly interconnected as to preclude some independent variability. Hence we expected all the scales to be intercorrelated, but only moderately. We could easily imagine that some men might be traditional on most values, yet modern on a few. Table 2 gives the empirical results; the correlation coefficients range from zero to .44.

[7] Readers without computers who wish to use the scales can weigh all items equally, and the rank order of respondents will not be changed very much.

Notes to Table I Continued

Bori; see her Chap. 10 in *Mobilidade e Trabalho,* ed. B. Hutchinson; and by Rosen, "Socialization and Achievement Motivation in Brazil," *American Sociological Review,* 27 (October 1962), 612-624.

2. Items 6, 7, 23, 28, and 29 from unpublished research in Peru by William F. Whyte, based on the earlier "Cornell Values Study."

3. Items 26 and 27 from unpublished research of Alvin W. Gouldner. See a similar scale, Morris Rosenberg, "Misanthropy and Political Ideology," *American Sociological Review,* 21 (December 1956), 690-695, and Rosenberg's *Occupations and Values.*

4. Items 30–35 suggested by the work of Daniel Lerner, *The Passing of Traditional Society.*

5. Items 44–48 suggested by unpublished work of Alex Inkeles.

6. Items 53–58 from Lawrence K. Williams, "The Measurement of Risk-Taking Propensity in an Industrial Setting" (Doctoral dissertation, University of Michigan, 1960). Also used by William F. Whyte in research in Peru.

It is interesting to note that the Williams instrument was originally constructed as a Guttman-type scale. We obtained a correlation of .87 between a factor-analytic scoring and a Guttman scoring of the same items. The former has slightly higher correlations with other variables, and thus we use it in our subsequent calculations.

7. The other items are my own, but were composed in consultation with my colleagues during the field work. (I first used the scales of Occupational Primacy and Stratification of Life Chances in research in Cambridge, Massachusetts, in 1953 in collaboration with James A. Davis.)

TABLE 2

Correlation Matrix of Value Scales

BRAZIL

		I	II	III	IV	V	VI	VII	VIII	IX	X	XI
I.	Activism	..	44	33	20	35	19	34	29	24	14	37
II.	Low Stratification of Life Chances		..	31	16	27	10	27	18	20	14	31
III.	Low Community Stratification			..	11	22	03	30	10	10	11	31
IV.	Low Occupational Primacy				..	07	15	14	08	22	-01	14
V.	Low Integration with Relatives					..	12	17	21	12	14	28
VI.	Individualism						..	09	17	14	10	15
VII.	Trust							..	17	14	-02	22
VIII.	Mass-Media Participation								..	15	-07	15
IX.	Anti Big Companies									..	-02	08
X.	Pro Manual Work										..	16
XI.	Preference for Urban Life											..

MEXICO

		I	II	III	IV	V	VI	VII	VIII	IX	X	XI	XII	XIII	XIV
I.	Activism	..	22	31	01	43	36	17	35	16	26	36	21	14	26
II.	Low Stratification of Life Chances		..	22	24	16	11	28	04	18	12	23	04	-02	13
III.	Low Community Stratification			..	09	22	16	29	11	15	12	32	07	07	11
IV.	Low Occupational Primacy				..	00	-02	26	-12	21	00	09	08	03	06
V.	Low Integration with Relatives					..	31	05	30	16	27	24	26	21	27
VI.	Individualism						..	06	20	24	20	20	19	14	20
VII.	Trust							..	05	18	04	25	07	01	16
VIII.	Mass-Media Participation								..	03	12	15	10	14	22
IX.	Anti Big Companies									..	06	12	13	08	10
X.	Pro Manual Work										..	12	12	04	08
XI.	Preference for Urban Life											..	15	13	12
XII.	Family Modernism												..	31	17
XIII.	Low Religiosity													..	16
XIV.	High Risk-Taking														..

A study of Table 2 shows that about half the variables have especially close interconnections, with coefficients from the twenties to the forties. In general, the same variables have high intercorrelations in both countries, a correspondence which suggests that there is a central "core" to the dimension of traditionalism-modernism.

However, instead of studying the core of modern values by arranging the coefficients in clusters, it is simpler to perform another principal axis factor analysis. The results of this second-order analysis (that is, one in which the value scales and not individual items were the variables) are shown in Table 3.

The results in the two countries are strikingly parallel. Take, for instance, the seven scales with loadings over .42 in Mexico: six of them have equally high loadings in Brazil.

The first seven scales in Table 3 can be considered the "core" of modernism. A "modern" man is an activist; he attempts to shape his world instead of passively and fatalistically responding to it. He is an individualist, who does not merge his work career with that of either relatives or friends. He believes that an independent career is not only desirable but possible, for he perceives both life chances and the local community to be low in ascribed status. He prefers urban life to rural life, and he follows the mass media.

There are some subsidiary values that are also associated with modernism, but to a lesser degree, as shown by their smaller loadings: trust in people, an attitude in favor of manual work, and a distaste for large companies.

Using our standard criterion of a loading of .35 or better for inclu-

TABLE 3

Factor Analysis of Value Scales: Modernism I

	LOADINGS, BRAZIL	LOADINGS, MEXICO
Activism	.76	.72
Low Integration with Relatives	.55	.65
Preference for Urban Life	.61	.56
Individualism	(.33)	.55
Low Community Stratification	.56	.51
Mass-Media Participation	.43	.44
Low Stratification of Life Chances	.66	.42
Trust	.54	.39
Anti Big Companies	.39	.39
Pro Manual Work	(.22)	.38
Low Occupational Primacy	(.34)	(.17)
Risk-Taking	. . .	.47
Family Modernism	. . .	.43
Low Religiosity	. . .	(.33)
Percentage variance controlled by common factor	27%	23%

sion, we note that one value predicted to be a part of modernism does not in fact fall within it in either country, namely, Low Occupational Primacy. We had expected it to be negatively related to the factor; it turns out to have a low but positive relation.[8] We had also expected modern men to be in favor of big companies, but the results were to the contrary; apparently, the individualistic sense of career keeps such men from accepting what is certainly a fact of contemporary life: bureaucratic organization. Finally, we must report that a scale of Integration with Friends (with items similar to those referring to relatives) which we predicted would indicate a modern perspective— for we thought of it as a contemporary alternative to close ties to relatives—failed to meet the criterion level in either country.

An index called Modernism I, based on the results shown in Table 3, was constructed. Each component scale was weighted in accordance with its loading, eliminating all that fell below the criterion of .35. The three scales used only in Mexico were not included in the index. The index score assigned to each man by this procedure was then related to other variables in ways which will be described in later chapters.

Stability of Modernism I in Subsamples

The suggestion was offered earlier that the particular pattern or syndrome of values which indicated a modern perspective might not be the same for middle-class as for working-class men, and we might add here, not the same for metropolitan as for provincial men. We tested this possibility by performing separate factor analyses for various subsamples.

We first divided the sample into equal thirds on a scale of socioeconomic status (SES) based on occupation, education, and self-identification, then computed the factor loadings shown in Table 4. The patterns are basically similar for all groups, but there are some varia-

[8] The scale of Occupational Primacy has been used in several investigations in the United States, and the pattern of results suggests that it measures an overt and "pushy" type of ambition that is characteristic of the upper levels of skilled workers and the lower levels of white-collar workers. Below those groups, apathy prevails; above those groups, a man takes success for granted, and does not express ambition in such open terms. This curvilinear relation to status is probably the reason why the scale does not fit into modernism, for the latter is positively related to status in a rectilinear manner. See my "Some Measurements of Achievement Orientation," cited in Table 1.

tions in detail.[9] In Brazil, Mass-Media Participation fails to reach the criterion loading within any of three levels of SES, and Individualism drops close to zero for the lowest status level. In Mexico, Low Religiosity is unrelated to Modernism I among high-status men, and Trust is unrelated to it among low-status men.

In Table 5, the loadings are shown for subsamples based on loca-

TABLE 4
Factor Analysis of Value Scales, by Socio-Economic Groups

BRAZIL			
	LOADINGS, HIGH SES	LOADINGS, MEDIUM SES	LOADINGS, LOW SES
Activism	.64	.72	.61
Low Integration with Relatives	.54	.63	.58
Preference for Urban Life	.57	.54	.50
Low Community Stratification	.51	.58	.51
Individualism	.35	.32	.08
Low Stratification of Life Chances	.47	.72	.56
Trust	.44	.27	.40
Mass-Media Participation	.10	.13	.01
Pro Manual Work	.32	.39	.42
Anti Big Companies	.23	.35	.27

MEXICO			
	LOADINGS, HIGH SES	LOADINGS, MEDIUM SES	LOADINGS, LOW SES
Activism	.64	.71	.56
Low Integration with Relatives	.53	.57	.55
Preference for Urban Life	.54	.58	.50
Low Community Stratification	.54	.44	.55
Individualism	.41	.63	.50
Low Stratification of Life Chances	.44	.44	.43
Trust	.41	.26	.08
Mass-Media Participation	.20	.31	.40
Pro Manual Work	.50	.42	.22
Anti Big Companies	.29	.26	.43
Risk-Taking	.33	.20	.30
Family Modernism	.25	.36	.28
Low Religiosity	—.01	.35	.22

[9] Insofar as there is a high correlation between modernism and SES, if there had not been stability of pattern within status levels, one would have feared that the syndrome of modernism was spurious, and represented in fact a syndrome of high-status values.

NORTHWEST MISSOURI
STATE COLLEGE LIBRARY
MARYVILLE, MISSOURI

TABLE 5
Factor Analysis of Value Scales, by Location

BRAZIL			
	LOADINGS, METROPOLITANS	LOADINGS, MIGRANTS	LOADINGS, PROVINCIALS
Activism	.72	.71	.79
Low Integration with Relatives	.62	.38	.58
Preference for Urban Life	.64	.62	.55
Low Community Stratification	.62	.54	.49
Individualism	.45	.10	.29
Low Stratification of Life Chances	.58	.73	.65
Trust	.52	.52	.50
Mass-Media Participation	.39	.10	.28
Pro Manual Work	.10	.65	.15
Anti Big Companies	.32	.41	.57

MEXICO			
	LOADINGS, METROPOLITANS	LOADINGS, MIGRANTS	LOADINGS, PROVINCIALS
Activism	.74	.65	.71
Low Integration with Relatives	.57	.65	.70
Preference for Urban Life	.59	.42	.51
Low Community Stratification	.56	.42	.44
Individualism	.52	.55	.65
Low Stratification of Life Chances	.46	.41	.38
Trust	.44	.41	.18
Mass-Media Participation	.32	.46	.49
Pro Manual Work	.44	.46	.21
Anti Big Companies	.32	.25	.53
Risk-Taking	.50	.52	.38
Family Modernism	.53	.34	.41
Low Religiosity	.26	.37	.35

tion: metropolitan men (those residing in Rio de Janeiro or Mexico City who were reared in large cities); migrants (those reared as young boys in small towns but who lived in the two capital cities at the time of the interview); and provincials (those who had always resided in small towns up to the time of the interview). Again, the stability of the modernistic syndrome is apparent, although some deviations appear among the Brazilian subsamples (Individualism and Mass Media are again the culprits).

How can these variations be interpreted? The relation of Mass-Media Participation to modernism turns out to be a spurious result of their mutual connection with SES. The other scales, however, hold up well as having a loading on modernism independently of SES. The lack of consistency of the other divergences from the results of the undivided national samples leads one to suspect that minor weaknesses in the measuring instruments and random variations in the sub-samples are at work, rather than that a theoretically meaningful fact of life is revealed.

Rotation of Axes

A final question remains about the structure of Modernism I: Can it be broken into meaningful subdimensions through the extraction of more than one factor and rotation of axes? Various attempts were made, and the only pair of values that could be separated from the entire syndrome was Family Modernism and Low Religiosity (in Mexico only; those scales were not used in Brazil). Those two values have an intimate relation to each other that goes beyond their saturation with the common factor of modernism.

Thus we conclude that for all practical purposes, the covariation which exists among the fourteen value scales, as shown in the matrix of correlation coefficients, is explained by a single underlying dimension of modernism-traditionalism. Yet it must be remembered that the common variation explained by this factor by no means exhausts the total variance of the separate scales, for each one has idiosyncratic variation unique to itself.

Modernism II

There are those who, seeking to find the structure of reality, like to use factor analysis as an inductive tool, throwing a large number of items into a "pot," followed by the extraction of multiple factors in a "blind" fashion. The procedures described so far indicate that I prefer to use the technique in a more deductive fashion, testing the "unidimensionality" of previously hypothesized scales. Nevertheless, it seemed worthwhile to try to replicate the fourteen values scales by purely inductive procedures, just to see what would come out of the "pot." Consequently, all the attitude items on the questionnaire—sixty-four in Brazil and sixty-seven in Mexico—were factored in one operation (each country kept separate, of course). Successive numbers of factors, up to a maximum of fifteen, were extracted and rotated by both orthogonal and oblique criteria.

The first principal axis factor turns out to be very similar in both countries.[10] The eight items that had the highest loadings in Brazil were the ones with the highest loadings in Mexico; they are shown in Table 6. Three of them are from the scale of Activism, one is from Low Stratification of Life Chances; and one each is from Individualism, Low Community Stratification, Low Integration with Relatives, and Preference for Urban Life. In other words, they come from the scales which make up the "core" of Modernism I.

We made up an index called Modernism II based on these items, with signs adjusted in the modern direction, and with each item weighted according to its loadings. The correlation between Modernism I and Modernism II was .83 in Brazil and .84 in Mexico, figures indicating that they are alternative measures of the same dimension. Their correlations with other variables turned out to be very similar.

The extraction of rotated multiple factors did approximate many of our fourteen value scales, but did not exactly reproduce them. The scales of Activism, Mass-Media Participation, Trust, Low Community Stratification, and Anti Big Companies replicated fairly well in both countries. Family Modernism, used only in Mexico, also appeared among the multiple factors.

To give just one example of this process (and it does not seem worthwhile to report more than that): the extraction of seven oblique factors in Mexico produced the following scales:

    I. Four items from Family Modernism, combined with Item 51 from Low Religiosity.

    II. Items 14, 15, and 16 showing High Occupational Primacy, Items 6 and 7 showing Activism (both stressing the importance of knowing plans in advance), Items 8 and 10 from High Stratification of Life Chances, and an item indicating that life is more interesting in big than small cities.

    III. Five of the six items from Trust.

    IV. The three items of Low Community Stratification.

    V. Five of the six items from Mass-Media Participation.

    VI. The three items of Anti Big Companies, combined (negatively) with three from a scale of Life Satisfaction, to be described later.

    VII. Five items from various scales.

[10] It controls 10 per cent of the variance of the sixty-odd items.

TABLE 6

The Eight Items with Highest Loadings:[1] Modernism II

ITEMS	LOADINGS, BRAZIL	LOADINGS, MEXICO
3) With things as they are today, an intelligent person ought to think only about the present, without worrying about what is going to happen tomorrow.	−.60	−.62
21) In order to be happy, one must behave in ways that other people desire, even if one has to suppress his own ideas sometimes.	−.51	−.61
13) This city is not too friendly a place; you can only make friends with people who are pretty much of the same sort as yourself.	−.63	−.59
1) Making plans only brings unhappiness, because the plans are hard to fulfill.	−.65	−.59
18) When looking for a job, a person ought to find a position in a place located near his parents, even if that means losing a good opportunity elsewhere.	−.60	−.58
43) People in a big city are cold and impersonal; it is hard to make new friends.	−.61	−.54
9) The son of a laboring man does not have a very good chance of rising into the liberal professions.	−.60	−.55
2) It doesn't make much difference if the people elect one or another candidate, for nothing will change.	−.60	−.52
Percentage variance controlled by common factor	36%	31%

[1] The loadings shown in this table are from a principal axis factor analysis based on *only* the eight items within the scale.

Conclusions

In this chapter I have presented in detail every step of our field operations. I explained how the items in the various scales were developed, combining knowledge from previous research with the ideas we got from our preliminary qualitative interviews. After pretesting, the items were then administered to large samples of men in Brazil and Mexico.

The first stage of statistical analysis of the answers produced a series of fourteen scales, each of which measured a basic value that had been hypothesized beforehand. The scales were "purified" by factor analysis, eliminating items that did not correlate sufficiently with the common dimension among all the items in that particular scale. Then a scale score was computed for each man.

The interrelations among the scale scores were further studied through a second-order factor analysis. It revealed a common dimension of "traditionalism-modernism" which closely matched the theoretical predictions. This result is fundamental. It shows that the syndrome of modernism posited in the theoretical literature can be demonstrated empirically. Measures can be contrived for each of its components separately, and then their tendency to hang together in a single perspective about the world can be clearly shown. Their *relative* importance within that perspective can be indicated.

Using these measures, we can rank order a sample of men according to their degree of modernism. Or, we can identify groups of men who, contrary to the average tendency for consistency, are modern on some values but traditional on others. Furthermore, the measuring instruments proved stable, in the sense that similar patterns were found in both Brazil and Mexico.

In the next chapter it will be shown how modernism is related to position in the social-status hierarchy and also to geographical location in metropolises or provinces.

CHAPTER III

Who Are the Modern Men?

A commitment to modern values about work is related positively to socio-economic status (SES). We used an index of SES based on occupation, education, and self-identification, as explained in Appendix A. The correlation coefficient between SES and Modernism I is .58 for Brazil; .56 for Mexico.[1]

But modernity is also related to one's being located in the metropolis. With the samples divided into three locality groups, namely, metropolitans (those reared in large cities and living now in Rio de Janeiro or Mexico City), migrants (those living in the metropolis now, but who were living in towns of fewer than 20,000 inhabitants at the age of ten), and provincials (those currently living in small towns), the zero-order correlation with Modernism I is .26 in Brazil and .24 in Mexico.

The multiple correlation of SES plus location as a predictor of modernism is no higher than the zero-order relation with SES alone. The partial coefficients are as follows:

	BRAZIL	MEXICO
SES and Modernism I, location controlled	.55	.53
Location and Modernism I, SES controlled	.14	.10

Thus, SES is much more powerful than location for the prediction of modernity in values.[2]

---

[1] The coefficients between Modernism I and education are: Brazil, .57; Mexico, .55. The coefficients between Modernism I and occupation are: Brazil, .50; Mexico, .48. The partial correlation of education with Modernism I is twice as high as the partial correlation of occupation with Modernism I (the coefficients jump from about .16 to .35).

[2] The Beta Weights are almost equal to the partial coefficients. SES explains about 33 per cent of the variance in Modernism I, while location explains 7 per cent, according to the method of Robert L. Hamblin, described in Chap. IV, note 17.

This finding is one of the central results of the research. It indicates that a modern perspective diffuses through society via the social-class hierarchy. People of upper-middle status are in intellectual contact with one another regardless of the geographical zones in which they live. Those who live in small towns are participants in modern life. Whether they have learned their contemporary values from school or by other means we cannot tell for sure, but the qualitative interviews indicate that education, constant travel to the metropolis, personal contacts with friends or relatives of high status in the bigger cities, and steady reading of newspapers and magazines all combine to influence their outlook. They know what is going on in the outside world, and they care about it.[3]

Men of lower status, regardless of location, tend more toward traditionalism. They feel less sure of themselves in the modern world, and cling to old-fashioned forms of personal relations for protection. They have more nostalgia for rural ways of living, more distrust of the people and the customs of the big city. Most particularly, they have a more fatalistic and apathetic attitude toward their own chances for successful careers. Having had less material success, they expect less.

Component Value Scales

Turning from a consideration of modernism as a whole to its component scales, we can ask whether they all show the same pattern of relation to status and to location. The answer is mostly, but not entirely.

The partial correlation coefficients of SES or location (holding the other constant) with each of the separate value scales are shown in Table 7. Activism, Low Integration with Relatives, Mass-Media Participation, and Risk-Taking all show high positive correlations with SES, and smaller ones with metropolitan location—that is, the same pattern as Modernism I. Preference for Urban Life has the highest relation to location; in Brazil, it is equal to the coefficient with SES.

Individualism and Anti Big Companies have low *negative* relations with metropolitan location. Since both of them express the general mood of petty entrepreneurship—working for oneself—it is not sur-

---

[3] It should be remembered, of course, that we are not talking about farmowners, but about small-town business and clerical people.

prising that the small-town men of the middle class show the highest scores.

Low Community Stratification, Trust, and Family Modernism show no relation to location. Pro Manual Work is the lowest of all the scales in its relation to SES; indeed, in Brazil it turns negative.

Comparisons between Brazil and Mexico: Modernism III

The correlations presented thus far indicated that social status had more impact on value orientations than did metropolitan location. But it would be useful to take a more detailed look at the data to find the particular level in the status hierarchy where the major change in values occurs, and also to see whether the pattern is exactly the same in both countries.

TABLE 7
Partial Correlations of Values with SES and Location

| | PARTIAL CORRELATIONS | |
	SES	METROPOLITAN LOCATION
Modernism I		
Brazil	.55	.14
Mexico	.53	.10
Activism		
Brazil	.38	.14
Mexico	.47	.05
Low Integration with Relatives		
Brazil	.26	.11
Mexico	.41	.15
Preference for Urban Life		
Brazil	.24	.25
Mexico	.24	.14
Individualism		
Brazil	.16	−.08
Mexico	.30	−.04
Low Community Stratification		
Brazil	.17	−.03
Mexico	.21	.02
Low Stratification of Life Chances		
Brazil	.31	.10
Mexico	.19	.09
Trust		
Brazil	.29	−.02
Mexico	.24	.01
Mass-Media Participation		
Brazil	.38	.11
Mexico	.31	.13

Pro Manual Work
Brazil	−.07	.09
Mexico	.13	.04

Anti Big Companies
Brazil	.26	−.13
Mexico	.23	−.05

Risk-Taking
Mexico	.38	.08

Family Modernism
Mexico	.29	−.03

Low Religiosity
Mexico	.18	.15

If we wish to compare specified groups of one country to similar groups in another, we cannot use the index of Modernism I, for it was "standardized" within each country; that is, the range of scores for individuals was divided into four approximately equal parts, and the correlation coefficients were computed in terms of a person's relative placement within one or another quartile of the distribution for his own country. That procedure is appropriate for comparing groups *within* a country, but would not be for comparisons *between* countries.

For cross-national contrasts, we needed an index that had some "absolute" meaning, independent of the distribution within a country, and the simplest procedure was to take the eight items that were used to define Modernism II,[4] and score the responses the way they were printed on the questionnaire: Agree very much (4); Agree a little (3); Disagree a little (2); Disagree very much (1). The answers for the eight items were summed; thus a man who replied that he strongly agreed with all of them received a score of 32, and a man who strongly disagreed with all of them received a score of 8. Since the items were all phrased in the direction of traditionalism, a high score indicated traditional views and a low score indicated modern views. We call this scale Modernism III.

The mean scores on Modernism III for both countries are shown in Table 8, along with breakdowns by education and location. Since the average of the standard deviations for the various cells in Table 8 is close to 5, we can use 2.5 as a rule of thumb to indicate a significant difference between two groups. If we contrast comparable cells from the two countries (that is, with education and location controlled),

---

[4] See Chap. II, Table 6. Modernism II weighted the items according to their factor loadings, then standardized the results within each country.

we note that in no instance is there a difference as large as 2.5. *Cell by cell, Brazil matches Mexico.*

Furthermore, the pattern within each country matches that of the other; that is, once men have reached secondary school, they have achieved a modern perspective—it makes relatively little difference whether they have had partial, complete, or postsecondary training.

In the provincial zones in both countries, the biggest difference in mean scores on modernism is between primary- and secondary-school men. The difference between those with partial and those with complete primary education is not as great. But among metropolitans in both countries, the reverse is true: there is a wider difference between the partial and the complete primary-school men than there is between men who have completed primary school and those who have a secondary-school education.

This pattern suggests that the rural primary school is not as efficient as is the urban as a socializing institution. The hold of traditional values on provincial men continues until they reach the secondary level. But apparently the metropolitan men are more ready for change—even a small amount of primary education turns them toward modernism.

Comparisons with the United States

Professor Lee Rainwater, of Washington University (St. Louis), and of Social Research Incorporated (Chicago) kindly obtained scores

TABLE 8

Mean Scores on Modernism III, by Education and Location[1]

	BRAZIL				
EDUCATION	ALL LOCATIONS	METROPOLITANS	MIGRANTS	PROVINCIALS	N
Postsecondary	13.8	12.7	. . .	15.0	50
Complete secondary	13.7	13.3	. . .	15.6	105
Incomplete secondary	15.3	14.9	16.4	16.2	108
Complete primary	18.6	17.1	19.2	20.1	168
Incomplete primary	21.2	20.0	20.9	22.4	196
All Educations	17.6	15.6	19.6	19.7	
N	627	311	132	184	

		MEXICO			
EDUCATION	ALL LOCATIONS	METROPOLITANS	MIGRANTS	PROVINCIALS	N
Postsecondary	14.3	14.1	15.7	14.1	108
Complete secondary	14.9	15.0	14.7	15.1	64
Incomplete secondary	15.6	15.6	16.1	15.5	160
Complete primary	18.5	17.9	17.3	19.0	159
Incomplete primary	21.7	22.3	21.4	21.6	249
All Educations	17.6	16.8	18.3	19.4	
N	740	344	126	270	

[1] The index of Modernism III is scored in the opposite direction from our usual practice; in this instance, a low number indicates high modernism. No cell with a mean score has fewer than ten cases.

on Modernism III for a sample of 503 housewives from medium-sized and large cities in the United States. When ranked by education, the scores were as follows:

College graduates	11.6
Postsecondary	12.4
Complete secondary	13.1
Incomplete secondary	14.9
Complete primary	18.4
Incomplete primary	19.7

The Rainwater sample contains no respondents from small towns, so we should compare it with our Brazilian and Mexican metropolitan groups. Holding education constant, in only one comparison does the difference between countries rise as high as two points (Incomplete primary, United States versus Mexico). And the range from high to low status among the North American women is just the same as it is from high- to low-status men in the Latin countries.

The North American data permitted a comparison of Protestants with Catholics, holding education constant. There were no significant religious differences on Modernism III, a finding which supports other recent studies indicating that Max Weber's historical analysis of the impact of the Protestant Ethic on occupational values no longer holds in the United States, where the common culture has institution-alized a set of values for each status level that overrides religious differences.[5]

Conclusions

Whether we use the complex index of Modernism I, or the simpler Modernism III, the pattern is the same: a modern-value perspective is strongly associated with social-status level, and weakly associated with metropolitan-versus-provincial location. Comparisons of groups from Brazil, Mexico, and the United States show no nationality dif-ferences when education and urban location are controlled. Within all three countries the pattern of scores by status level is the same. *The regularity of the cross-national results gives additional weight to the reliability of the instrument.*

These results support the position of Alex Inkeles that social struc-ture tends toward convergence in industrial (or industrializing) countries, creating sets of cultural values that reflect status positions and the exigencies of life that are associated with them, regardless of previously different national traditions.[6] This point of view does not imply that national cultures are all becoming identical. But it does imply that with respect to those beliefs most closely associated with the world of work, there is emerging a world-wide set of insti-tutions reflecting industrial and bureaucratic modes, and that all modernized cultures accommodate themselves in parallel ways to these institutional requisites.

The range of difference in modernism from the top to the bottom of the status hierarchy is sufficiently great to require that in all studies of value differences among men and women—be it contrasting Brazilians with Mexicans with North Americans, or small-town with large-city residents, or the native-born with immigrants, or satisfied with frustrated men, etc.—we must hold socio-economic status con-stant. *The most significant use of our tools for measuring values will thus become the contrast between men of similar status whose values are different.* If we can find some causes for those differences (which

---

[5] See Raymond Mack, *et al.*, "The Protestant Ethic, Level of Aspiration, and Social Mobility," *American Sociological Review*, 21 (June 1956), 295-300; and An-drew M. Greeley, *Religion and Career: A Study of College Graduates*. A contrast-ing perspective is given by Gerhard Lenski, *The Religious Factor.*

[6] Alex Inkeles, "Industrial Man," *American Journal of Sociology*, LXVI (July 1960), 1-31.

will naturally be rather small, once the variance associated with status level is controlled), and can trace their effects upon behavior, we will advance our understanding of the social process. In the chapters which follow, a few essays in that direction will be attempted.

CHAPTER IV

Modern Values, Education, and Occupation

David Lockwood has written:

> The middle-class orientation of the clerk is further manifested in two other measurable indices of social status: family size and attitudes toward education. A relatively small family and a strong desire for the educational success of one's children have been the hall-marks of middle-class status since the closing decades of the nineteenth century. Taken together they represent a concern with social mobility through individual achievement, and a conscious discounting of the present against the future.[1]

If we add that some modern men of the working class also share the values of small family and educational success for one's children, we have found the theme for this chapter and the next one. First I shall show the way schooling determines job, and then shall explore the reasons why some boys get more education than others. In the next chapter, the determinants of family size will be studied. In both instances, the strategy will be to measure the impact of modernism, with both social status and geographical location controlled.

From School to Job

Industrialization increases the importance of formal education: men prepare for work in school rather than through informal apprenticeship. Yet this does not mean that the correlation coefficient between education and occupation necessarily is higher in modern society. In fact, theory would argue the reverse, for in traditional society both secondary and higher education are very uncommon, and are determined by family background. That is, only members of the middle and upper classes customarily go to secondary school, and they automatically assume nonmanual jobs. And members of the

[1] *The Black-Coated Worker: A Study in Class Consciousness*, p. 128.

lower classes usually are either illiterate, or have a few years of primary education; they automatically assume manual jobs.[2]

The change that takes place is one which distributes education much more widely throughout the hierarchy, makes it possible to use education as a stepping stone to a better job than the one held by a man's father, and turns education toward more technical content related to work, in place of the traditional content stressing the literary values of an established, landed elite.

The process through which a given education leads to a given occupation is one that involves a sequence of steps through time.[3] When a man leaves school and starts his first regular job, he presumably seeks one that is appropriate to the type of career he plans for himself. Of course, he may not find the "right" kind of job at first. Furthermore, experience on the job itself will have some effect on what happens to both his aspirations and his successes: he may learn new things and move up beyond his original expectations, or he may turn out to be inefficient and remain stuck at a job that was originally taken as a first step to something higher. If education is fundamentally important, it should turn out to be more useful as a predictor of *later* occupational level than it is of the *first* job, for the latter has elements of accident in it that a long-term plan can partly overcome.

Correlational analysis does show that education is a better predictor of current occupation (the one held at the time of the interview) than it is of the first job a man gets. Apparently the latter does contain some elements of experiment. This is also shown by the fact that education is more likely than the first job to predict the current one (see Table 9).

However, the effect of education on occupation is not uniform at all levels of society; thus the correlation coefficient, being an average, covers up interesting variations. Let us dichotomize the sample into those who have up to a complete primary-school education(which is five years in Brazil and six years in Mexico) versus those who have at least some secondary education. And let us dichotomize occupation into manual versus nonmanual levels.

---

[2] Once again, fact does not support theory: the correlation between occupation and education is higher for our respondents (by thirteen points in both countries) than it was for their fathers, and it is about the same in provincial towns as it is in capital cities.

[3] The insights of my former research assistant Stanley M. Davis, now teaching in Harvard Graduate School of Business, have been particularly helpful in preparing this section.

It will be seen from Table 10 that a primary education almost *certainly* leads to manual work, but that a secondary education does *not* necessarily guarantee white-collar work. The value of a secondary education in obtaining white-collar work on the first job is greater in Brazil than in Mexico; 71 per cent of the Brazilians with secondary training started as nonmanual employees, whereas only 52 per cent of the Mexicans had equally high jobs. On the other hand, lack of secondary schooling seems even more of a handicap in Mexico than in Brazil, for 88 per cent of the Mexicans with only a primary education started as blue-collar workers, compared to 82 per cent of the Brazilians.

How can these differences be explained? We can guess that because secondary education is more common in Mexico, it is a little less valuable in guaranteeing a high job; yet since education is also a little more common, those without much of it are even more firmly held at the bottom.

Over a period of time, the power of education makes itself more clearly felt on a man's life, and seems to exceed experience on the job itself as the main factor that controls career. By the time of the interview those with secondary education were ensconced in white-collar jobs 85 per cent of the time in Brazil, and 67 per cent of the time in

TABLE 9

Correlations of Education, First Job, and Current Occupation[1]

	BRAZIL	MEXICO
Zero-order coefficients		
Education & First Job	.60	.56
Education & Current Occupation	.72	.65
First Job & Current Occupation	.61	.53
Partial coefficients		
Education & Current Occupation,		
First Job constant	.55	.54
First Job & Current Occupation,		
Education constant	.32	.25
Multiple coefficients		
Education & First Job with Current Occupation	.75	.70

[1] The Beta Weights are almost equal to the partial coefficients. The combination of Education & First Job explains about 55 per cent of the variance in Current Occupation; about 38 per cent is explained by Education, and 17 per cent by First Job.

Mexico (increases of about seventeen percentage points over the figures for the first job). The percentages regarding those with primary education in manual jobs did not shift much between the first job and the current job.

A Brazilian with a secondary education who starts as a manual worker has a 57 per cent chance of later on climbing into the white-collar ranks, whereas a man with a similar first job but less education has only a 7 per cent chance. For Mexicans, the corresponding figures are 63 per cent versus 17 per cent.

In Mexico one-half—in Brazil slightly more—of those few men with a primary education who somehow manage to start their careers with white-collar jobs will slip down to manual work later on. Yet less than 5 per cent of those with secondary education who start with high jobs will lose them.

The influence of education on career is indeed pervasive long after a man leaves school.[4]

How Much Is an Education Worth?

Let us look a little more closely at the "worth" of a given amount of education—its rewards in terms of occupation and income. Here we shall concentrate on the current occupational position of the respondent at the time of the interview.

Table 11 gives the detailed cross-classification of occupation by education. Absolute numbers are presented so that the reader may calculate percentages either horizontally or vertically, since both are meaningful. Table 11 does not add much to the discussion presented in the preceding section except for three observations: (1) the foremen are better educated in Mexico than in Brazil; (2) there is an especially wide range of educational accomplishment within the clerical and supervisory groups; (3) the skilled workers in Brazil are better educated than the unskilled, but in Mexico there is not much difference.

[4] For North American data that are similar (but not exactly comparable), see S. M. Lipset and F. T. Malm, "First Jobs and Career Patterns," *American Journal of Economics and Sociology*, XIV (1955), 247-261; also S. M. Lipset and R. Bendix, *Social Mobility in Industrial Society*, Chaps. V–VII. In a study in Oakland, California, they found that postsecondary education led to white-collar work on the first job 67 per cent of the time, complete or partial secondary 35 per cent of the time, and primary education only 20 per cent of the time. Their correlation coefficients between education and first job, and between education and current occupation were somewhat lower than those in Brazil and Mexico, but their coefficient between the first job and current occupation was somewhat higher.

TABLE 10
First Job, by Education

| | BRAZIL | | | | MEXICO | | | |
| | NON-MANUAL | MANUAL | TOTAL | | NON-MANUAL | MANUAL | TOTAL | |
			%	N			%	N
Total sample[1]								
Secondary education	71	29	100	263	52	48	100	332
Primary education	18	82	100	364	12	88	100	408
Metropolitans only								
Secondary education	67	33	100	187	51	49	100	212
Primary education	23	77	100	124	10	90	100	132
Provincials only								
Secondary education	81	19	100	54	55	45	100	65
Primary education	20	80	100	130	12	88	100	205

[1] Migrants are included in the total sample but are not shown in metropolitan and provincial breakdowns.

A postsecondary education is worth about twice as much in income as an incomplete primary training. Executives earn about two-and-a-half times as much as unskilled workers. The ratios are almost the same in both countries. The data are presented in Table 12 which computes income in terms of ratios, taking provincials in unskilled jobs as a standard base equal to unity.[5]

When we related occupational accomplishment to educational preparation within regions for each country, we found little difference between the capital and the provincial cities, except for the fact that a complete primary education brings, on the average, somewhat higher jobs in the provinces. But when we related education to income, a regional difference did appear among those who had not completed secondary education: metropolitans earn more than provincials. Since there is not much regional difference among those who com-

[5] It is important to note from Table 12 that income is linearly related to education, but not to occupation, since foremen have a relatively low education but high income; the implications of this fact will be developed in Chapter VI.

pleted secondary school or went beyond it, the net result is a wider range of income in the provinces than in the capital cities when educational groups are compared. The same is true in Mexico when occupational groups are compared on income, but the reverse holds in Brazil.

The pattern is interesting. Among those with complete secondary education or more (and thus, nonmanual jobs), the money value of their training does not vary much by the size of the city where they work. Apparently, white-collar jobs, especially at the higher levels, are roughly standardized in pay. But at lower levels of education, and mainly among manual workers, regional differences appear: in the provinces, a given education brings a slightly higher job but much less pay. Since living costs are higher in the metropolis, my advice to a rational economic man would be this: If you are well

TABLE 11

Occupation, by Education

	BRAZIL						
	OCCUPATIONAL GROUP[1]						
EDUCATION	A	B	C	D	E	F	TOTAL
Postsecondary	0	3	3	19	5	20	50
Complete secondary	2	2	1	65	5	30	105
Incomplete secondary	6	18	3	53	11	17	108
Complete primary	44	71	15	27	6	5	168
Incomplete primary	112	58	15	10	1	0	196
Total	164	152	37	174	28	72	627

	MEXICO						
	OCCUPATIONAL GROUP[1]						
EDUCATION	A	B	C	D	E	F	TOTAL
Postsecondary	3	1	9	19	16	60	108
Complete secondary	2	10	6	14	14	18	64
Incomplete secondary	16	36	25	40	25	18	160
Complete primary	40	57	8	28	22	4	159
Incomplete primary	93	134	12	7	3	0	249
Total	154	238	60	108	80	100	740

[1] A = Unskilled or semiskilled manual.
   B = Skilled manual.
   C = Foremen.
   D = Clerks or salesmen.
   E = Supervisors, fewer than five subordinates.
   F = Executives, more than five subordinates.

TABLE 12
Income Ratios,[1] by Education and by Occupation
(Monthly income is expressed as a multiple of the average
earned by unskilled workers in provincial towns.)

	BRAZIL				MEXICO			
EDUCATION	ALL	METROPOLITANS	MIGRANTS	PROVINCIALS	ALL	METROPOLITANS	MIGRANTS	PROVINCIALS
Postsecondary	2.7[2]	2.9	...	2.5	2.6	2.5	2.4	2.7
Complete secondary	2.3	2.3	...	2.1	2.2	2.3	2.3	2.0
Incomplete secondary	2.1	2.1	2.5	1.8	2.0	2.0	2.1	1.7
Complete primary	1.7	1.8	1.9	1.2	1.7	1.8	1.7	1.5
Incomplete primary	1.4	1.6	1.5	1.2	1.3	1.5	1.5	1.1

	BRAZIL				MEXICO			
OCCUPATION	ALL	METROPOLITANS	MIGRANTS	PROVINCIALS	ALL	METROPOLITANS	MIGRANTS	PROVINCIALS
Executive	3.1	3.3	...	2.3	2.8	2.8	2.8	2.6
Supervisor	2.5	2.8	...	...	2.1	2.4	2.5	1.8
Clerk or salesman	1.9	1.9	1.7	1.8	1.8	2.0	1.7	1.7
Foreman	2.2	2.8	2.3	1.6	2.2	2.1	2.2	2.2
Skilled manual	1.6	1.9	1.9	1.1	1.5	1.8	1.9	1.2
Unskilled or semiskilled manual	1.3	1.3	1.4	1.0	1.2	1.4	1.2	1.0

[1] The income of the top categories is underestimated, since the responses were coded as "over" a certain sum and not in exact terms; thus the extremely high incomes were not influential in the mean scores.

[2] Every cell with a ratio contains ten or more respondents.

educated, go to the provinces, but if you are poorly educated, go to
the capital city.

Why Do Boys Stay in School?

In the preceding pages statistics have been presented that show the
relation between the number of years a boy stays in school and the
type of job he eventually gets. The relation is a close one, as indicated
by the correlation coefficient of about .70 between education and job
at the time of the interview. However, the detailed tables indicate
that the prediction is very good at the extremes, but not so good in
the middle of the status hierarchy. Men with incomplete primary
education are almost certain to have low-level manual jobs; yet men
with complete primary training or a little more fill a wide range of
occupational posts.

But the statistics are one thing, and a common knowledge of such
facts by the men involved might well be something quite different.
Do men realize how important education is in controlling life chances?
The qualitative interviews give a clear answer in the affirmative.

One man, a textile worker in a small town in Mexico, said that
his father was a farmworker and did not like it, but "with the little
background that he had, what could he have done about it?"[6] The
father had finished only two years of primary school.

The father wanted his children to escape from the countryside, and
he educated them for that purpose. But with six children and small
resources, the best he could do was the barest minimum. Two of the
children (including our informant) managed to finish primary school
and get a year or two of secondary education; they were the younger
siblings and were helped out by the older ones who had left school
and gone to work. The family remains solidary; the brothers and
sisters see each other, or, for those who have gone to work in Mexico
City, maintain contact by mail or occasional visits. The informant
lives in his father's house.

The informant has been married six years and has two children.
He is a semiskilled worker in the textile factory, and likes it fairly
well, but is somewhat restless. He feels that his current income will
not be sufficient to educate his children (he wants a total of four),
and the work is not demanding enough on his skills and interests as a
mechanic. So he talks about studying by correspondence to be a

---

[6] "Con la poca cultura que tenía, ¿qué podía hacer?"

skilled mechanic, and shifting to some other employment that will provide advancement. He feels that his present job offers no hope for promotion.

Speaking of his ideas for the upbringing of his children, he says:

"I want to train them to be moral—to be good men who work, who work with honesty, sincerity, honor. Schooling gives children the chance to improve themselves, including dropping bad ways of doing things that people do from habit and ignorance—it opens a better future.

"When my children reach an age in which they can judge for themselves, they can choose a professional career or a job that pleases them—it depends on them."[7]

We showed this informant a set of drawings of men doing various kinds of work and asked him to comment on the jobs and to indicate whether he would like such jobs for himself or his children. In this way we stimulated him to be a bit more specific in his attitudes toward occupations of different levels of skill and training.

He commented that a truck driver had an ordinary job—it could be all right, but was not very good. He would not want such a job for himself or his children.

When he saw the picture of a man working at a lathe, he found that much more interesting. "It's a job that pays better, it's not just a low common job; it's specialized and requires study in order to get ahead. Anybody can be a truck driver, but a lathe operator has to be somebody with a precise character so that his work will be precise, because any variation in the work and it's no good."[8] He thinks this might be a good job for his children.

Regarding a man sitting at a desk shuffling papers, he thought poorly of that, for sitting indoors all day is bad for the health. But when he saw a sketch of a man in a laboratory with test tubes, he

[7] "Una educación desde luego donde influye mucho la moral. Ser hombres de bien que obran, que obran en una forma con rectitud—sincera, honrada. La instrucción escolar así les dá margen para valerse a sí mismos, inclusive de deshechar muchas cosas que por la ignorancia se adhieran como hábito y porque tienen otro porvenir mejor.

"Ellos llegan a una edad en que se valen por sí mismos, incluso escogen carrera o empleo o meta que llenen particularmente; pero eso más bien depende de ellos."

[8] "El tornero—sí, porque su trabajo es un trabajo más remunerado, no es un trabajo bajo común, es especializado que requirió estudio y más bien es necesario para ascender. El de chofer, puede ser cualquiera persona, el tornero necesita ser una persona con un carácter preciso para que su trabajo también sea preciso, porque cualquier desvariación del trabajo, pues no le sirve."

said: "It's a chemist mixing solutions. I can't really judge the conditions of life of such a man because he's above my level, but it seems to be a man of science—a good thing, it helps medicine and many other things."[9] He says such a job would be beyond him, but he'd like it for his sons.

In three generations of one family we see the gradations from traditional farming to modern industry and technology. The father of the informant, a farmworker with practically no education, did not like his work, and encouraged his children to escape it through education. However, his economic circumstances did not allow him to go very far: partial or complete primary school for four children, a bit of secondary for two of them.

The family was close-knit, and the values of the father were readily absorbed by the son, who sees education—particularly technical or vocational training—as the key to advancement. His own job is reasonably satisfying to him, but he dreams of a little more. He sees his route to advancement through more training in mechanics (though at the moment he is doing nothing about it). He hopes his children will get more instruction than he had—therefore, he desires to limit his family to four children, and to help them stay in school as long as possible. But since he recognizes the degree to which they must choose for themselves in terms of their own interests and capabilities, he sets no exact goals for them. He does not glorify "paper work" in the traditional way, but rather sees a better route through modern industry and science. Indeed, at one point, when asked which group he thought would contribute most to the progress of Mexico, he replied: "The scientists and technicians, I think, because the technicians make it possible for an industry to advance. The scientists in order to collaborate with the technicians."[10]

A family structure which forms strong character and transmits ambitions and values; an educational system that opens new opportunities (but limited ones, since family resources usually allow each generation to climb only one step above its predecessors); expanding industry that provides jobs—these are the intertwined factors that

9 "Es un químico, porque está mexclando soluciones. Las condiciones de vida de este señor no las puedo yo juzgar pues creo que está sobre el nivel de mi vida, superficialmente le diré que es un hombre de ciencia. Es muy bonita, ayuda mucho a la medicina y para infinidad de cosas."

10 "Los científicos y técnicos, creo yo, porque en primera, los técnicos dan margen a que una industria vaya para arriba. La ciencia por colaborar con los técnicos."

modernize the labor force. Men who come from disorganized families often fail to develop a character structure that allows self-discipline for future goals. Children from poor families—especially large ones— usually are forced to go to work sooner than they or their parents would like, but even so many can climb a notch or two above their fathers. Boys who grow up in rural areas where schools are scarce have less chance, although occasionally they go to live with relatives in some larger town where a school is available.

Some of the men talk of advancement as coming primarily through intelligence and hard work instead of formal education, but they are a minority (if we had included independent entrepreneurs in our sample, we might have caught more of them). The perception among most of our respondents is very clear: schooling sets the basic level of a man's life, and his diligence and luck have an additional minor effect by determining his precise status within that general level. They perceive a hierarchy of jobs and a hierarchy of education that are closely matched. And they know where they themselves fit.

Over and over again, we find that the informants talk of the effect on them of the ambitions of their parents. And over and over again, they tell us that the education of their own children is their central responsibility and purpose in life.

These themes, which are perfectly clear to most of the informants, can be readily measured in our statistics.

The Prediction of Education by Father's Status and by Size of Town

The best single predictor we have of the education of an informant is the socio-economic status of his father: in both countries the correlation coefficient was .58 (see Appendix B). The average education for sons of high nonmanual workers was complete secondary; about half had gone beyond it. The typical schooling for sons of low nonmanual workers as well as sons of high manual workers was incomplete secondary; the typical education for sons of low manual workers was incomplete primary (see Table 13). Naturally, these facts refer to happenings of some two decades ago; the sons of our informants will do a little better.

However, the size of the town where the informant grew up did exert considerable influence on the schooling he obtained. In almost all instances, those in medium-sized cities received significantly more training than those in small towns, and those in large cities did even better.[11]

I have already reported that when we measure values, the differences between small town and big city men are noticeable but usually not very great, if socio-economic status has been controlled. But here we see an instance in which the behavior differences in different locations are quite substantial, and probably have an important influence on the social process. Because of their greater access to formal education, and their greater interest in taking advantage of the schools that are available, boys in cities have a decided advantage over their provincial cousins, an advantage that increases their opportunities for occupational success.

This is one way that a school system breaks down a traditional social order, for in that order high status is based on rural landholdings, and is directly inherited. But as the modern occupational system develops, it demands modern education, and provincial boys get less schooling. Thus, with the exception of the minority of provincial boys who make a special effort to get a good education, the position of the provincial elite is slowly weakened in favor of newer groups from the bigger cities.[12]

The values which keep provincials from taking full advantage of modern educational opportunities are so vividly illustrated in the interview with an office manager in a small Brazilian city, quoted in Chapter I, it is worth repeating here. The respondent was talking about his wife's brothers, who are medium-scale farmers:

"They are typical of farmers hereabouts, they don't educate themselves; secondary school is a lot for them, and they return to the farm. They don't give much value to study, even about agricultural matters; a farm that provides a living is what they want; they don't even learn modern methods of agriculture. Yes, they would like more income, but they are so fixed in the traditions of their fathers and grandfathers that they don't want to try innovations. Today it is getting a little better, because the farmer vaccinates his cattle and bathes them, but even so, it is still very primitive."[13]

---

[11] With the exception of the sons of high nonmanual workers from large cities, and sons of low manual workers in medium-sized cities, the differences between countries are negligible.

[12] For North American comparisons, see Lipset and Bendix, *Social Mobility in Industrial Society*, Chap. VIII.

[13] See Chap. I, note 18, for the Portuguese.

Values and Education

There are two ways to think about the role of values in the sorting-out process which distributes men into various educational and occupational positions: as an aspect of socio-economic status, and as an additional factor beyond status. If we concentrate on the former, we see a process in which the status of the father as measured by objective indices determines to a large degree the status of the son, but partly

TABLE 13

Education[1] of Respondent, by Father's Occupation and Size of Town

FATHER'S OCCUPATION, AND SIZE OF TOWN WHERE RESPONDENT LIVED AT AGE 10	EDUCATION OF RESPONDENT			
	BRAZIL		MEXICO	
	MEAN	N	MEAN	N
High nonmanual				
Large (city over 100,000)	3.8	48	4.3	38
Medium (city from 5,000 to 100,000)	3.8	19	3.5[2]	19
Small (farm or town under 5,000)	...	2	...	7
All towns	3.8	69	4.0	64
Low nonmanual				
Large	3.1	93	3.3	105
Medium	2.7[2]	86	2.9[2]	81
Small	2.2[2]	38	2.5[2]	66
All towns	2.8	217	3.0	252
High manual				
Large	2.7	83	2.7	92
Medium	2.2[2]	52	2.5	42
Small	1.8	24	1.7[2]	110
All towns	2.4	159	2.2	244
Low manual				
Large	2.2	29	2.1	48
Medium	1.5[2]	71	2.1	30
Small	1.3	69	1.3[2]	92
All towns	1.5	169	1.7	170

[1] Educational code:
    1 = Incomplete primary.
    2 = Complete primary.
    3 = Incomplete secondary.
    4 = Complete secondary.
    5 = Postsecondary.

[2] Difference between this figure and the one immediately above it is significant at .05 level.

Primary education lasts six years in Mexico, five years in Brazil. Secondary education lasts five years in Mexico, seven in Brazil.

through the intervening effect of values. That is, a high-status man teaches his son values appropriate for leading the son to stay a long time in school and to behave on the job in an ambitious manner, thereby obtaining for himself a high status similar to that of his father. From this point of view, values are built into objective statuses. Certainly all our data do show high correlations between status level and values.

But an alternative approach is to see values not just as part of status but also as independently influential. Here it is recognized that the socialization process is not automatic: sons do not always turn out to be junior replicas of their fathers. They take on different values as a result of latent psychological aspects of family life, or through contacts with peers at school or at work, or from the mass media, or through some process of private creativity that we cannot see. They then behave differently from what we would predict solely from the status of their fathers.

In a sense, values as an aspect of status can be thought of as important for succession, and values as additional influences can be thought of as important for mobility.

Only longitudinal studies that follow men through a period of time can properly sort out the various ways in which values influence succession and mobility, and unfortunately we are confined to a questionnaire instrument that was administered at only one point in time. Questions about sequences of events in the past are hard for a man to answer, and it is harder still for us to have much faith in the accuracy of his reconstructions. We know that there is a close relation between values and current occupational status, but we cannot tell for sure whether a man became successful because he believed in achievement values, or whether he came to believe in achievement values because he was successful and associated with men who asserted such convictions. It is hard to tell which came first, the values or the success.

However, there are several indirect clues in our data. Let us start with the fathers of the respondents. We have no direct measure of their values, and we are inclined to view with suspicion any report about beliefs of fathers that comes to us from their sons, for it is hearsay evidence. Yet one question may serve, since it is phrased to elicit information about the father that was called directly and positively to the attention of the son: "Did your father have a definite idea about the amount of schooling he wanted you to have?" About

5 per cent of the respondents answered that they did not know. And about 50 per cent replied that their fathers had no particular idea in mind. The remainder could distinguish between primary and secondary school versus university as the goals held by their fathers. We call this measure "Father's School Pressure."[14]

The data are given in Table 14. Considering first only the difference between pressure toward primary or secondary schooling versus pressure toward university training, we note that there are insufficient cases among the sons of high nonmanual fathers to make a test. But in all other groups, there is a significant difference in the actual educational attainment of the sons according to the perceived pressure from the fathers. Thus, with status constant, we can infer that the expressed wishes of the father did in fact influence the behavior of the son.[15]

What about the large number of respondents who reported that their fathers had no particular goal in mind? At the top level of status, the sons of such fathers did as well as or better than those whose fathers explicitly pushed toward a university education. Here we can guess that university education was so standard a goal among the entire social group—fathers, sons, relatives, and friends—that no open pressure was necessary, or if it existed, it was not felt as something special by the sons. Perhaps we can call this the lack of a "contrast effect": only the unusual is clearly noticed and long remembered.

At lower levels of status, we note that the group reporting no pressure achieved an amount of education intermediate between those reporting primary or secondary schooling and those reporting university training. Here the respondents probably include more than one subtype, producing an intermediate average. For instance, these re-

---

[14] For an indication of the power of this concept, see J. A. Kahl, "Educational & Occupational Aspirations of 'Common Man' Boys," *Harvard Educational Review*, XXIII (Summer, 1953), 186–203. Subsequent research confirmed the propositions in that early paper; see the data and the references in Richard L. Simpson, "Parental Influence, Anticipatory Socialization, and Social Mobility," *American Sociological Review*, 27 (August 1962), 517–522.

[15] Note from Table 14 that among high nonmanual fathers, almost all of those who expressed a goal indicated university-level training; among low nonmanual fathers, somewhat more than half chose university; among high manual fathers, somewhat less than half; and among low manual fathers, about one-fifth indicated university. And also note that the proportion that exerted no pressure noticeable to their sons increased markedly with a decrease in status. Thus, there is a clear relation between status and parental goals, which we must control in order to extract the influence of these goals on sons that goes beyond status.

spondents probably include some who so completely agreed with their fathers that they noticed no pressure; thus the father's actual goals were influential but not clearly evident. And these respondents may include some sons who found their own paths in life just because their fathers left them alone (or were not even present in the household).

But where the father had a goal, and it was perceived by the son, the son's behavior was clearly influenced by the expressed goal.

Now let us switch the time perspective from the past to the future. Do the values of the respondents influence the amount of education they expect their sons to have? The answer is Yes.

Our question was: "Many fathers have dreams for the future of

TABLE 14

Education[1] of Respondent, by Father's Occupation
and Father's School Pressure

| FATHER'S OCCUPATION AND FATHER'S SCHOOL PRESSURE | EDUCATION OF RESPONDENT | | | |
| | BRAZIL | | MEXICO | |
	MEAN	N	MEAN	N
High nonmanual				
University	3.8	32	3.8	32
Primary or secondary	...	6	...	2
None	3.8	31	4.3	30
Low nonmanual				
University	3.4	67	3.6	86
Primary or secondary	2.1[2]	57	2.0[2]	26
None	2.8[2]	93	2.7[2]	140
High manual				
University	3.2	30	2.9	53
Primary or secondary	2.0[2]	44	1.7[2]	62
None	2.3	85	2.1[2]	129
Low manual				
University	2.4	13	2.7	11
Primary or secondary	1.3[2]	42	1.5[2]	43
None	1.5	114	1.6	116

[1] Educational code:
   1 = Incomplete primary.
   2 = Complete primary.
   3 = Incomplete secondary.
   4 = Complete secondary.
   5 = Postsecondary.
[2] Difference between this figure and the one immediately above it is significant at .01 level.

their children, but, as you know, the realities of life don't always permit us to realize our dreams. Therefore, we ask you about your realistic expectations for your sons, and not your dreams of a perfect life. How much education do you think your sons will get?" In Brazil, men without sons were eliminated. In Mexico, men without sons were asked to imagine what their expectations would be if they had sons.

The picture is shown in Table 15, which gives the mean scores for the expected education of sons by subgroups based on the occupations and the values of the respondents. Once again, it appears that among the top-status men the expectation of university training for their sons is so widespread that even the few who are less committed to modernism share the same high goals. But among all other groups of men, the role of values is clear: *modernists push their children higher than do traditionalists.* (Notice that comparisons between coun-

TABLE 15
Expected Education[1] of Sons, by Occupation and Modernism I

RESPONDENT'S OCCUPATION AND HIS RANK ON MODERNISM I	EXPECTED EDUCATION OF SONS			
	BRAZIL		MEXICO	
	MEAN	N	MEAN	N
High nonmanual				
High Modernism I	3.0	26	3.0	71
Medium Modernism I	2.9	12	2.9	25
Low Modernism I	. . .	. .	. . .	. .
Low nonmanual				
High Modernism I	2.8	47	2.8	83
Medium Modernism I	2.6[2]	32	2.5[3]	58
Low Modernism I	2.4	15	2.3	33
High manual				
High Modernism I	2.6	28	2.6	72
Medium Modernism I	2.2[3]	39	2.2[3]	94
Low Modernism I	1.8[2]	43	2.0	106
Low manual				
High Modernism I	. . .	. .	2.3	15
Medium Modernism I	2.1	18	2.0[2]	43
Low Modernism I	1.8	41	2.0	81

[1] Code for expected education of sons:

    1 = Primary.

    2 = Secondary.

    3 = University.

[2] Difference between this figure and the one immediately above it is significant at .05 level.

[3] Difference between this figure and the one immediately above it is significant at .01 level.

tries show negligible differences in educational goals, when status and modernism are both controlled.)

Of course, we cannot prove from our material that the expectations of our respondents will in fact control the behavior of their sons, but it is highly likely.[16] After all, the expressed wishes of the fathers of the respondents had a clear influence on their sons.

The data in Table 15 showed that both occupational status and modernism influenced the expected education of sons. Furthermore, we would surmise from what we found earlier (Table 13) that geographic location would also have an effect, with metropolitans expecting more schooling than provincials. The *relative* importance of the three independent variables can be seen from the partial correlation of each variable (the other two held constant) with expected education of sons:[17]

	BRAZIL	MEXICO
Modernism I	.21	.17
SES	.41	.40
Metropolitan Location	.19	.18

The multiple correlation of all three independent variables with expected education of sons is .63 in Brazil and .60 in Mexico. The partials show that SES is the most important single predictor; after it is controlled, modernism and location have about equal weight as secondary influences.

The pathways of causation—the exact ways in which the three independent variables interact to influence the dependent variable— will be explored in more detail in the next chapter; for the moment,

[16] The data from Puerto Rico neatly demonstrate the point: Melvin M. Tumin, *Social Class and Social Change in Puerto Rico*, Chaps. III and IV.

[17] We switch in regression analysis to SES instead of occupation, since being a slightly more powerful index, it lessens the heterogeneity of status that exists within broad occupational strata.

The Beta Weights are almost equal to the partial coefficients. In a series of simulation experiments on the electronic computer, my colleague Robert L. Hamblin found that the usual method of calculating explained variance in multiple-partial correlation has the tendency to underestimate it when there are several independent variables with low correlations with the dependent variable. He has prepared a new method (not yet published) that is more accurate. Using the new method, we arrive at the following percentages of explained variance: for the multiple coefficient, .56 in Brazil and .54 in Mexico. The relative percentages for each independent variable separately are approximately .13 for Modernism I, .30 for SES, and .12 for Metropolitan Location.

it is enough to repeat that values are "built into" status and location, and are also "something more."[18]

Conclusions

In this chapter we have moved from the study of modern values in and of themselves to an examination of the role of values in predicting educational attitudes and behavior. First I established a framework by showing the importance of formal education in modern society—indeed, even in the semitraditional society represented by our provincial towns. Education is the key factor which sorts men out into the many occupational positions that exist in a complex division of labor. To gain high occupation (and income), one needs advanced education.

But what determines the amount of education that a boy gets? Most importantly, the socio-economic status of his father. But two other factors of importance were measured: the metropolitan-versus-provincial context in which a boy grew up, and also the values held by his father. In other words, *within* a given status level, men differ in their views about the importance of education for their sons, and those differences can in part be explained by geographic location and values. This process was studied twice: once in terms of the respondent and his father, and once in terms of the respondent and his son.

It should be noted that the patterns in both countries were practically identical. Therefore, the differences between Brazil and Mexico that will be demonstrated in the next chapter concerning ideal family size are especially striking.

[18] For an additional variable—that of democratic family structure—and an intriguing cross-national analysis of five countries which includes Mexico, see Glen H. Elder, Jr., "Family Structure and Educational Attainment," *American Sociological Review*, 30 (February 1965), 81-96. See also Bernard C. Rosen, "Socialization and Achievement Motivation in Brazil," *ibid.*, 27 (October 1962), 612-624.

CHAPTER V

Modern Values and Fertility Ideals

The "demographic transition" has customarily been described by means of relations between socio-economic and demographic variables, relying primarily on those which can be measured by official national statistics. Thus we are told that the initial stages of economic development produce a drop in mortality, and that this is followed (usually a generation or two later) by a reduction in fertility. The latter is said to be brought about by the combined forces of urbanization and the emergence of a large middle class.

It is recognized, of course, that the decision to have children or, more precisely, to attempt to avoid having children, is a personal one made by married couples, and that a great many factors influence them. "Urban residence" or "middle-class status" are merely shorthand phrases that somewhat summarize those factors. Implicit are many intervening variables. It is assumed that people who live in cities, and especially those who belong to the urban middle class, adhere to certain values and perceive their life circumstances in certain ways which lead them to restrict fertility.[1] But attempts to make direct measurements of the effects of those subjective variables upon fertility have not been common and have not yet produced important results.[2]

Recent statistics from Latin American countries show that the supposed fertility reduction is not everywhere occurring on schedule. Specifically, Mexico is now one-half urban; Mexico City and its environs contain some six million people, many of them belonging to

[1] It is now recognized that in the most advanced countries, the urban middle-class way of life begins to diffuse throughout the entire population, annulling (and occasionally even reversing) the earlier class differences in fertility.

[2] The most famous investigation is the Indianapolis study: see Clyde V. Kiser and P. K. Whelpton, "Summary of Chief Findings and Implications for Future Studies," *Milbank Memorial Fund Quarterly*, 36 (July 1958), 282-329.

the middle class; yet the national birth rate has not decreased, and indeed may even be going up.[3] We can, then, appreciate the urgency for new studies that measure the intervening variables affecting fertility in a direct manner, rather than leaving them hidden and implied. What makes Mexico different from the United States, or Argentina, or Spain, all of which have low birth rates? Why does urbanization have different results in different countries?

Consequently, although our study was not originally designed as a research on fertility, and the sampling procedures and questionnaire are far from ideal for that purpose, it nevertheless seems worthwhile to analyze the relevant data. We do have direct measurements of values, and these are distributed throughout the population in precisely the way one would expect from theories of the demographic transition which emphasize the importance of urban residence and middle-class status. We can, therefore, use our measures of values as direct indices of the implied values that are presumed to intervene between position in the social structure and fertility.

Fertility Ideals

As our samples included men of various ages, it would not be practical to use as the dependent variable the number of children they had in fact produced at the time of the interviews, for many had not yet completed their families. Better to use as a guide is the response to this question: "How many children do you think ideal for a family of our times?"

The modal answer was two children among Brazilians and three among Mexicans; the mean was 2.6 for the former, and 3.9 for the latter. The desire for larger families among Mexicans was consistent among all subgroups by occupational status and by metropolitan-versus-provincial residence, as shown in Table 16.

This difference between countries in the size of family desired startled us for two reasons: (1) the national birth rates for the two countries are similar, and (2) our other findings showed that the two countries were remarkably similar on most values and aspirations. Thus the sharp difference on fertility ideals became a serendipitous finding that was a definite challenge, and we squeezed our data as hard as possible in a search for understanding.

Actually, the data in Table 16 show not only a difference in average

[3] Andrew A. Collver, *Birth Rates in Latin America.*

TABLE 16
Ideal Family Size, by Occupation and Location

| OCCUPATION OF RESPONDENT AND HIS LOCATION | IDEAL FAMILY SIZE (PREFERRED NUMBER OF CHILDREN) | | | |
| | BRAZIL | | MEXICO | |
	MEAN	N	MEAN	N
High nonmanual				
Metropolitans	2.4	46	3.5	72
Migrants	...	8	3.6	14
Provincials	2.9	14	3.4	13
All locations	2.5	68	3.5	99
Low nonmanual				
Metropolitans	2.2	118	3.6	86
Migrants	2.7[1]	18	3.5	24
Provincials	3.2	59	3.8	64
All locations	2.5	195	3.6[3]	174
High manual				
Metropolitans	2.1	84	3.7	100
Migrants	2.6[2]	38	4.2[1]	47
Provincials	3.4[2]	59	4.4	125
All locations	2.6	181	4.1	272
Low manual				
Metropolitans	2.3	50	3.8	63
Migrants	2.7	62	4.2	25
Provincials	3.3[1]	39	4.1	51
All locations	2.7	151	4.0	139
Grand average	2.6	595	3.9	684

[1] Difference between this figure and the one immediately above it is significant at .05 level.

[2] Difference between this figure and the one immediately above it is significant at .01 level.

[3] This mean differs significantly at .01 level from the mean for High Manual workers for all locations.

number of children desired among Brazilians as compared to Mexicans, but also a difference in the pattern of impact of independent variables that influence fertility norms. In Mexico there is a small negative relation between status level and the desired number of children, but it is not noticeable in Brazil. And in Brazil, there is a strong negative relation between metropolitan residence and desired family size, but in Mexico that relation is weak.

Thus, middle-class status seems to be the main influence toward the small-family norm in Mexico, whereas metropolitan residence seems to be the main factor in Brazil. If these results were rashly generalized to predict national trends, we would have to surmise that metropolitanization will reduce the birth rate more in Brazil than in Mexico, for in Mexico any reduction that occurs in the large cities could be supposed to come more from a redistribution toward the middle class than from metropolitan residence per se.

Furthermore, we might conjecture that the large difference in fertility ideals between countries will soon produce a difference in behavior—that is, we can assume that the Brazilian ideals have already moved toward smaller families, and this will before long be reflected in the birth rates. However, various circumstances intervene between norms and behavior, so we had best not bet too heavily on that prediction.[4]

Since most demographic field studies put their questions to women, one wonders whether the answers our men gave would correspond to the ideas of their wives about childbearing. Fortunately, Professor Raúl Benítez Zenteno, of the National University of Mexico, with the sponsorship of the United Nations Latin American Demograph Center, Santiago, Chile (commonly known as CELADE), studied an excellently representative sample of about twenty-four hundred women in Mexico City in 1964. Table 17 shows the ideal family size indicated by the women of his sample, along with that of the men of our sample, in both instances according to educational level. A comparison of results shows that the men prefer slightly smaller families at all educational levels, but the range by education is parallel in both sexes.

Is there any evidence from census data that can be used to check these patterns to see whether actual behavior is related to statements about "ideals"? A recent article by Carmen A. Miró,[5] director of CELADE, summarizes the available evidence. She reports that the national crude birth rates in the two countries are estimated to be similar (between 43 and 47). Estimated urban birth rates, standardized for age, are also very similar (33 to 35), but rural rates are quite different, with the Brazilian rate higher (50 compared to 43). She further shows that when age-specific rates are calculated for women who have completed their families (over forty-five years old), there

---

[4] In Lima, Peru, the relation between status level and fertility norms was found to be positive, but the relation between status level and actual fertility behavior was negative; see J. Mayone Stycos, "Social Class and Preferred Family Size in Peru," *American Journal of Sociology*, LXX (May 1965), 651-658.

[5] "The Population of Latin America," *Demography*, Vol. I, No. 1 (1964), especially pp. 34-38.

TABLE 17
Ideal Family Size, by Education of Respondent
(Mexico City: Men and Women)

YEARS OF SCHOOL COMPLETED[1]		IDEAL FAMILY SIZE MEN	WOMEN
Incomplete university:	12 or 13 years	3.4	3.8
Preparatory:	10 or 11 years	3.4	3.7
Secondary:	7 to 9 years	3.7	3.8
Complete primary:	6 years	3.8	4.2
Partial primary	4 or 5 years[1]	3.9	4.2
Beginning primary:	1 to 3 years[1]	4.2	4.7
None:	0 years		5.0

[1] For men only, 1 to 4 years were coded as "beginning primary," and 5 years as "partial primary." The data for women are from a preliminary tabulation by Professor Raúl Benítez Zenteno (see text).

is a clear indication that younger Brazilian women in urban areas have had fewer children than did older ones, but the same trend is *not* noticeable in Mexico. Indeed, among women in their thirties, urbanites have had more children in Mexico than in Brazil, but ruralites have had fewer.

In other words, the census data support the general idea that there is now a larger rural-urban differential in Brazil than in Mexico, and suggest that it is fairly recent, a differential reflecting a declining Brazilian urban birth rate and a stationary and very high rural one. In Mexico, both rates appear to be stationary. Now, our own data are for "metropolitans" versus "provincials," and the latter are urban by census definition. But they come from small towns which are partly rural in their cultures. Thus the census data and our sample data are commensurate with respect to the major trends, though obviously they cannot be compared in detail as to absolute levels of fertility desired or achieved.

The Role of Values

What about the impact of modern values? Again controlling by occupational level, and then contrasting the modernists with the traditionalists, we note the pattern in Table 18. It shows that with the exception of the high nonmanual workers, the modernists prefer somewhat smaller families than do the traditionalists. The effect of values is most marked among the upper-status manual workers. Once again we see that in every instance, even with occupation *and* values controlled, Mexicans prefer larger families than Brazilians. But it is possible to substitute for Modernism I three other scales of values that are more directly relevant to family life: Low Integration with Relatives, which measures an orientation of independence from the extended-family network, and is available for both countries; Family Modernism, which indicates a contemporary attitude toward the roles within the nuclear family, available for Mexico only; and finally, Low Religiosity, used only in Mexico. The tables for these scales, paralleling Table 18, are not shown here, since the same patterns appear as for Modernism I; however, the significance of the differences goes up slightly.[6]

TABLE 18
Ideal Family Size, by Occupation and Modernism I

| | IDEAL FAMILY SIZE | | | |
| OCCUPATION OF RESPONDENT AND HIS RANK ON MODERNISM I | BRAZIL | | MEXICO | |
	MEAN	N	MEAN	N
High nonmanual				
High Modernism I	2.8	40	3.5	71
Medium Modernism I	2.3	20	3.5	25
Low Modernism I	...	8	...	3
Low nonmanual				
High Modernism I	2.4	94	3.5	83
Medium Modernism I	2.5	68	3.8[1]	58
Low Modernism I	2.7	33	3.7	33
High manual				
High Modernism I	2.4	46	3.5	72
Medium Modernism I	2.5	58	4.0[2]	94
Low Modernism I	2.8	77	4.6[2]	106
Low manual				
High Modernism I	2.6	19	3.5	15
Medium Modernism I	2.6	50	3.8	43
Low Modernism I	2.8	82	4.1	81

[1] Difference between this figure and the one immediately above it is significant at .05 level.

[2] Difference between this figure and the one immediately above it is significant at .01 level.

[6] For items in the scales, see Table 1, Chap. II. For Mexico, the zero-order correlations with Ideal Family Size are as follows: Modernism I, —.22; Low Integration with Relatives, —.27; Family Modernism, —.25; Low Religiosity, —.27. The zero-order coefficients with some other variables are: Activism, —.15; Individualism, —.15; Trust, —.02; Low Stratification of Life Chances, —.01; Expected Education of Sons, —.23; SES, —.24; Metropolitan Location, —.18; Occupation, —.17; Education, —.26.

Research in other countries has often shown that when other status variables are held constant, income has a low positive correlation with family size. In other words, the cultural values and family structures that are associated with occupation and education produce a general norm for an appropriate family size, but when members of a given family have a little more money, they can afford to have perhaps one child more than the group norm. (Of course, the zero-order relation between income and fertility is usually negative.)

Our data show that with SES controlled (occupation, education, and identification), the partial correlation of income with ideal family size is −.12 in Brazil and −.02 in Mexico. Here the usual pattern does not hold—if anything, income is acting as an additional status variable adding to the effects of occupation, education, and identification, rather than counteracting them.

Let us estimate the *relative* weights of SES, location, and modernity in values as influences on ideal family size. We will use Low Integration with Relatives as our measure of values, since it has a slightly more powerful effect on fertility ideals than the more abstract scale of Modernism I.

The multiple correlation of all three independent variables with the dependent variable is −.36 in Brazil and −.31 in Mexico. The partial correlation of each predictor with ideal family size (holding the other two constant) is as follows:

	BRAZIL	MEXICO
Low Integration with Relatives	−.10	−.17
SES	−.05	−.12
Metropolitan Location	−.31	−.09

Once again we see the big difference between countries: location is the most important predictor in Brazil, whereas status and values are relatively more important in Mexico.[7]

---

[7] The Beta Weights for the three independent variables are almost equal to the partial coefficients. The percentage of variance explained by each variable (using the method of Hamblin described in Chapter IV, note 17) is:

	BRAZIL	MEXICO
Low Integration with Relatives	.08	.15
SES	.04	.11
Metropolitan Location	.25	.07
All three	.37	.33

Family Structure in Brazil and Mexico

Why is there a substantial difference between Brazil and Mexico concerning fertility ideals, but practically none at all concerning educational ideals, or the distribution of modernism among various status and regional strata, as shown in Chapter III?

I cannot "explain" this difference with firm data, but I can speculate about it. I have lived for a year in Brazil, and longer than that in Mexico, sometimes as a paying guest in middle-class homes. It is possible, therefore, to offer an impression: the conjugal family system in Rio de Janeiro appears to be more "modern" than the family system in Mexico City. My experience in the provinces is much more superficial, but my impression is that there is less difference between the provinces of the two countries than between their large cities.

In Rio de Janeiro, I found it easier to make friends than it was in Mexico City, for the contacts I made among professional colleagues quickly led to invitations home to dinner, or for a week-end at the family cottage in the country. Mexicans seem more reserved; with patience, one's professional contacts slowly turn into warm and loyal friends, but absorption into the family circle is much less common.

Furthermore, I sensed that women have a more modern role in Rio de Janeiro; the family structure, at least in the middle class, seems more equalitarian, with less male dominance. Brazilian psychoanalysts do not follow the current fashion of their Mexican colleagues in writing books about *machismo* (exaggerated masculinity).

I suspect that these differences are related to some old traditions within the Portuguese and Spanish cultures that were transferred to the New World, and possibly to some differences between the Negro contribution in Brazil and that of the Indian in Mexico. In Brazil interpersonal relations of many types seem somewhat more relaxed and less formal than in Mexico; for instance, the use of first names is much more common. Therefore, despite my feeling that many phases of the world of work are more modern in Mexico than in Brazil, I believe that in Rio de Janeiro conjugal roles more closely approximate the usual urban-industrial mode than in Mexico City, especially in the middle class.[8]

[8] For the world-wide pattern, see William J. Goode, *World Revolution and Family Patterns*. Writing before the turn of the century, Emile Durkheim understood the basic trends; see his "A Durkheim Fragment," *American Journal of*

All of this is to suggest that the family is modernizing more rapidly in Rio de Janeiro than in Mexico City, whereas the provincial zones of the two countries are more alike (although not identical). If true, we would expect a wider difference between provincial and metropolitan fertility norms in Brazil than in Mexico, and that is what the statistics show.

Supporting Evidence on Family Structure

Can we muster any questionnaire data to support this impression of the difference in family styles? Unfortunately, the scale most appropriate to the task—Family Modernism—was not used in Brazil (in Mexico, it showed a moderate correlation with SES, but none with location—see Table 7). Hence we must concentrate on the next-best instrument, the scale of Low Integration with Relatives.[9]

To compare the two countries, we cannot use the "standardized" scale scores (that is, quartile divisions for each country), but must look at the absolute levels of agreement and disagreement with the items. Let us examine all three items:

1. When looking for a job, a person ought to find a position in a place located near his parents, even if that means losing a good opportunity elsewhere.

	AGREE VERY MUCH	AGREE A LITTLE	DISAGREE A LITTLE	DISAGREE VERY MUCH	TOTAL %
BRAZIL	20	11	13	56	100
MEXICO	15	11	15	59	100

2. When you are in trouble, only a relative can be depended upon to help you out.

BRAZIL	17	15	24	44	100
MEXICO	13	14	22	51	100

Sociology, LXX (March 1965), 527-536. For aspects of conjugal-role structure in the United States that affect fertility, with social status held constant, see Lee Rainwater, *Family Design*. Some contrasting Mexican attitudes can be found in A. F. Corwin, "Contemporary Mexican Attitudes toward Population, Poverty and Public Opinion," *Latin American Monographs* (University of Florida), No. 25 (September 1963).

[9] The insights of Mrs. Marilyn Merritt have been particularly helpful in preparing this section.

3. If you have a chance to hire an assistant in your work, it is always
   better to hire a relative instead of a stranger.

BRAZIL	20	14	17	49	100
MEXICO	33	26	20	21	100

On the first two items, the distributions are similar. But on the last
item we note a reversal: Mexicans are much more inclined to hire a
relative on the job than are Brazilians. Here is some support for the
idea of a tighter family structure in Mexico.[10]

In order to seek the pattern by SES and location, we made up a
simple Likert sum scale from the three chosen items (following the
logic for cross-national comparisons discussed in Chapter III with
respect to the scale for Modernism III). Although Brazilians in the
metropolitan zone turned out to be slightly less tied to relatives than
their Mexican counterparts, the differences were not great. The big
differences showed up among migrants and provincials of medium and
low SES: in each of these strata, the Brazilians were considerably less
tied to relatives than the Mexicans.

That finding is somewhat mixed with respect to our theory. It
supports the idea that Brazilians are less tied to relatives, as we
expected. But it puts the differences among provincials and migrants,
whereas we expected them mainly among metropolitans.

However, a revision of the hypothesis seems possible that would
come closer to both the finding on ties to relatives, and also the general
trend of the fertility data. In Brazil, metropolitans and migrants are
very much alike with respect to their values about relatives, whereas
provincials are markedly more traditional and familistic. In Mexico,
the migrants are exactly intermediate between metropolitans and
provincials. The idea then emerges that Rio de Janeiro may be able
to socialize its migrants more readily to city values than does Mexico
City. If so, the birth rate would be lower in Rio de Janeiro.

Nonfamily Relationships

My qualitative impressions suggested that some of the difference
in family structure in the two countries was related to the over-all

---

[10] One other related item in the questionnaire shows sharp differences between
countries, despite the over-all tendency for most items to have similar distributions:
"Businessmen have good connections that make it easy for their sons to become
successful." Although there is more agreement than disagreement in both countries,
acquiescence is much stronger in Mexico than in Brazil.

quality of interpersonal relationships, with the Brazilians being more relaxed and open, and the Mexicans more constrained and even suspicious with strangers (and, concomitantly, more confined to the family for emotional support).[11] Bolstering this idea are two pointed items (one from the scale of Trust, the other from Preference for Urban Life):

1. People help persons who have helped them not so much because it is right but because it is good business.

	AGREE VERY MUCH	AGREE A LITTLE	DISAGREE A LITTLE	DISAGREE VERY MUCH	TOTAL %
BRAZIL	13	08	11	68	100
MEXICO	41	41	11	07	100

2. People in a big city are cold and impersonal; it is hard to make new friends.

BRAZIL	30	17	14	39	100
MEXICO	33	25	19	23	100

Here we note the extraordinary contrast on the first item, and the somewhat weaker contrast on the second; in both instances, the Brazilians show up as seeing interpersonal relationships with nonfamily members as warmer and safer than do the Mexicans.

To give an extreme example of the distrust of people which is characteristic of some Mexicans, particularly those with traditional values, I quote a provincial factory worker. He was born a bastard, never knew his father, and was reared by his uncle. His first job was as a shepherd; then he worked in a bakery, and finally entered a textile mill. This man was so suspicious that he did not even keep up contacts with his brother—in itself unusual, for the distrust of strangers often drives a man closer to his relatives. He had confidence only in his wife. Asked if he visits relatives or friends, he replied:

"No, miss, I don't like to visit relatives or friends. I like to go from work to home. For recreation I only go to the movies with my wife and the little boy. My uncle, the one who sent me to school, was the person who taught me that I ought to avoid friends, that they only make trouble in life; the best friend is the one who will be the traitor.

[11] For a penetrating account by a Mexican of the reserve characteristic of his countrymen, see Octavio Paz, *The Labyrinth of Solitude*.

The only friendship a man should have is with his wife. It's much better to amuse yourself with your wife than with friends."[12]

A Theory of Causation

It is necessary to explore somewhat further the possible paths of causation that link modern values to both regional and status position, and in turn to link all three to specific attitudes and behavior about education and fertility.

It is easy to understand a theoretical framework which treats values as dependent on both location and status—that people who live in large cities tend to be modern, and also that people in upper levels of socio-economic status tend to be modern, their modernism following as a direct consequence of their position in physical space and social plane. Furthermore, one can readily accept the notion that location and status have a *cumulative* effect upon values, though not with equal strength at all status levels. In more specific terms, one can absorb the data in Chapter III which show that SES predicts modernism to a high degree, and that metropolitan location also produces modern answers, but only among people of lower status.

But then we have to get more cautious, and consequently, more complex in our thinking. We note that the correlations between status plus location on the one hand, and values on the other, are significant and important, but certainly not completely decisive in size: together, the two independent variables predict slightly less than one-third of the variance in the dependent variable. Now, since we are using rough-and-ready measurements, we can assume some slippage, and feel confident that the "real" relations are somewhat higher. But even with perfect measures, much variance would remain unaccounted for.

Further reflection welcomes that finding, for observation of our friends tells us that not all people at a given status level in a given location are completely alike in beliefs, despite the fact that on the average they are more similar to one another than to people in other

[12] "No, Srta., no me gusta andar visitando ni parientes ni amigos. A mi gusto es de mi trabajo a mi casa. Diversiones solamente al cine, llevar a mi esposa y al chiquito. Mi tío—él que me envió a la escuela—fué quien me inclucó que yo no debía andar de amiguero. Que siempre se presentan casos en la vida. El más amigo es el traicionero. La única amistad que puede uno tener es con su esposa de uno. Distraerse con la esposa de uno es mucho mejor que los amigos."

positions. *What produces the variation?* Here we have to fall back on a multitude of small influences, most of which are difficult to catch in our net of measurements: differences in "background," which mean that people who are now similar in status and location were different some years, or some generations, ago; differences in personal contacts of a wide variety, including friendship with persons of divergent values; differences in "personality," reflecting idiosyncratic aspects of life histories that may well include influences of a psycho-dynamic sort that demand Freudian explanation; and so on.

Our measures of values are useful precisely because they relate to position in physical space and social plane in a way which corresponds to common-sense observation, but at the same time catch some of the residues of variations in personal experience that go *beyond* such position. Values are part of status, and yet something more. They thus should be useful in predicting mobility: people of a given status level whose beliefs are similar to people of a higher level should attempt to behave in ways that help them (or their children) to climb up the ladder. Our data on expected education of sons and on ideal family size support this perspective.

And yet, one aspect of parsimony eludes us. It would be convenient to think of values as a perfect intervening variable, such that SES, plus location, plus personal-life experience, produce general values, and they in turn (in combination with other influences) produce specific attitudes toward education and fertility. If that were the case, values would have a higher correlation with specific attitudes than would status and location. The symmetry of theory, alas, is more elegant than the symmetry of life: status has a higher relation to expected education of sons than does modernism. And in Brazil, metropolitan location has more influence on ideal family size than do values. However, in Mexico the pattern of relations to fertility ideals matches the theoretical model.

The explanation for the divergence of the coefficients from the theoretical model may lie in the parenthetical phrase used above— "in combination with other influences." Clearly, values *alone*, even if they intervened between physical and social position and behavior, would not be enough. A man with a given set of values is also a man faced with the realities of his environment. He needs money to express his values in action; he needs friends to help him; he needs intelligence and will power and discipline to act in accordance with his ideals.[13] Now, some of these aspects of reality, if not most of them, are in turn reflections of status and location. Thus, the latter factors have another influence on behavior that goes beyond their impact on values, and in this way show up in the correlation coefficients for a second time.[14]

Unfortunately, we cannot further untangle this web of influences, since we have no adequate measures of the other factors of life experience which are tied to status and location and to the specific attitudes we are trying to predict, and which operate independently of values. And we do not know how much of the variance is escaping us simply as a consequence of the crudity of our instruments.

Those readers who enjoy diagrams are invited to follow the arrows in Figure 1.

Conclusions

In this chapter we continued the examination of the role of modern values as an independent variable, a predictor of attitudes and behavior. In the previous chapter, the effect of modernism on educational aspirations and accomplishments was shown. Here, its effect on fertility ideals was studied.

We found one major difference between Brazil and Mexico, a result contrary to the over-all results of the research, which disclosed very few differences between the two countries. Brazilians prefer smaller families than do Mexicans. Furthermore, it is particularly in the metropolitan zone that the small-family ideal is widespread in Brazil. But in Mexico, provincial-metropolitan differences are small, whereas social-status differences are large. Modern values are of help in predicting ideal family size in both countries (with SES and location held constant), but of much more help in Mexico than in Brazil.

The implications of these findings are quite important. Most studies of fertility behavior have used socio-economic status and location as the predictors—indeed, with census data, there are no alternatives. Those few studies that have attempted to measure values and add them to the basket of predictors have generally not achieved success.

[13] One particular economic fact may make a difference: secondary education is mostly private and expensive in Brazil, and mostly public and free in Mexico.

[14] The logic here is similar to that used in Appendix B in the discussion of the influence of father's status upon son's status, which is shown to have two routes: a major indirect influence via the son's education, and a minor direct influence above and beyond that education.

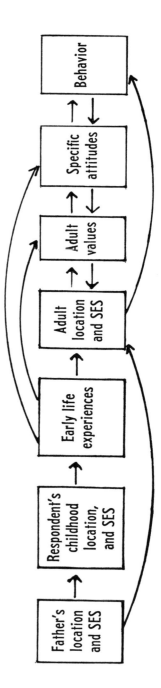

Figure I

Some Paths of Causation

Here I have demonstrated a way of using direct measures of values with profit.

"Socio-economic status" is a crude descriptive category. It implies that people with the same status will think, feel, and act alike. But that is true only "on the average." Some people at a given objective status level think like the average of another level. Furthermore, it is obviously the thoughts and feelings that produce actions, not the mere objective position by itself. Therefore, to understand the actual process by which status influences behavior, we must fill in the picture with the intervening variables that are *predicted* by status but that directly *cause* behavior. Thereby we not only increase our understanding of the average situation, but also can begin to find out why some individuals deviate from the average. I have shown that modern values are a useful intervening variable when used in this way. They predict both educational and fertility norms in a pattern which is consistent with our knowledge of the stratification system, but which goes beyond it.

Some such approach based on the study of values will be necessary to explain the striking differences on fertility ideals that we discovered between Brazil and Mexico. These differences cannot be adequately understood through the usual notions of stage of economic development, degree of urbanization, or emergence of a new middle class. The two countries are quite similar concerning those characteristics. But in Brazil, urban location is the key predictor of the modern small-family ideal, and SES makes no additional difference. In Mexico, however, both location and SES have a relatively equal but smaller impact, and values a much larger one, and in general, big families are still the norm.

Not having designed this study as primarily a research on fertility, we did not gather enough additional data to give a satisfactory explanation of these cross-national differences. But using qualitative impressions, and tidbits of questionnaire material, we advanced a hypothesis: certain general traits of Brazilian culture are more conducive to the small-family system, so that once urbanization sets in, a rapid transition occurs. But since these traits are lacking (or weaker) in Mexico, city life has less impact.

Specifically, I posit that a more relaxed style of interpersonal relationships in Brazil, more confidence in nonfamily ties, less dependence on relatives, and less emphasis on male dominance all lead to a conjugal family structure approximating the modern urban mode.

Parents see their lives as participants in the wider society; they wish to give their children an important boost (through education) toward success in that society. They plan their families as they plan their careers, in both instances depending more upon individualistic efforts than upon nepotistic favors. A small, rather than large number of children helps them gain success, just as it helps the wife participate more actively in life outside the home.

These are "average" statements about Brazil and Mexico. Obviously *some* Mexicans share the more modern view of family structure, and they should therefore prefer fewer children, whether they live in the capital city or the provinces. The partial correlation between our measures of values and those of fertility norms indicate precisely that fact.

CHAPTER VI

Personal Satisfaction and Political Attitudes

Satisfaction with life has long been a central concept in the theory of the political aspects of development. It is usually seen as a consequence of a man's level of living: the more luxurious the life style, the more content he is thought to be. And it is usually believed that satisfaction with one's lot in life leads to approval of the current social system, or an attitude of political conservatism. Thus, personal satisfaction is assumed to be an important intervening variable between economic circumstance and political action.

Marx argued that the trend of economic development was such as to impoverish manual workers—first, driving them from their traditional roles in agriculture to less adequate positions in urban factories and slums, and second, lowering factory wages to bare subsistence. The result, he said, would be discontent, eventually producing revolution.

Recent historical experience with the more mature stages of industrialization suggests a curvilinear pattern: there may well be some deterioration of the position of manual workers at the beginning of the process, but as capital accumulates, machines get more efficient. Eventually the rate of population growth declines, and a much larger product receives a more equitable distribution, so both the absolute and the relative positions of the manual workers improve.[1] This trend is often used as an explanation of the decline of organized radical protest in the United States and Western Europe since the end of the Second World War.[2]

One of the unsolved problems in this general theory is the question of absolute-versus-relative levels of living as determinants of satisfaction. Do people become content once they have passed from some

[1] See Gláucio Ary Dillon Soares, "Economic Development and Political Radicalism" (unpublished doctoral dissertation, St. Louis, Washington University, 1965). Also Torcuato S. Di Tella, *La teoría del primer impacto del crecimiento económico.*

[2] At the moment of writing, there continues to be a persistent group of perhaps 20 per cent of the population in the United States that is not sharing in the general

objectively determinable level of poverty to a level of comfort? Or do they constantly compare themselves to others, and thus continue to feel unfortunate if most others are better off than they are, regardless of their absolute level of comfort?[3]

Another unsolved problem of relativity in judgments concerns the importance of very recent changes. It is sometimes argued that men are constantly evaluating their present circumstances by comparisons with the recent past and the near future, so that they become discontent if things are getting worse, or threaten to get worse, or if promised gains are about to be denied. According to this view, long-term and stable poverty leads to resignation, but short-term losses produce protest.

Although I shall in passing touch upon a few of these general themes of political sociology, I mention them mainly to indicate a background. My main purpose here is a narrow one: to present three alternative measures of personal satisfaction, and several attempts to link them to level of living on the one hand, and political attitudes on the other. I seek to test the relative utility of these three measures, rather than prove a theory of political protest. The measures are: Job Satisfaction, Career Satisfaction, and Life Satisfaction. Let us begin with the first two of them.

Job and Career Satisfaction

When a man evaluates his job, he can take a short- or a long-term perspective. The short-term perspective emphasizes concrete characteristics of the job: the adequacy of the pay in relation to the particular type of job; the temperament of the boss; the congeniality of the workmates; the distance to be traveled each day from home; the specific nature of the tasks. The long-term perspective, however, is more likely to relate the job to the individual's over-all career pattern: Is the pay adequate for the family's needs at this stage of the life cycle? Is the job a step forward? Does it lead toward where the man wants to go? Is it about what he had anticipated in advance that he

---

affluence, but it is subdivided into politically ineffective segments—old people, adolescent unemployed, marginal farmers, and so on—who react more with apathy than protest. Only when combined with racial discrimination does poverty produce protest in the contemporary American home.

[3] Evidence on percentage of family income saved supports the relative theory, since that percentage remains constant even though average family income keeps rising through time. See James S. Duesenberry, *Income, Saving and the Theory of Consumer Behavior.*

would have achieved at his current age? Is it appropriate for a man of his background?

To take a sharp example: a man with high ambitions to be an executive may be willing to take a low-level clerical or sales job when he first gets out of school and starts to work, so long as he feels that the job is merely a temporary preparation for something better—in other words, if it fits into his scheme of "working his way up in the company." But if he still has the "temporary" job twenty years later, he will think of it as a dead-end which symbolizes failure.

Immediate job satisfaction is obviously not the same thing as long-term career satisfaction. Nevertheless, we should expect the two attitudes to have some relation to each other, especially if we are measuring them for a large sample of men. For instance, there will be some men without any long-term ambitions; they are likely to respond to a question about career satisfaction with a short-term perspective, similar to their response to a question about their particular job of the moment. And for many men, the two questions will intertwine: their feelings about their current job and their feelings about their lifelong careers will influence one another.

Our data confirm these speculations, insofar as Job Satisfaction and Career Satisfaction are related, but only moderately.

Career Satisfaction was measured by one question: "Compared to your hopes when you first started to work, would you say that you have gotten further than you expected, or not as far?" There were three precoded answers; figures indicate the percentage of men giving each response:

	BRAZIL	MEXICO
1) Not as far as I expected	16	10
2) Equal with what I expected	35	22
3) Further than I expected	49	68
Total	100	100

Job Satisfaction was measured by three separate questions:

"Are you satisfied with your present job?":

	BRAZIL	MEXICO
1) Not at all	03	06
2) A little	23	38
3) Somewhat	36	31
4) Very much	38	25
Total	100	100

"Which of these phrases comes closest to your opinion about your present job?":

	BRAZIL	MEXICO
1) It's a bad job	02	02
2) It's a job, like any other	18	28
3) It's a good job	53	56
4) It's a fine job	27	14
Total	100	100

"What is your plan for the future?":

	BRAZIL	MEXICO
1) Remain in the job I now have in this company	20	21
2) Try to get a promotion in this company	47	37
3) Look for a better job in another company	07	11
4) Start a business of my own	26	31
Total	100	100

A glance at the distribution of responses to the items shows that most men are quite satisfied with their jobs and with their careers. The differences between the two countries are small but interesting: the Mexicans, as compared to the Brazilians, rate a little higher on Career Satisfaction but a little lower on Job Satisfaction: perhaps long-term success raises short-term expectations.

Between half and two-thirds of the men indicated that they like their jobs more than just a little, and that they have gotten further in life than they expected. However, comparative studies show that men usually will respond favorably to questions of this type, so that the percentage of contented respondents should not be taken as a sign of special euphoria in Brazil and Mexico.[4] What we are really interested in are the *reasons* why some men are satisfied and some are not —that is, in the differences in attitudes toward work among various groups of men.

We naturally have more confidence in a measure that combines information from several attitude items than in a measure consisting of only one, for a multi-item index is a more reliable instrument, canceling out some of the idiosyncratic reactions to the wording of a given question. Unfortunately, for Career Satisfaction we have but the one question; however, the three questions concerning Job Satisfaction were combined into a single index after factor analysis in-

[4] See Robert Blauner, "Work Satisfaction and Industrial Trends in Modern Society," in *Labor and Trade Unionism*, ed. W. Galenson and S. M. Lipset.

dicated that they reflected a single dimension. The range of scores on that index was then divided into three approximately equal groups in each country, which I shall hereafter call Low, Medium, and High on Job Satisfaction.[5]

Life Satisfaction

We have one question on a general appraisal of life chances that was used in both countries (again, figures indicate the percentage of men giving each response):

"If things continue as they are, do you think that you will have opportunities to improve your life?":

	BRAZIL	MEXICO
1) Yes, many	13	26
2) Yes, some	38	41
3) Few	31	23
4) None	18	10
Total	100	100

Two additional items, suggested by Tumin's[6] work in Puerto Rico, were added in Mexico:

[5] In Brazil (but not Mexico) the last question was dichotomized, and men who intended to stay in the company were classed as "satisfied," and those who intended to leave as "dissatisfied." For Brazil, the three items had loadings of .81, .79, and —.56, respectively, on a principal axis factor; the scale score weighted each item in proportion to its loading. For Mexico, the loadings were .83, .82, and —.50.

[6] Melvin M. Tumin, *Social Class and Social Change in Puerto Rico*, Chap. 10. Tumin found a generally high level of life satisfaction, and attributed it to special aspects of Puerto Rican development and politics. But the Brazilians and the Mexicans show up as satisfied with the state of things as Puerto Ricans, if not more so. The generally high level of satisfaction in Brazil and Mexico is also shown by the following questions:

In Brazil, respondents were asked whether they now live in a place different from the one where they lived at age ten. Then, those who had moved were asked whether the move had made life better or worse. The answers, by percentage:

49 had not moved
02 life got worse
08 life didn't change
25 life got a little better
16 life got much better.

In Mexico, those in the provinces were asked whether life had changed in recent years, and if so, were the changes good for them:

16 changes were bad
15 were no changes
62 changes were good
07 changes were very good.

"Do you think you have more, the same, or fewer opportunities than the majority of people in Mexico to get the good things in life?":

1)	More	36
2)	The same	52
3)	Fewer	12
	Total	100

"Compared to the average, do you think life has been good for you?":

1)	Good	53
2)	Fair	45
3)	Bad	02
	Total	100

The three items used in Mexico intercorrelated with one another in the twenties, and produced a common factor with loadings of .71, .74, and .66, respectively. A composite scale was constructed from them, using the factor weights and reversing signs, then dividing into quartiles; I call it Life Satisfaction.

Relations among the Three Indices of Satisfaction

In both countries, men who had gotten further ahead in their careers than they themselves had anticipated scored high on Job Satisfaction about 40 per cent of the time. By contrast, men who had not gotten as far as expected were highly satisfied with their jobs only 20 per cent of the time. The correlation coefficient between the two measures was .24 in Brazil and .25 in Mexico.

The Mexican migrants to the capital city were asked whether the move had made their lives better or worse:

05	much worse
12	a little worse
12	neither better nor worse
46	a little better
25	much better.

Those who were born in and still lived in the capital city were asked whether life had changed in recent years, and if so, were the changes good for them:

04	changes were bad
14	were no changes [or no answer]
67	changes were good
15	changes were very good.

The limited variance on these responses and lack of comparability between countries kept us from using them in subsequent calculations.

In Mexico, Life Satisfaction correlated .25 with Job Satisfaction, but only .11 with Career Satisfaction.

Satisfaction, Occupation, and Location

Alex Inkeles has collated data from six countries on job satisfaction as a function of occupational level.[7] He reports that in general the relation is positive—the higher the level of a man's job, the more he likes it, a finding which might appear to be nothing more than a confirmation of the "obvious." But there is a hint of one slight reversal in the pattern: where the data are detailed enough to show separate categories for skilled manual workers and low white-collar workers, the latter are slightly less satisfied than the former, despite the fact that they are usually thought to occupy a somewhat higher position in the occupational hierarchy.[8]

Inkeles also compiled comparative data for thirteen countries on a question almost identical to ours on career satisfaction, and these data are much less regular than those for job satisfaction. That is, men with high occupations tend to be more satisfied than those with low positions, but the differences are not pronounced, and indeed, in some countries the white-collar workers are the least satisfied of all men.[9] Here the facts begin to depart from the "obvious."

The Brazilian data are even more at variance with the "obvious." On Job Satisfaction, there is no noticeable correlation with occupational level, and on Career Satisfaction, the correlation is small but negative ($-.17$). In Mexico, there is a small positive correlation between occupation and Job Satisfaction (.21); none between occupation and Career Satisfaction; and a more marked positive relation of .31 between occupation and Life Satisfaction.

The mean scores shown in Table 19 give a more detailed portrait. Inspecting the average for "All locations," and comparing the four occupational strata with one another, one sees no clear linear relation between status and all the measures of satisfaction, although it exists for Job Satisfaction and Life Satisfaction in Mexico. Indeed, for some of the scales there is a definite nonlinear relation: the high nonmanual and the high manual men are somewhat more content, and the low nonmanual and low manual men are somewhat less content (when

[7] Alex Inkeles, "Industrial Man," *American Journal of Sociology*, LXVI (July 1960), 1-31.
[8] *Ibid.*, Table 1.
[9] *Ibid.*, Table 7.

TABLE 19

Satisfaction, by Occupation and Location

OCCUPATION AND LOCATION	MEAN SCORE ON JOB SATISFACTION		MEAN SCORE ON CAREER SATISFACTION		MEAN SCORE ON LIFE SATISFACTION
	BRAZIL	MEXICO	BRAZIL	MEXICO	MEXICO
High nonmanual					
Metropolitans	2.3	2.4	2.1	2.5	3.3
Migrants	...	2.4	...	2.7	3.4
Provincials	1.6	2.7	2.1	2.5	3.3
All locations	2.2	2.4	2.1	2.5	3.3
Low nonmanual					
Metropolitans	1.7	2.2	2.0	2.6	2.9
Migrants	2.0	1.8	2.3	2.6	2.6
Provincials	1.9	2.0	2.3	2.6	2.5
All locations	1.8	2.1	2.1	2.6	2.7
High manual					
Metropolitans	2.0	2.1	2.4	2.6	2.6
Migrants	2.4	2.1	2.6	2.7	2.6
Provincials	1.9	1.7	2.6	2.6	2.0
All locations	2.1	1.9	2.5	2.6	2.3
Low manual					
Metropolitans	2.0	1.9	2.3	2.6	2.5
Migrants	2.3	1.8	2.5	2.7	2.0
Provincials	1.8	1.7	2.5	2.6	1.9
All locations	2.0	1.8	2.4	2.6	2.2
All men	2.0	2.0	2.3	2.6	2.5

NOTE: Job Satisfaction and Career Satisfaction range from a low of 1 to a high of 3, but their distributions are markedly different, as described in the text; thus scores on one of them should not be compared to the other. Life Satisfaction is a quartile scale.

foremen are singled out from other high manual workers, they often show exceptionally high satisfaction scores). And even more surprising is the lack of parallel between the two countries on any given satisfaction scale. There may be two simultaneous but contradictory forces at work: (1) a tendency for satisfaction to grow in a linear manner with absolute status level; (2) a tendency for relative judgments to take place *within* the manual and nonmanual categories, so that a man at the bottom of either group feels deprived, and a man at the top of either one feels elated.

If occupation shows no clear and consistent power to predict satisfaction, what about location? Are migrants to the big city suffering from disorganization and *anomie*? Or do they find the city more rewarding than the countryside? Do provincials reflect the quiet contentment of integrated communities? Or, by contrast, do provincials feel stuck at the margins of an exciting new society and respond with discontent? Our data do not give a consistent series of answers. Depending upon the measure of satisfaction one chooses, the level of occupation within which to make comparisons, or the country, the observer can answer any of the contradictory questions in the affirmative. For example, among high nonmanual workers, the metropolitans are higher on Job Satisfaction than the provincials in Brazil, but the reverse is true in Mexico. Or, among high manual workers, the migrants are happier about their jobs and their lives than are provincials, but show no difference in judgments about their careers.

Obviously the three measures of satisfaction do not all reflect a single dimension of well-being. Job Satisfaction and Career Satisfaction include questions that ask a man about his own specific feelings, whereas Life Satisfaction queries him about his rewards *relative* to the average in his country. Therefore, the latter should more closely reflect objective facts: a man at the lower end of the hierarchy, even if he likes it, will tend to recognize that others have more than he does. But because the scales of Job Satisfaction and Career Satisfaction ask directly about a man's own feelings, some men of objectively low position may (for reasons we shall explore) report that they are contented.

Furthermore, the experiences of men in general strata such as "high manual workers in metropolitan areas" are not likely to be homogeneous. Some will have had success after success; others will have suffered a series of failures. Therefore we must deal with the specific personal situations of more homogeneous types of men in order to get a better understanding of the paths to contentment.

In other words, we need a theory of satisfaction more complex than the "obvious" one that objective facts like occupational level (or geographic location) automatically determine a subjective feeling of satisfaction with job, career, and life.

Thus, one conclusion can be presented at this point: Theorists who generalize about the subjective experiences of such strata as "migrants" or "new industrial proletariats" or "emerging urban middle classes" have a burden of proof that there is an empirical reality that corresponds to their abstractions.

Time Sequence: Satisfaction Relative to Aspiration

A promising line of analysis would seem to emerge from the well-known fact that a feeling of satisfaction is the result of the ratio between reward and desire. Satisfaction does not reflect achievement in a direct fashion, but only in terms of the original goals that a man set for himself. Therefore attitudes are developed as a consequence of experiences in life that succeed one another in time.

This more complex approach to the explanation of satisfaction—relating rewards with expectations—is supported by a study by Form and Geschwender.[10] They questioned manual workers only (545 of them in Lansing, Michigan, in 1950-1951). They found that mobility was positively associated with satisfaction, and the relation held up whether they measured the mobility of the respondent by comparing his position with that of his father, or his brothers, or his peers (other men of the same level of origin).

However, Form and Geschwender do not conclude from this that a man starts with a given level of aspiration and judges all subsequent experience by that original goal. Indeed, they posit that goals change under the impact of experience, so that manual workers eventually come to believe that white-collar positions are beyond their reach, regardless of what they may have dreamed of as youths, because they see that most manual workers do not climb out of that category. And the authors posit that those few manual workers who experience some mobility, or see it around them among men who are close enough to them to influence their thoughts—such as their brothers—will begin to raise their sights toward higher positions. If they fail to advance toward these new goals, they will then feel frustrated and dissatisfied. The evidence presented is indirect, and is based primarily on the observation that older manual workers are more satisfied than younger ones, an observation which appears to indicate that they have adjusted their aspirations to gloomy reality.[11]

Studies by Samuel A. Stouffer and associates during the Second World War add strength to this line of reasoning, for they found that military units with higher *actual rates* of promotion were the ones

---

[10] William H. Form and James A. Geschwender, "Social Reference Basis of Job Satisfaction," *American Sociological Review*, 27 (April 1962), 228-230.

[11] In our data, there is no correlation between age and satisfaction.

with higher *expectations* of promotion and therefore with higher felt frustration, since the hopes outran the reality.[12]

We face here a difficult problem of measurement: the aspirations of men, particularly at a point of time long before the interview took place. We tried a direct question:

"When you started to work, just after leaving school, did you have some special occupation that you wanted to follow? What was it?"

Exactly one-quarter of the Brazilians and an astonishing two-thirds of the Mexicans reported that they had no particular occupation as a goal in their youth. If we concern ourselves only with those who did state some occupation as a goal, and compare their current occupations with their original goals, we get a measure of Career Realization. Strangely enough, it had no significant relation to the direct question on Career Satisfaction ("Compared to your hopes when you first started to work, would you say that you have gotten further than you expected, or not as far?"). We must conclude, then, that direct questions about early aspirations are of little use.

Why should the subjective awareness of success be unrelated to the actual course of a man's career accomplishment? It seems that the original goals were not very realistic, and therefore perhaps are no longer kept in mind as bench marks of achievement. For instance, almost all of those manual workers who had any goals at all in mind indicated skilled work as their aim; only four men in the whole Brazilian sample, and twenty-five in the Mexican sample, indicated unskilled or semiskilled work as a goal, despite the fact that about a quarter of the men were holding such jobs. Similarly, a substantial number of white-collar men indicated professional work as their original goal, even though most of them did not have the needful university education.

As we had no success in realistically measuring the youthful aspirations of our sample by a direct question, we tried indirect measures. We assumed that a man learns his aspirations about life from his family orientation. The simplest version of this assumption (which we shall follow for the moment) is that a man seeks goals in life proportionate to the achievements of his father. A more complex

[12] Samuel A. Stouffer, *Social Research to Test Ideas*, Chap. 2; originally published in *The American Soldier* (Princeton, N.J., Princeton University Press, 1949). Durkheim's classic analysis of *anomie* among the mobile members of society also supports the theoretical position I am taking in the text; see his *Suicide* (1897).

version (which we will explore later) is that his father's teachings may include ambitions for the son to achieve what the father himself failed to reach.

If a man's goals start with his father's style of life, then men who have climbed above their fathers should feel a special sense of accomplishment and satisfaction. We thus measured Intergenerational Mobility—the difference between a man's current job level and that of his father—but found that there was *no* relation to Job Satisfaction, Career Satisfaction, or Life Satisfaction.

Measuring the level of a man's current job against his first job produces an index of Career Mobility. It was *not* related to the measures of satisfaction.

When we take a shorter time span into account, the prediction is somewhat better. In both countries, improvement in level of living within the past five years (as judged by the respondent) has a correlation of about .25 with Job Satisfaction and Career Satisfaction, and a coefficient about half that size with Life Satisfaction.

Education, Occupation, and Satisfaction

There is one indirect measurement of aspiration that should be a realistic index of early goals: education. In modern society, formal education is designed to prepare men for jobs. Primary schooling leads to manual occupations, and secondary schooling to white-collar jobs. The tight relation between education and occupation is shown by the correlation coefficients of .72 in Brazil and .67 in Mexico. We can assume that a man enters the occupational world with ambitions roughly commensurate with his formal education. Furthermore, since a father expresses his ambitions for his son by encouraging him to achieve a certain level of education, the son's education is probably a better measure of the aspirations he learned at home than is the occupational level of the father; the son's education is a result of both his father's status *and* his father's mobility aspirations for his son.

Men with *low* education and *high* job level should be the most satisfied, for they have reached positions beyond what they were trained to have; those with high education, in relation to their job level, should be the least satisfied.

We can test these hypotheses with the data shown in Table 20. Starting with white-collar men who have had at least some secondary education, there are six possible comparisons on Job Satisfaction. In each instance, the high nonmanual workers profess more Job Satis-

TABLE 20

Satisfaction, by Education and Occupation

EDUCATION AND OCCUPATION	MEAN SCORE[1] ON JOB SATISFACTION		MEAN SCORE[1] ON CAREER SATISFACTION		MEAN SCORE[1] ON LIFE SATISFACTION
	BRAZIL	MEXICO	BRAZIL	MEXICO	MEXICO
Postsecondary					
High nonmanual	2.1	2.4	2.4	2.5	3.4
Low nonmanual	1.6[2]	1.9[2]	2.1	2.4	3.1
Complete secondary					
High nonmanual	2.2	2.6	2.0	2.6	3.4
Low nonmanual	1.7[2]	2.1[2]	1.9	2.4	3.1
High manual	...	1.9	...	2.6	2.8
Incomplete secondary					
High nonmanual	2.3	2.4	2.1	2.7	2.9
Low nonmanual	1.9[2]	2.0[2]	2.1	2.7	2.5
High manual	1.7	2.1	2.2	2.5	2.8
Low manual	...	1.4[2]	...	2.4	2.6
Complete primary					
Low nonmanual	2.2	2.2	2.4	2.7	2.5
High manual	2.1	1.9	2.5	2.6	2.3
Low manual	2.0	1.9	2.4	2.7	2.2
Incomplete primary					
Low nonmanual	2.0	2.1	2.6	2.6	2.4
High manual	2.1	1.9	2.6	2.7	2.1
Low manual	2.1	1.9	2.5	2.7	2.2

[1] All cells with mean scores contain ten or more respondents.

[2] Difference between this figure and the one immediately above it is significant at 0.5 level.

faction than the low nonmanual workers. With respect to Career Satisfaction, four of the six comparisons show a small (nonsignificant) trend in the expected direction, and two are tied. The three comparisons on Life Satisfaction are in the expected direction. Thus thirteen of fifteen contrasts support the hypothesis that a higher degree of objective job success is related to a higher degree of satisfaction, provided education and, we assume, original aspirations are held constant.

Let us turn to manual workers.[13] For those with incomplete second-

[13] It should be kept in mind that our samples include only steadily employed men; the underemployed men in the construction trades and petty services, who constitute a substantial proportion of the very poor in Latin American towns and cities, are excluded.

ary or complete primary training, the pattern holds (albeit weakly) as expected in both countries (there is one reversal). For those with only partial primary education, the data are inconclusive.

Consequently, we can conclude that to this point there are some trends in the results which support the theoretical perspective of relativism in satisfactions, but the data are far from conclusive.

Income and Satisfaction

As reported earlier in this chapter, zero-order correlations between the three measures of satisfaction and occupational level produced small and inconsistent coefficients; indeed, the relations were not consistently linear. If we substitute either education or identification for occupation, the patterns are equally confusing. But if we use income, there is a more consistent result; with one exception, the correlations are positive, and they are slightly higher than they were in the other status indices. The zero-order coefficients with income are:

	BRAZIL	MEXICO
Job Satisfaction	.16	.33
Career Satisfaction	−.06	.04
Life Satisfaction	...	.44

Apparently our respondents are rather materialistic: they sense the good life when they have money in their pockets. This is especially true among nonmanual workers, for by comparison with manual workers, income predicts their Job Satisfaction with coefficients that are about ten points higher.

But again we must ask whether the reaction to a given income is the same for all persons, or on the contrary, whether the size of the paycheck is evaluated in terms of the status level of the respondent. Theory would suggest that each status group is likely to have its own idea of an "appropriate" income, and react accordingly in terms of felt satisfaction.[14]

---

[14] The problem of a man's relative ranking on different status hierarchies—education, occupation, identification, income, etc.—is referred to in the literature as "status crystallization" or "status consistency." Lenski found that lack of crystallization tends to produce somewhat more radical political opinions, and Jackson has related it to mental stress. See Gerhard E. Lenski, "Status Crystallization: a Non-Vertical Dimension of Social Status," *American Sociological Review*, 19 (August 1954), 405-413; and Elton F. Jackson, "Status Consistency and Symptoms of Stress," *ibid.*, 27 (August 1962), 469-480.

To test that idea, we will once again use education as our measure of initial aspirations, and assume that the men in each educational level expect rather similar rewards from life. If we control for education, the partial correlations with income become:

	BRAZIL	MEXICO
Job Satisfaction	.25	.33
Career Satisfaction	.07	.13
Life Satisfaction	. . .	.31

Notice that controlling for education improves the prediction of satisfaction. Thus, by comparison with the zero-order coefficients, the partial coefficient between income and Job Satisfaction goes up .09 points in Brazil, though it stays the same in Mexico. The partial coefficient between income and Career Satisfaction increases .13 points in the positive direction in Brazil and .09 points in Mexico.

But the partial correlation between income and Life Satisfaction in Mexico decreases. Is that a contradiction to my theory? Not at all, since I have said that the measure of Life Satisfaction is quite different from those of Job Satisfaction and Career Satisfaction. The latter two measures ask in fixed (or absolute) terms: Are you satisfied? Life Satisfaction, by contrast, asks: Are you well off *in comparison to the average?* Thus, this measure should more closely reflect a respondent's actual position in the status hierarchy; *regardless* of his initial aspirations, he should be able to look around him and recognize how his rewards compare with those of others. People high in the status system should report ample rewards; people low in the status system should report deprivation. Therefore, if we subtract the effect of one status index (education) from another (income), we should reduce the power to predict satisfaction. The partial coefficient should be lower than the zero-order coefficient, as in fact it is.

What is the effect of modernism? We expected that it too would be an index of aspirations. Thus we predicted that the relation between income and Job Satisfaction and Career Satisfaction would go up if modernism was controlled, but the data did not support the hypothesis.[15]

---

[15] However, one scale within modernism showed a consistent connection with Job Satisfaction and Career (not Life) Satisfaction: men who were opposed to big companies were less satisfied. Perhaps all three scales tap the same general dimension of discontent.

Measures of Radical Orientation

As measures of a radical posture toward the social and political order, we developed two indices.

The first index included two items:

"With respect to foreign capital, what is your opinion?":

1) Foreign capital *is necessary* for the development of Brazil (Mexico), and Brazil (Mexico) ought to do everything so that foreign companies would come to the country.

2) Foreign capital *could contribute* to the development of Brazil (Mexico), and Brazil (Mexico) ought, with some care, to act so that some selected foreign companies would come to the country.

3) Foreign capital *could be harmful* for the development of Brazil (Mexico), and Brazil (Mexico) ought not to permit other foreign companies to come to the country.

4) Foreign capital *is very harmful* to the development of Brazil (Mexico), and Brazil (Mexico) ought to nationalize all the foreign companies that now exist and not permit others to come.

The percentage distributions of responses in the two countries were:

	BRAZIL	MEXICO
...is necessary	16	28
...could contribute	44	45
...could be harmful	10	09
...is very harmful	15	17
...no opinion	15	01
Total	100	100

"What is your opinion with respect to the role of government in economic life?":

1) The government ought not to mix in economic life, and ought to leave it to private enterprise.

2) The government ought not to have industries, but ought to control the activities of private enterprise.

3) The government, besides controlling private enterprise, ought to own basic industries.

4) The government ought to own the majority of industries and control all economic life.

The percentage distributions of responses in the two countries were:

	BRAZIL	MEXICO
. . . not mix	06	13
. . . control	26	36
. . . own basic industries	21	23
. . . own most industries	23	25
. . . no opinion	24	03
Total	100	100

The two items intercorrelated .15 in Brazil and .20 in Mexico, and factor analysis indicated that they reflected a single dimension. Furthermore, their pattern of relation to other variables was identical. Therefore we combined them into a single index which we call Radicalism.[16] In this instance, the concept of a radical orientation means an emphasis on socialism *and* nationalism. In Latin America, the two are almost always joined together, since capitalism is identified with North American "imperialism."

Radicalism correlates about $-.25$ with socio-economic status in both countries; it makes no difference whether status is measured by the index of SES, or occupation, or education, or income; the relation to identification is slightly lower. The pattern is linear.

In Mexico, we had two additional items indicating protest toward the system (percentage distributions of responses):

"Which statement do you prefer?":

1) Mexico is much better off today because we had the Revolution.	78
2) The Revolution hasn't solved our problems.	22
Total	100

"Do you believe that the political parties that exist now are providing adequate solutions for the problems of Mexico?":

1) Always	23
2) Sometimes	47

---

[16] The items were written by Gláucio A. D. Soares. It could be argued that the term "Radicalism" for this scale is a misnomer, since government participation in the economy is not seen by many Latin Americans as being very radical. Yet in world-wide perspective, the items have a left-wing, though certainly not a revolutionary, flavor. Let the reader remember the operational definition, and not allow other connotations of the word "radical" to distract him.

3) Rarely	21
4) Never	9
Total	100

These two items were intercorrelated with a coefficient of .19. Because factor analysis, and the pattern of relation to other variables, indicated that the items reflected a common attitude, they were combined into an index called Anti-the-Revolution. Since only one political party, the official organ of the Revolutionary movement, carries any weight in the country, a disillusionment with parties mainly symbolizes a withdrawal from that movement.

The ideology of the Revolution is proletarian and socialistic, but many of its actual practices aid native capitalists. So one wonders whether those who reject the present system are more likely to be working class or middle class; in a "revolutionary" society that is fifty years old, who is in the opposition? There is a negligible correlation of .04 between SES and Anti-the-Revolution, which shows that this attitude measure is not a reflection of low position in the status hierarchy, thus does not indicate the usual form of political protest. Indeed, there is no noticeable correlation between Anti-the-Revolution and the scale of Radicalism.

The relation of the two scales to the reported voting behavior of the Mexican respondents shows their validity and clarifies their meaning. There are three active political parties in Mexico, although only the official one gets many votes: PAN, the Catholic and conservative "Party of National Action," which is to the right of the government; PRI, which is the official government "Institutional Revolutionary Party"; and PPS, the "Popular Socialist Party," to the left of the government.[17] The supporters of PAN averaged 2.2 on our quartile scale of Radicalism; the supporters of PRI averaged 2.6; and the supporters of PPS averaged 3.2—all differences significant at the .01 level. We can conclude that the scale of Radicalism accurately predicts voting behavior.

Interestingly enough, the scale of Anti-the-Revolution showed that supporters of both PAN and PPS rejected the official institutions to about the same degree, but supporters of PRI were significantly more in favor of them. Hence the fact that the scale is sensitive both to the

[17] Among our sample, PRI received 70 per cent of the vote in the previous election, PAN received 12 per cent, and PPS received 4 per cent. The other 14 per cent of respondents voted for smaller parties, stayed home, or declined to answer.

usual form of radical protest of a left-wing sort and also to conservative protest of a right-wing variety explains its lack of linear correlation with either SES or Radicalism.

Status, Satisfaction, and Radicalism

We return now to the original hypothesis that dissatisfaction with one's economic success is at the root of political protest.

I have already noted that Radicalism has a negative and linear relation with all the status indices, as does Life Satisfaction. But Job Satisfaction follows a more complex pattern. As noted in the discussion of Table 19, there may be some tendency for a linear relation to status, but it may be obscured by feelings of relative deprivation within each half of the manual-versus-nonmanual dichotomy: people of low status within each stratum may feel deprived. If so, then high manual workers might end up with a greater sense of satisfaction than low nonmanual workers. This pattern would be a particular version of lack of status crystallization. Until we see the parallel patterns of all the attitude measures in relation to the objective status measures, we cannot properly assess the influence of one attitude (satisfaction) upon another (Radicalism).

An additional point must be made: the radical ideology of a low-status group in society does not necessarily reflect dissatisfaction of each and every individual in the group. Once ideology emerges as a collective force, it is taught by working-class newspapers, by political and union leaders, and by group discussions on the job, and thus will be absorbed to some extent even by those who do not feel particularly unhappy. A man's attitudes reflect what Durkheim calls the "collective conscience" of his group just as much as do the particular facts of his personal life history. Therefore, with status controlled, the relation between measures of dissatisfaction and measures of Radicalism should simply show the small additional effect of private misery—the unhappy man's especial susceptibility to protest. Here one faces another of the peculiar problems of testing with cross-sectional survey data a general idea that emerged from a theory of history.

The details in Table 21 help us unravel the complexities of the situation. The table shows the patterns for Job Satisfaction and Life Satisfaction, but ignores Career Satisfaction because no consistent pattern emerged for the scale (which consists, in contrast to the others, of only a single question with limited variance). Table 21 also gives parallel mean scores for the two scales of political protest, and it

TABLE 21
Activism, Satisfaction, and Political Ideology
by Education and Income[1]

EDUCATION AND INCOME	ACTIVISM		JOB SATISFACTION[2]		LIFE SATISFACTION	RADICALISM		ANTI-THE REVOLUTION
	BRAZIL	MEXICO	BRAZIL	MEXICO	MEXICO	BRAZIL	MEXICO	MEXICO
Secondary school								
High income	3.2	3.3	2.2	2.4	3.3	2.1	2.1	2.4
Upper-middle income	*2.9[3]	**3.0	**1.7	**1.9	**2.8	2.1	*2.3	2.4
Lower-middle income	2.9	*2.7	1.5	1.8	**2.4	**2.8	2.5	2.4
All secondary	(3.0)	(3.0)	(1.8)	(2.1)	(2.9)	(2.3)	(2.3)	(2.4)
Primary school								
Upper-middle income	2.5	2.2	2.2	2.3	2.7	2.7	2.7	2.3
Lower-middle income	**2.0	**1.9	2.1	**1.9	**2.0	**3.0	*2.9	2.2
Low income	1.9	1.9	**1.8	*1.7	*1.8	2.9	2.8	2.3
All primary	(2.2)	(2.0)	(2.1)	(1.9)	(2.2)	(2.9)	(2.8)	(2.3)

[1] Income is defined as follows: the respondents in each country were first dichotomized by education, then divided into approximate thirds by income within each educational stratum.

[2] Job Satisfaction is a tercile scale, the others quartiles.

[3] Significance test with next higher figure in the column: * = .05 level; ** = .01 level.

adds information about Activism.[18] Income is varied, and education is controlled.

The combination of education and income predicts Activism in a way that produces a linear decline for both countries in mean scores from the top to the bottom of Table 21. The difference between the top group and the bottom group is very large, and despite the overlap

[18] Modernism as a whole shows the same pattern as Activism, but not all subscales within it; to emphasize that point, Activism is used here.

in incomes between some primary-school men and some secondary-school men, the linearity of belief is not affected. Here is our strongest evidence for group culture, for "collective conscience," in which both education and income, in a *cumulative* manner, define group membership, which in turn produces value orientation. (When Table 21 is dichotomized into manual and nonmanual workers, instead of primary and secondary education, the results are the same.)

The scale of Life Satisfaction behaves in a manner parallel to that of Activism, except for a reversal which puts men at the bottom of the secondary-education group somewhat behind those at the top of the primary-education group, a reversal which suggests a hint of relative deprivation added to the over-all linear relation.

The contrast with Job Satisfaction is most illuminating. Bear in mind that the questions here are the most subjective of all: they ask a man whether he is satisfied or not, without specific reference to his objective position relative to other men in the status hierarchy. Yet his judgments obviously show that he uses a certain relative sense of reward or deprivation, and that it operates only *within* his educational stratum, not all the way across the status hierarchy. There is *no* difference, *on the average*, between men with secondary and those with primary educations. Yet within each educational stratum, income and satisfaction go hand in hand. And occupation can be substituted for education with identical results.

What about political ideology? Radicalism shows a predominantly negative and linear relation to socio-economic status; it is more similar in pattern (though in reverse direction) to Activism and Life Satisfaction than it is to Job Satisfaction. On the average, secondary-school men are conservative, and primary-school men are radical. We see here the effects of group culture. Within each stratum, low income adds somewhat to radical views.[19]

The scale of rejection of the Revolutionary institutions in Mexico is not related to either education or income.

The patterns in Table 21 are especially interesting, for they show the way position in the social structure affects attitudes and values in a complex manner. Some of the latter are linearly related to socio-economic status, and some are not; some are influenced by lack of consistency between educational and income levels, some are not. But

[19] The partial correlation of income with Radicalism, controlling education, was —.17 in Brazil and —.10 in Mexico. The zero-order correlation of either income or education with Radicalism was approximately —.25 in both countries.

these differences are not random; indeed, they are perfectly under-standable. General values like Activism are rather direct reflections of status, and each status variable simply adds to the cumulative effect. Life Satisfaction behaves similarly (though with an added possibility of relative deprivation), for the very content of the items asks a man to relate his rewards in life to the general average for his country, and most men can recognize the objective reality of their own position. And Radicalism behaves in a similar way.

But Job Satisfaction is much more subjective; the items ask a man whether he likes his job or not. Here the objective facts about the job are deeply intermingled with each man's expectations. A man who has some status characteristics—like education, or membership in a general occupational category—that lead him to expect high rewards, but in terms of other status characteristics—like income—receives puny returns, is going to be an unhappy man. Thus, instead of a linear pattern when education and income are combined as predictors, we find no contrast between broad educational strata, but a linear pattern by income within those strata.

So far I have been predicting each value or attitude directly from status characteristics. There remains one question: Does one attitude directly affect another? Does dissatisfaction with one's job lead to a radical disposition, *with status position controlled?*

For this question, partial correlations can be used. Let us control for income, and vary Job Satisfaction. If the latter has a direct influ-ence upon Radicalism, it should show up in the partial-correlation coefficients. But in fact the partials with Radicalism are negligible: .03 in Brazil, and .05 in Mexico. Therefore it appears from the data that an attitude of political radicalism can best be predicted directly from status position, without using Job Satisfaction as an intervening variable. And Life Satisfaction can be substituted for Job Satisfaction with similar results.

Mexican Manual Workers

Many of the items used in Mexico concerning politics and union activities have a clearer meaning for manual workers than for white-collar workers, for the latter less often participate in unions, and their view of the social system tends to be somewhat different. Therefore let us examine the zero-order correlations between our two scales of

TABLE 22
Zero-Order Correlations between Political Ideology
and Various Characteristics: Mexican Manual Workers

| | CORRELATION COEFFICIENTS | |
	RADICALISM	ANTI-THE-REVOLUTION
Age (older)	.03	.10
Income (higher)	−.17	.03
Metropolitan Location	−.13	.02
Modernism	−.24	−.05
Activism	−.19	−.03
Anti Big Companies	−.01	.07
Individualism	−.13	.01
Low Stratification of Life Chances	−.16	.02
Pro Urban Life	−.14	−.11
Trust	−.02	−.05
Risk-Taking	−.09	.02
Ease of finding another job	−.13	−.03
Prefers foreign firm	−.16	.09
Bad opinion of unions	−.12	.06
Participation in union activities	.16	−.03
Job Satisfaction	−.04	−.01
Career Satisfaction	.12	−.09
Life Satisfaction	−.08	−.09
Radicalism	. . .	.05

political attitudes and a series of other variables, *taking only Mexican manual workers into account.*[20] The coefficients appear in Table 22.

What can we learn from the list of coefficients? First of all, it should be noted that none of them is very large, so let us take a correlation of .10 or more as large enough to be worth noticing; although it is not sufficient to control much of the total variance, it is adequate to predict the views of men at the extremes of the distributions, and is statistically significant for samples of this size.

Older manual workers are a bit more disillusioned with the progress of the Revolution than younger ones, but not more radical in the usual socialist-nationalist sense of the term. Poorer workers are more radical than richer ones, as we would expect, but their position stays within the official institutions—in other words, they would like to

[20] For those measures which were also used in Brazil, the patterns were identical.

push the present system a little more toward socialism. (It is the absolute size of the income that counts, for recent changes in it do not affect ideology, despite their influence on the measures of satisfaction.)

Workers in Mexico City are more conservative than those in the provinces, a fact which will surprise many observers of Mexican life. This may reflect the fact that they get higher incomes in the capital.

Modernism, which had no consistent relation with the scales of satisfaction, does relate to Radicalism negatively. But when the sub-scales within modernism are examined, it is clear that not all of them relate to Radicalism in the same way. The Radicals, as expected, are collectivistic rather than individualistic in viewpoint, and they see life chances as highly stratified, giving the individual little chance for personal progress. But contrary to much theorizing, they are fatalistic and rural in orientation. (Such values as Trust and Anti Big Companies have no ties with Radicalism.)

Radicals are pessimistic about the chances of finding another job if they lose their present one; they prefer to work in Mexican (especially government-operated) rather than foreign firms; they believe that unions help their members, and tend to belong to them and participate in their activities.

The over-all picture is consistent—although I must reiterate that we are dealing with trends based on very small correlation coefficients: our radical manual workers are men who have become involved with the industrial system but get the least from it. In comparison to our conservative manual workers, they receive smaller wages, feel less secure about steady employment, are more likely to live in the provinces (and prefer provincial life), see little chance for personal progress, are collectivistic and union-oriented, and view the world fatalistically. They want the government to improve their lives.

By contrast, highly successful manual workers (i.e., those with the highest incomes) are likely to be middle class in viewpoint: they are prepared to pursue success as individuals in a system which they view as open to personal advancement through merit. Indeed, though it is not shown in Table 22, they are in fact more likely to identify with the middle class.[21]

In a preceding paragraph the phrase "*our* manual workers" was used as a device to remind the reader that our samples deliberately eliminated marginal men at the bottom of the blue-collar world. We

---

[21] For further details on class consciousness, see Appendix A.

included no part-time construction workers, no servants, no ditch-diggers. Even our poorest manual workers were men with steady jobs in stable enterprises. The point is important, for it would be dangerous to project our correlations outside the limits of our sampling frame, and conclude in general terms that the poorer a worker is, the more likely he is to be radical in the sense of expecting the government to help him out.

Indeed, the evidence is to the contrary. For example, Pablo González Casanova explains that the marginal man in Mexico is a traditional and submissive and apathetic man: he may have occasional fantasies of protest, but he knows that he will lose more than he gains if he raises his voice. Thus he belongs to no organizations, does not participate in elections, does not adopt a radical ideology, has little faith that the government will do anything for him. In fact, his only hope for a little gain is to have a rich or powerful *patrón* who will, as a personal favor, help him out.[22]

Thus there seems to be a curvilinear pattern: the most successful manual workers have more faith in their own efforts than in the government; those in the middle hope for government action in their behalf; those at the bottom expect little from either the government or their own actions.

Mexican Nonmanual Workers

A parallel study of white-collar workers in Mexico produces these results: age makes men a bit more conservative, as does a higher income. Activism is related negatively to Radicalism, but the same is not true of the other scales within the general complex of modernism. Urban location, or preference for urban life, has no effect on Radicalism. Radicals do not expect to find another job easily, they would rather work in Mexican firms, and they participate a little more in union activities. In other words, they tend to belong to the lower part of the nonmanual sector.[23]

Those who are Anti-the-Revolution are those with a bit more education but not more income; they have a low opinion of unions and do not participate in them, and have a high opinion of foreign firms; however, in general, they dislike large companies. In other words, they are old-fashioned free enterprisers of a *petit-bourgeois* variety.

[22] *La democracia en México*, Capítulo VII. See also Oscar Lewis, *The Children of Sánchez*.
[23] Those measures which were also used in Brazil produced similar results.

The Ambivalent Mexican

When Mexicans view the government and the political process, they are ambivalent men. In an abstract way they support the Revolution and its institutions—indeed, 78 per cent of our respondents reported that the country was better off because it had the Revolution. They say that things are slowly improving, for they see "progress" around them in the form of new schools, hospitals, roads, and industries. And yet, they are very cynical about politicians and "leaders" of various types, who seem always out to help themselves rather than the people at large. For example, 59 per cent of the respondents said that union leaders are not really interested in the ordinary workers. Mexicans support the system, but not the officials in it.[24]

Let me report an example from an interview with a foreman in a small-town textile mill. He had had four years of primary education and had worked his way up in the factory to his present position. He is more articulate and ambitious than the average among factory workers. Asked what he thought about the national elections, he responded:

"For me, the national elections are a myth, because when all is said and done, the government itself chooses the one who will be President. Everything spent on campaigns and tours should be spent to help the people with hospitals, places to find work, instead of spending millions and millions of pesos uselessly. If the government is going to pick the man who will be President, why not just say so openly?

"Besides, I'm not a follower of any party, nor do I think any of them are legal or any good. They're not serious. Just take a look at Sr. ———, director of PRI; he has his bunch of friends, and from them, chooses So-and-So to be mayor, and so on. Unfortunately, in small towns the behavior of those fellows is notorious. They don't help the progress of the towns at all.

"Once I entered PRI, because I was a supporter of the campaign of

---

[24] Our materials are consistent with those in the most detailed available survey of Mexican political attitudes, part of the comparative study of five nations conducted by Gabriel A. Almond and Sidney Verba, *The Civic Culture*; see especially Chapter XIV. For an excellent interpretation of these results in the light of Mexican society and political institutions, see Robert E. Scott, "Mexico: The Established Revolution," in Lucian W. Pye and Sidney Verba (eds.), *Political Culture and Political Development*.

Sr. ——— for governor; I liked him. He was the best governor we have had.

"I left politics because it is a dirty business. I had bad experiences; So-and-So promises a lot, but when he gets the job, he forgets everything.

"But the future of Mexico, as everybody knows, it is developing rapidly. But for me, there are still lots of defects. Mexico isn't yet a completely democratic country, because it doesn't respect the will of the people. Here in our town recently we've had a hundred men fired because the factory is modernizing. We've sent committees to Mexico City to the different government departments, but they just closed the doors on us. No other industry is coming. And there are lots of unemployed people here.

"Yet, the future of Mexico is very good in general, because Mexico in every respect is a forward-looking country and is ahead of all the others in Latin America. It is, taking into account all the countries of the world, for its doctrine, for its politics, for its mission in favor of peace and neutrality and respect for the rights of others . . ."[25]

[25] "Para mí las elecciones nacionales son un mito. Porque al fin y al cabo, el propio gobierno designa a quien va a ser el mandatario. Todo lo que se gasta en propagandas, en giras políticas, debía de emplearse en beneficio del pueblo: hospitales, centros de trabajo; y no gastar miliones y miliones de pesos infructuosamente. Si el gobierno decide quien será el mandatorio, ¿por qué no decirlo abiertamente?

"Además ni soy adicto a ningún partido, ni considero que ningún partido sea legal, ni es correcto. No hay nada de seriedad. Simplemente mire Ud al Sr.———, director del PRI; que se forma un grupo de íntimos amigos, y por capricho, de aquellos elementos, a Don Fulano para presidente municipal, etc. Desgraciadamente en los pueblos chicos es más notoria la representación de estas gentes. No ayudan para el progreso de los pueblos.

"Pues, en una ocasión si anduve metido en el PRI, precisamente que era muy simpatizador de que fuera gobernador el Sr.———, tuve muchas simpatías por él. Pues que para mí fué el mejor gobernador que ha tenido el estado.

"Salí de la política porque la política es desgraciadamente muy cochina. Tuve malas experiencias; Don Fulano promete mucho, pero llega al puesto y entonces se olvida de todo.

"Pero, el futuro de México, pues es completamente notorio, se va desenvolviendo rapidamente. Pero para mí, hay muchos defectos todavía. México no es todavía un país completamente demócrata, porque no respeta propiamente la voluntad del pueblo. Aquí en nuestro poblado hemos tenido últimamente el despido de más de cien obreros, a causa de la modernización. Se han formado comisiones, en donde han ido al Patrimonio Nacional, a Economía, a distintas dependencias, y se les han cerrado las puertas, porque no ha habido otra industria, otras personas que venga a poner una industria más. Y fíjase, hay un porcentaje grande de gente con desempleo.

"Pues, el futuro de México es muy bueno en general, porque México en todas sus ramas es un país completamente adelantado y supera casi a la totalidad de los de

This man believes that Mexico is moving forward, and he approves of general government policies. He believes that the government should take an active hand in developing industries and other benefits for the people. And yet in every personal experience with politicians he has found them crooked or useless, except perhaps for the one governor he supported. Thus he believes in a government whose representatives he distrusts.

The ambivalence of this man is quite typical, and is found at all levels of society. It is explained in part by the general cynicism which pervades Mexican culture, as discussed in the previous chapter. Since a Mexican expects everybody to be out for himself, he is not outraged by self-seeking politicians and union leaders. Nor would he anticipate that things would be very different if the political system were changed. Therefore, he does not blame the Revolutionary institutions for the chicanery of his fellow-citizens, which he sees as merely a reflection of the Mexican temperament.[26]

Conclusions

This chapter began with a query about the relation between discontent with one's lot in life and the desire for government action to improve things. It is commonly stated that discontent or frustration flows from low rewards of money and prestige, and that it leads to radicalism (in the usual sense of the term).

I developed three different measures of satisfaction (contentment with job, career, and life as a whole), and showed that not all of them relate the same way to economic rewards. A simple prediction that the richer would be the most content was not borne out by the data. Indeed, the more subjective and personal the measure of satisfaction, the more it was related to the ratio of reward to expectation. Not all men seek the same rewards, and they judge what they get in terms of what they expect to get. These subtle differences among men must be viewed in the light of a rather high average sense of satisfaction in both countries.

I developed two different measures of political protest: a scale of Radicalism, which contains a socialistic-nationalistic bent, and was

---

América Latina. Es, tomando en cuenta en todos los países del mundo—por su doctrina, por su política, por su misión pro-paz, y la neutralidad y respeto a derechos ajenos . . ."

26 For the historical roots of the Mexican temperament, see Samuel Ramos, *Profile of Man and Culture in Mexico.*

used in both countries; and a scale of Anti-the-Revolution, which was particular to Mexico. The two scales were unrelated, for the first measured proletarian protest and desire for government aid, and the second measured disillusionment with the official Mexican institutions that came from both right- and left-wing sources, and was thus not predictable from low socio-economic status (it seemed most common among those who clung to the highly individualistic values of a *petit-bourgeois* type).

Radical protest of the socialistic-nationalistic variety seems to reflect group position and group ideology more than personal frustration. The more radical men come from the lower ranges of our manual-worker respondents, plus a few low-level clerical workers. The values associated with Radicalism are collectivistic, fatalistic, and rural-oriented, and are connected with a perception of the social system that includes high Stratification of Life Chances. They are the values of traditional men who are just beginning to become involved with the industrial system, and just beginning to break out of old forms of passivity. The more successful manual workers, and the majority of nonmanual workers, are more individualistic, activistic, and urban-oriented, and see the world as open to personal advancement; they are politically more conservative.

When position in the social structure is controlled, *no additional connection between dissatisfaction and Radicalism can be noted.* Thus each of the two attitudes can be predicted directly from social structure, but one attitude does not seem to influence the other, despite much theory to the contrary.

Why are our radical men more likely to be traditionalists than modernists (holding social status constant)? There are two possible explanations. The first would be that our own concept of modernism contains some biases; the stereotype of the modern man from which it was derived referred to an urban, middle-class man who sought personal advancement through individualistic effort. Such a man is heir to Weber's Protestant businessman, although in modern times he is just as likely to be a striving bureaucrat in a socialist enterprise, or a skilled worker in a large factory. The man who does not see himself in this role, who senses that he is stuck in a fixed position at the lower ends of the hierarchy, will, therefore, according to our definitions, be both radical and traditional.

The second possible answer would be that the trends of economic development are such as to explain our findings. Before economic development begins, a traditionalist is a rural man who fatalistically accepts his position in life, and that goes for the poor as well as the rich. The poor receive little but expect little; they are conservative and traditional.

Early development shakes things up; men are dislodged from the countryside and flock to the urban factories. They get new aspirations, but the rewards are still rather small; even though they live somewhat better than before, they are still at the bottom of the hierarchy within the factory system, and they become conscious of the richer and more powerful men around them. They are still somewhat traditional in values, since they glance back toward rural ways and they continue to have a strong dose of fatalism about their personal chances. But they have changed just enough to desire advancement. Through unions and the mass media they learn about new possibilities of protest; they seek to remove the blocks to their advancement by political means. They combine old traditionalism with new Radicalism.

But those men who have been more successful in terms of their original aspirations—which means most white-collar men, and those blue-collar men with the highest incomes—react with conservative acceptance of the new system, and modernistic values of activism and personal striving.

Eventually, economic development reaches the point where there is enough for almost everybody. Education becomes more widespread, and through it, the sense of mastery over life increases. People become more satisfied with the system, and see it as open to their manipulation. A man who has unfulfilled desires tries to actively strive for advancement within the existing system. Radicalism as a whole declines; the majority of men become middle class in viewpoint.

I believe that both answers contain some truth. My definition of modernism is biased toward the middle-class view of the world, but the trend of economic development is in fact moving us slowly in that direction. Socialist protest declines in Europe and the United States; and there are even "bourgeois" trends toward "individualism," "mass consumption," and "conservativism" within the Soviet Union. A new individualism based on the competition of educated men for advancement in bureaucratic hierarchies becomes the unifying theme that replaces the old dichotomy between owners and workers with sharply different ideologies.

Only the marginal men are left out. In the United States they are now a small minority. But in Brazil and Mexico, they still outnumber the participants. They are the base for possibly violent protest movements that combine values of equalitarian solidarity among the poor, charismatic leadership of a powerful *patrón*, and magical redress of unjust exploitation. They combine traditionalism and radicalism, and represent the potentialities for sudden reversals of mood among normally passive and submissive men when they feel pushed beyond the limit of tolerance.

CHAPTER VII

Work Attitudes

Let me recapitulate to remind the reader that the general level of satisfaction with job, career, and over-all life circumstances was quite high in both countries, as measured by a series of questions shown in the previous chapter. More than 80 per cent of the men in both countries said that they had gotten at least as far in their careers as originally anticipated when they first started to work; more than 70 per cent called their jobs "good" or "fine"; about two-thirds indicated that the general trend of social changes was more in their favor than against it. And these indications of contentment were roughly similar among lifelong metropolitans, migrants to the capital cities, and provincials.

One further question can be added to show the tendency toward satisfaction among our men; the Mexicans were asked how hard it would be to find another job if they lost the one currently held. Fourteen per cent said "very hard"; 30 per cent said "rather hard"; 37 per cent said "rather easy"; and 19 per cent said "very easy"—thus the majority thought it would be easy to get another position. The nonmanual workers were the most optimistic, for 69 per cent of them, as against 48 per cent of the manual workers, thought it would be easy to find a new job.

To get a better framework for the interpretation of survey questions, let us now turn to some of the qualitative interviews about work satisfaction.[1]

---

[1] Additional qualitative studies of attitudes toward work in Brazil and Mexico can be found in J. A. Kahl (ed.), *La industrialización en América Latina*, Segunda Parte, "La fuerza de trabajo."

The Wide Range of Views

The qualitative interviews show clearly the amount of subjectivity that enters in when a man evaluates his job. Depending upon his past experiences and his accumulated expectations, he sees his work in personal terms. What looks like a good job to one man appears bad to another. For instance, a semiskilled worker in a textile factory in a small town in Mexico said:

"Well, for me it's a good job—because if it rains or thunders I don't get wet, and my wages come in safe and sure. It's different with a farmworker—if it rains, he can't work. In the factory the worker can always do his job."[2]

This man speaks from experience, for he started working as a shepherd when he was a boy, then worked long hours in a bakery before entering the factory. He says the factory is easy.

But others say that to have a factory job is to have a dull job. One man, who works in the same place as the fellow quoted above, said:

". . . it's just a routine job that I have, that my father has, that anybody has who is with us in the factory."[3]

Yet he readily admits that it is better than working as a farm laborer because the income is greater. His ambivalence is such that he occasionally studies commercial subjects like typing and bookkeeping in hopes of getting out of the factory, but he doesn't stick to his studies with enough regularity to accomplish the goal. He has finished primary school, whereas the first worker has not.

There is another man in the same factory who had only four years of primary school, but is a hard-driving, ambitious man who managed to work himself up to a foreman's position. However, despite his relatively high position he is unsatisfied, for he dreams of even more:

"Well, no, I don't really have the job that I had wanted, because I wanted to be more. My ambition is not to be satisfied with what I

---

[2] "Pues, para mí es un buen trabajo—porque yo no me mojo, si llueve o truene; yo tengo mi salario a corriente, seguro. No es igual con él del campesino, que si llueve no puede trabajar. En la fábrica sí, porque el operario siempre puede estar con su trabajo."

[3] ". . . es la rutina que tengo yo, que tiene él (su padre), y cualquiera que estamos allí en la fábrica."

am. With luck maybe I'll get ahead and get a job with more prestige.
. . . The job I have now I got by my own efforts and merits; I have
confidence in myself. I have thought of having a business separate
from my job—to leave and be completely outside the factory."[4]

Given the amount of personal subjectivity in these views of work,
it should not be expected that the questionnaires would reveal many
neat statistical patterns. But a few trends did appear, and we now turn
to them.

Specific Job Attitudes

In the questionnaire interviews the men were asked, "What do you
like *best* about your present job?" The distributions of responses are
shown in Table 23, and indicate that the possibilities of promotion,
and the opportunity to learn new things—both indicating an eye to
the future—are prevalent reasons for contentment in both countries,
and among both manual and nonmanual workers. Indeed, in Mexico
they are the most prevailing answers. However, the Brazilians are
relatively more concerned about good relations with the bosses (especially the blue-collar men) and good working conditions (especially
the white-collar men). A check indicated that scale scores on neither
Modernism I nor Job Satisfaction helped predict the particular reasons
for contentment with the present job.

When the direction of the question was reversed—"What do you
like *least* about your present job?"—the pattern of responses was
similar in both countries. The number of men who said "Nothing" or
"Don't know" jumped way up to 30 per cent in Brazil and 18 per
cent in Mexico. (It was about 1 per cent on the previous question.)
Money came to the forefront, for in both countries approximately 22
per cent of the respondents said that low salary was the prime cause
of complaint. The three other major causes of discontent were lack
of a chance to learn new things, the difficulty of promotion, and the
possibility of being dismissed.

Next, the men were asked what they considered to be the one most
important method for getting ahead in their careers. The distribution
of responses is given in Table 24, and shows that there are interesting

---

[4] "Pues, propiamente no tengo el trabajo que deseaba, porque yo quisiera todavía
ser más. Mi ambición es no conforme con lo que soy. Ojalá y tenga la suerte de
escalar y conseguir un puesto de categoría. . . . Mi ocupación que actualmente de-
sempeño ha sido por mí propia capacidad, cumplimiento y méritos—tengo confianza. He pensado de un negocio separado del puesto de empleo—separarme y ser
completamente ajeno a la empresa."

TABLE 23

Like Best about Present Job

| | PERCENTAGE | | | | | |
| | BRAZIL | | | MEXICO | | |
	ALL MEN	NONMANUAL	MANUAL	ALL MEN	NONMANUAL	MANUAL
The work is easy	03	03	03	08	03	11
Good working conditions	22	27	19	07	05	09
Good relations with bosses	24	18	29	06	07	06
Steady employment	05	07	03	16	10	20
Satisfactory salary	05	05	04	04	02	05
Interesting work	05	04	05	12	18	09
Possibilities of promotion	16	20	13	24	30	21
Opportunity to learn new things	19	15	22	22	26	19
Total	99	99	98	99	101	100

differences between countries, but practically no differences between nonmanual and manual workers. The Brazilians stress being loyal to the boss, working carefully on the job, and being friendly with work-mates, whereas the Mexicans stress saving capital to start a new business, learning new skills on the job, and working carefully. Thus the Brazilians are inclined to be more concerned about interpersonal relationships, and the Mexicans with efficient techniques and capital formation.

We were interested in determining which of these attitudes toward advancement reflected "modernism," and which ones reflected "traditionalism," so we computed the mean score on Modernism I for the men who chose each alternative. The differences were rather small, but we found that among nonmanual workers in both countries, those who chose learning new skills on the job and introducing new methods of work tended to be modernists, and in Brazil, the same was true of those who stressed working carefully on the job.

Among manual workers in both countries, those who chose introducing new methods of work and learning to deal with the public were more likely to be modernists, and those who chose loyalty to the boss, making friends with important people, and being friendly

TABLE 24

Method for Advancement

	BRAZIL			MEXICO		
	ALL MEN	NONMANUAL	MANUAL	ALL MEN	NONMANUAL	MANUAL
Be loyal to boss	26	22	28	04	02	05
Make friends with important people	03	03	03	04	05	03
Save capital and open a business	04	03	06	28	24	31
Learn to deal with public	04	05	03	02	02	02
Work carefully on job	24	27	21	20	22	19
Learn new skills on job	10	13	08	15	16	15
Get good education	05	05	05	08	10	08
Introduce new methods of work	08	11	06	10	17	06
Be friendly with workmates	16	11	20	08	03	11
Total	100	100	100	99	101	100

with workmates were traditionalists. This latter syndrome is what one would expect, since it represents the classic picture of the traditional man of low status. The neatness of the pattern is spoiled, however, by one other favorite choice—for some strange reason, Brazilians (of both status levels) who emphasized a good education were more likely to be traditionalists than modernists.

We asked the men to pick from a list the one phrase which best described themselves. The results are given in Table 25, which shows both the distribution of responses and the mean score on Modernism I for the men in each cell.

Here again, the Brazilians are more inclined to stress interpersonal relationships, and the Mexicans to stress technical efficiency. Compared to these differences between countries, the differences between white-collar and blue-collar workers are slight.

We had predicted that the answers listed in Table 25 would form a scale, with the most traditional ones at the top of the list, and the most modern ones at the bottom. To test the idea, we compared the mean scores on Modernism I for the men who gave each response. Our prediction held up in Mexico, but not in Brazil.

Similar results were obtained from a question about the type of boss that was preferred. The Mexicans (of both status levels) emphasized preference for a boss who taught new techniques, whereas the Brazilians were more likely to stress preference for a boss who was friendly and who gave orders so clearly that everyone could understand.

The respondents were asked whether or not they felt handicapped in their jobs because they had received inadequate education. As seen from Table 26, most Mexicans replied "Yes": about half of the highest group on SES, to about three-quarters of the lowest group on SES, replied that they felt a handicap. But the Brazilians felt much better prepared: fewer than a third of them reported an educational handicap. (Only the migrants of high SES diverge from the pattern.) The differences between countries are quite striking, and suggest that

TABLE 25

Self-Image as a Worker:

Percentage Distribution and Mean Score on Modernism I[1]

| | BRAZIL | | | | MEXICO | | | |
| | NONMANUAL | | MANUAL | | NONMANUAL | | MANUAL | |
	%	MEAN ON MODERNISM I	%	MEAN ON MODERNISM I	%	MEAN ON MODERNISM I	%	MEAN ON MODERNISM I
Respectful to orders of boss	30	2.8	29	2.1	05	2.7	11	1.8
Prefers friendly place	18	3.0	17	2.0	08	2.7	11	2.0
Methodical; prefers orderly and unchanging environment	12	3.5	16	2.0	20	3.0	28	2.0
Thinks up new ways on job; likes efficient place and latest techniques	32	3.2	20	2.2	44	3.2	30	2.3
Studies technical books about job	08	2.8	18	2.1	23	3.2	20	2.3
Total	100		100		100		100	

[1] Modernism I is a quartile scale, with a mean of 2.5 for the total sample in each country.

TABLE 26
Percentage Who Feel Handicapped in Job Because of
Inadequate Education, by SES and Location

	BRAZIL	MEXICO
High SES		
Metropolitans	16	53
Migrants	50	33
Provincials	18	55
Medium SES		
Metropolitans	35	69
Migrants	35	62
Provincials	40	64
Low SES		
Metropolitans	23	73
Migrants	33	74
Provincials	31	69
All men	28	64

industry and commerce in Mexico are raising the requirements for their personnel faster than in Brazil, thus creating a sense of inadequacy among employees.

Finally, I report the results of a projective question: "If you won some money in the lottery, what would you do with it?" (Only one answer was permitted.) Since the differences between white-collar and blue-collar workers were small, the results can be given without separating the groups. Responses are in percentages:

	BRAZIL	MEXICO
Pay my debts	10	06
Buy clothes, appliances, a car, or travel	05	04
Get a better house or apartment	44	19
Open a business of my own	20	28
Use it for the education of my children	14	18
Save it or invest it	07	25
	100	100

Here inflation and the intense housing shortage (especially in Rio de Janeiro) may combine to put better housing as the first choice for Brazilians, and saving as close to the last choice. By contrast, Mexicans are more interested in saving and in opening a business. (Perhaps it is worth adding that among nonmanual workers in both countries, the reply which is most often given by men with the highest mean score on Modernism I is "saving or investment.")

The desire for purchase of consumer goods is remarkably low on the priority list in both countries. This will surprise some theorists who maintain that one of the obstacles to development in Latin America is a tendency for the people to prefer immediate pleasures to future gains —especially among the new middle class. By contrast, a somewhat similar question asked in March of 1961 by the Gallup Poll in the United States indicated that the purchase of consumer goods and payments on installment debts would be the main uses of new income, far ahead of all the other possibilities.

Rating by the Boss

With the one exception reported now, our entire study dealt with the statements of the respondent about himself. Therefore I have been confined to analyzing the relations between one attitude or value and another, or the relations between those attitudes and certain background characteristics of the respondent, such as his education.

But we did get one independent bit of information. We asked the immediate supervisor of each man to rate him as a worker, on a four-point scale ranging from routine, through good, very good, to wonderful. Thus we have a measure of the behavior of the respondent as viewed and evaluated by his boss.

We predicted that there would be a positive relation between occupational status and the boss' rating, since we expected the higher-level workers to be better motivated and hence more likely to satisfy their superiors. The results confirmed the hypothesis, but only *within* the white-collar ranks and *within* the blue-collar ranks, not between them. Once more we get evidence of the sharp split between manual and nonmanual workers: each represented a separate world of work, and judgments were made within each level and without reference to the other one. The foremen, at the top of the blue-collar hierarchy, got the highest ratings of any men. Skilled manual and unskilled manual workers got lower ratings, in that order. And the high white-collar workers received higher ratings than the low white-collar workers. The data are shown in Table 27.

Furthermore, we had hoped that with occupational level controlled, there would be a positive relation between boss' rating and modernism, on the hypothesis that the more modern men would be better workers.

TABLE 27
Boss' Rating,[1] by Occupation

| | MEAN SCORE[2] ON BOSS' RATING | |
	BRAZIL	MEXICO
High white-collar	3.1	2.4
Low white-collar	**2.6	**1.6
Foremen	**3.1	**2.7
Skilled manual	**2.5	**1.9
Unskilled manual	**2.1	*1.6
All men	2.5	2.3

[1] Scale for Boss' Rating of respondent:
  Wonderful = 4
  Very good = 3
  Good   = 2
  Routine   = 1
[2] Using two-tailed test:
  ** Difference between this figure and the one immediately above it is significant at .01 level.
  * Difference between this figure and the one immediately above it is significant at .05 level.

The data supported the hypothesis for white-collar workers in Mexico and blue-collar workers in Brazil. The white-collar workers in Brazil and the blue-collar workers in Mexico showed no consistent pattern.

Conclusions

There was a common theme running through these various questions about work: the Brazilians were more likely to stress interpersonal relations of a traditional kind (loyalty to boss, friendliness with workmates), whereas Mexicans were more likely to be interested in technical efficiency and learning new procedures, emphases which are related to a modern approach toward work. That is probably why the Mexicans felt more handicapped by inadequate education: the technical demands of their jobs were increasing faster than the educational system could satisfy them.[5] These differences between countries were more impressive than those between status levels.

[5] Judging by the proportion who had attended secondary school, Mexican manual workers were *better* educated than their Brazilian counterparts, but there was not much difference among nonmanual workers. However, a subjective feeling of inadequate education may well be most common in societies where educational opportunities are actually growing, creating a competitive situation that constantly reminds a man that his own education may be insufficient.

The Mexican stress on capital formation and the opening of a business of one's own may reflect a modern orientation toward career, but it may also be a consequence of the relatively stable value for the peso which makes such saving possible. The Brazilian cruzeiro has suffered so much from inflation that it would be irrational to put money in the bank, and most humble citizens do not have practical opportunities available to them for direct investment in businesses that profit from inflation.

Throughout this monograph I have reported results which show little difference between Brazil and Mexico: for instance, the facts of geographical and status position predict scores on modernism with equal accuracy in both countries, and the patterns of educational aspirations for sons are also the same. But in two chapters I have reported divergences: here, concerning specific job attitudes, and in Chapter V, concerning fertility ideals.

Yet the very divergences seem to present a paradox: the Brazilians prefer smaller families, which we call a "modern" perspective, and at the same time the Mexicans are more likely to stress technical efficiency and the learning of new procedures at work, which we also call "modern." Can the Brazilians be more modern in one sphere of life, and the Mexicans in another?

My answer is "Yes," for two reasons. (1) From the beginning, I have used a theory of profiles in value orientations which predicted a statistical tendency for a series of modern values to hang together, but which also expected considerable independent variability among them. (2) The particular contrast on values between the two countries which seems to make Brazil more modern on the size of family desired and Mexico more modern concerning work may not be as paradoxical as it seems.

Let us explore the second statement. In attempting to explain the Brazilian interest in smaller families, I analyzed certain themes in the culture of that nation which stressed a willingness to enter into interpersonal relationships with people who were not relatives, and a concomitant tendency to put somewhat less emphasis on the family network as the only one where intimate ties were possible or safe. It was suggested that this openness with people outside the family circle somewhat weakened the strong familism which is customary in Latin America and which is related to the pattern of having many children. But perhaps the same general attitude toward interpersonal relationships applies at work, and therefore is not really a special sign of modernism in Brazil. Indeed, in Brazil a man's score on Modernism I was not as good a predictor of his specific work attitudes as it was in Mexico.

In Mexico, the more restrained tone of interpersonal relationships seems to pervade both family and work life. Within the family, it may be connected with a more traditional style of male dominance and large numbers of children. At work, this very restraint with other people may lead men to distrust the possibilities of advancement through good relations with bureaucratic colleagues, and distrust the fairness of an abstract and universalistic set of rules for promotion. Therefore an ambitious man would be pushed toward advancement through a personal technical skill which he can control, and a private business which he can own.

Obviously we need more research which will seek various alternative types of modern men, rather than speak as I have throughout most of this report of only the general contrast between men who are modern and those who are traditional on all values simultaneously. Now that the general contrast has been accomplished, the interesting quest will be to discover men who are modern on some values but traditional on others—in a systematic, not a random way. If we can find them, and predict behavior patterns as a result, we will deepen our understanding of the complex process of modernization of societies.[6]

---

[6] Our original design was deficient in that it did not contain enough criteria or dependent variables (such as desired family size, or political attitudes) to be predicated by variations in profiles of modernism. However, some students of mine are pursuing the theme of diverse types of modern (and transitional) men by secondary analysis of the data.

CHAPTER VIII

Conclusions: Modernism and Development

"A book of exposition should state in the first chapter what it intends to do; in the middle chapters it should carry out its intention, and in the last chapter it should point out what it has done."[1] To this rule from Homans, one might well add an addendum: in the last chapter the author should be allowed to relax the restraints of statistical caution, and allow his imagination free (but prudent) rein.

This book started with a question: To what degree does industrialism create a common way of life for all peoples? It was suggested that once the stage of high industrialism has been reached, any society is likely to have developed features which make it quite similar to all other highly industrialized nations. Similarity is not, of course, identity. Those basic features which tend toward similarity are: a division of labor with a low percentage of agricultural workers, and a high percentage not only of industrial workers but also of skilled technicians of many shades of skill and prestige; sophisticated technology based upon current scientific knowledge; a degree of urbanization that puts the bulk of the population in large metropolitan areas; an economy based on specialization rather than subsistence, with trading links between all regions and sectors of the nation and also with world markets; a system of social stratification with many statuses and blurred lines between them; a thriving system of public education, with the bulk of the population having studied to a point well beyond the minimum of literacy; channels of mass communication that tie most people instantly into national modes of thought; and finally, values of modernism stressing the rational and secular choice of experimental means toward materialistic aims. To a degree that has not

[1] George Casper Homans, *The Human Group*, p. 440.

yet been determined, these features of industrial society are mutually reinforcing.

Our particular methodological problem was to create measures of those values which form a key part of the industrial way of life. Then our substantive problem was to use the measures in ways that would relate modern values to other aspects of contemporary society, and if possible, to throw some light on the process of transition from traditionalism to modernism.

Our working laboratories were Brazil and Mexico. More than six hundred men in the first country and more than seven hundred in the second were subjected to questionnaires. In addition, some twenty-five men in each country were asked to sit beside a tape recorder and tell us of their world view in free interviews. The men were divided between inhabitants of the (then) capital cities of Rio de Janeiro and Mexico City, and those who lived in small provincial towns of fewer than 10,000 people. Both manual workers and nonmanual employees were included in the samples.

The Value Scales

Pursuing the methodological goal, we invented or borrowed a large number of attitude items of the form commonly used in social surveys which seem to reflect the core values of a modern orientation toward life, and more specifically, toward work and career. These items were arranged in groups; each of the groups was thought to reflect a single basic value. Using factor analysis as a device for scale-building, we tested the homogeneity of the items within any given group and discarded those that did not fit. This procedure produced fourteen scales, each constructed as a unidimensional measure of one distinct value; each scale could vary from the traditional pole to the modern pole.

Further statistical analysis showed that seven of these scales were closely tied to one another: they composed a single pattern or syndrome which we have labeled the "core" of modernism. They are: Activism, Low Integration with Relatives, Preference for Urban Life, Individualism, Low Community Stratification, High Mass-Media Participation, and Low Stratification of Life Chances. The data showed that a man who believed strongly in some of these values was likely also to acquiesce to the others: although each had its own identity, and varied to some degree independently of the others, in general they were sufficiently related to hang together in a single syndrome.

The Typical Modern Man

We can describe the typical modern man by his answers to the items in the seven core scales. A modern man is an activist; he believes in making plans in advance for important parts of his life, and he has a sense of security that he can usually bring those plans to fruition. Unlike the fatalistic peasant who follows the routines of life and shrugs his shoulders to indicate that much of what happens will be beyond his control, the industrial man attempts to organize the future to serve his own purposes.

To carry out these plans, the modern man is willing to move away from his relatives and to depend upon his own initiative. For him, nepotism is more a burdensome responsibility than a mechanism of security. Similarly, he is an individualist who avoids extreme identification with people in his own work group. Therefore he says that he would prefer to express his own ideas and make his own decisions even if his peers disagree.

The context in which the modern man prefers to carry out his plans is the open scene of the big city. He finds that the stimulation of urban life and its opportunities is strong, and he develops sufficient skill with urban modes to feel at ease in making new friends in the city.

He perceives the city as a place which is not rigidly stratified—that is, he sees it as open to influence by ordinary citizens like himself. Similarly, he sees life chances or career opportunities as open rather than closed; a man of humble background has a chance to fulfill his dreams and rise within the system. He participates in urban life by actively availing himself of the mass media. He reads newspapers, listens to the radio, discusses civic affairs.

Thus the modern man, through the way he *perceives* the world around him and its opportunities for himself, and through the way he *chooses* which paths to follow, is a man who seeks to control his life, plan his future, climb up a bit in the status hierarchy, and improve his material circumstances—because these ends are desirable and also because they are seen as obtainable.

The traditional man is the opposite. He perceives himself as permanently stuck in a life which does not change and which cannot be controlled to any great extent. Therefore he seeks little and expects to gain little; he takes what the fates may bring; he pursues security through close personal ties, primarily with relatives but also with a few friends and with *patrones* in high positions who will protect him so long as he stays in his place. To this exchange he brings resignation and gains safety.

We can add a few subsidiary characteristics of the modern man—those which appear with less frequency. The modern man is willing to let his friends and relatives into the secrets of his life, for he does not fear they will take advantage of him. He trusts others and does not constantly fear their purposes. He is, however, somewhat suspicious of large companies and rather prefers smaller places of work where the individual has freer expression. He does not frown upon manual work but recognizes it as a worthy contribution to life. He is willing to take risks to gain useful ends. He feels that within the family, women should be allowed to make many of their own decisions and that children should be permitted on occasion to disagree with their parents.

Where Is the Modern Man?

Once we had this portrait of the typical modern man, we decided to ignore temporarily the variations which exist within the real world. That is, we put aside the subtypes of men who would be modern on some of these values but traditional on others, and concentrated only on the tendency for these values to hang together in a single pattern. Thus we constructed a general scale of modernism which combined information from the separate scales just enumerated. Using it, we sought to find out where the modern man lives. Of course, we found him more often in the metropolis than in the provinces, but somewhat to our surprise, we discovered that he is quite common in the middle strata of society in small provincial towns. The results of the questionnaires showed that geographic location made a difference in modernism as expected, but that socio-economic status made much more difference. Taking into account that our samples did not include peasants, and also that we had deliberately excluded men from the very top and the very bottom of the status hierarchy, we concluded that about a third of the measured variation in modernism was accounted for by socio-economic status, and slightly less than a tenth by metropolitan-versus-provincial location.

This is a suggestive result. It indicates that the middle classes in the small towns are not so stodgy as some authors portray them to be. Intellectually they are already participating in the national life and share the national goals, even though in many ways their economic opportunities are still limited. Given the chance by objective economic circumstances, they are prepared to move forward. They more closely resemble the people described by Charles Erasmus in *Man Takes Control*, who inhabit a progressive part of the Mexican hinterland, than the people described by Marvin Harris in *Town and Country in Brazil*, who inhabit a backward part of the Brazilian hinterland.

There are hints both from our questionnaires and from our free interviews that the provincial middle classes learn modern values because they are not in fact completely isolated in the small towns in which they live. They travel, they go to school, they read the newspapers and magazines that come from the metropolis; they listen to the radio. They may not be participating physically in the life of the big city, but to a considerable degree they are sharing its mentality. They have begun to disengage themselves from the fixed and traditional local patterns; they are experiencing "anticipatory socialization" toward urban patterns through empathy, in a process that has been vividly described by Daniel Lerner.[2]

Validity of the Tools

These first results of the research gave us a methodological as well as a substantive conclusion. The patterns in Mexico and Brazil were identical. The influence of urban residence and socio-economic status upon values was the same in both countries. Furthermore, the items which clung together to form the separate value scales, and beyond that, the way in which the separate scales clung together to form the over-all pattern of modernism, were the same in both countries. Thus we gained some confidence in our instruments and in our style of research.

We reinforced our initial belief that something as abstract as an orientation in life toward a modern perspective, an idea which has been discussed at length by philosophers and novelists, could in fact be handled sympathetically by the tools of empirical sociology. The important step was to break up the ideal type of modernism in values into its separate components, and then develop scales to measure each component in as pure or homogeneous a way as possible. Only in a later step did we relate those components to one another statistically. We tried to avoid the trap of theoretical pigeonholes. Instead of cross-classifying our separate dimensions in advance, thereby creating

[2] *The Passing of Traditional Society.*

complex tables with cells representing each possible combination of elements, we interrelated our dimensions by means of correlation coefficients. The burden on the memory was reduced; the many pigeonholes with few cases could be ignored; only the major central tendencies needed emphasis. The fact that these central tendencies were repeated almost identically in both countries indicated that we were dealing with a reflection of social reality and not an artifact barely significant at the .05 level.

Indeed, there was even a hint that the same pattern appears in the United States. We did not have available a sample of respondents in the United States exactly parallel to the samples we had in Brazil and Mexico, but we did have a sample of urban women who could be ranked by education and could then be compared to the men in Brazilian and Mexican metropolitan areas. The range of responses turned out to be about the same: urban primary-school graduates were just about as traditional in the United States as they had turned out to be in Brazil and Mexico, and those who had gone to secondary school or attended colleges or universities for some years turned out to be as modern in the one country as they had been in the other two.

Since this portrait of the modern man closely resembles the official image in the literature of sociology and anthropology, cynical friends have accused me of laboring mightily to prove the obvious. I think we have gone somewhat beyond that. First, let us remember that empirical research often shows inherited wisdom to be mistaken, so confirmation is not "obvious." Second, since we did find some contradictions to our predictions, the official image was only partially confirmed: (1) the scale of Occupational Primacy, which depicts overt striving for worldly success, did not prove to be within the core of modernism (indeed, there was a hint of the opposite); (2) the modern men were opposed to, rather than content with, large companies; (3) the modern men were not significantly different from the traditionalists in their religious views and behavior. Yet despite these contrary findings, the weight of the evidence was in favor of the standard sociological portrait of the modern man, a portrait more often repeated than verified in the literature.

And third, our tools are flexible enough not only to permit measurement of variations in modernism as a whole, but also to seek out those men whose style of modernism is somewhat atypical, namely, those who are more modern on some values than on others. Therefore, I submit that we started with the official portrait, verified its main outlines (but not all its details), and then provided an improved camera which will permit more accurate recording in the future.

Values and Education

Having perfected our instruments, the next step was to use them to study the role of values in the general process of transition to modern society. The first exercise concerned education. All observers recognize the key significance of formal education in modern society. It is the sorting mechanism which prepares men for their adult work roles. It both reinforces the existing status system and provides for movement within it. The schools reinforce the system because parents of high status are able to give their sons an education to a degree which is not available to most sons who come from lower parts of the status hierarchy. But once a widespread system of public education is available, *some* sons from the lower strata manage to take advantage of it and thereby gain entrance into higher-status jobs.

Formal education often appears before other features of an industrial society. Public-school systems have been developing in Latin America for fifty years—and the roots are older than that, since Church and even State schools and universities first appeared in the sixteenth century, although they did not become widespread. Thus education has a long tradition in Latin America, but it has mainly been education for a tiny elite that trained students in traditional ways which emphasized theological and literary and legal scholarship. Only in very recent years has the school system begun to change toward mass education for all the people, with curricula stressing technical education as preparation for industrial careers. The old and the new intermingle and conflict; the year I was in Brazil, 1960, was a time when the Congress was debating with great passion some reforms in the educational system which most outsiders considered long overdue. The strength of the resistance to these reforms was quite remarkable.

This debate symbolized one of the special features of Latin America which appears to me to be crucial and yet is often neglected by those who generalize broadly about the developing societies by classifying them together as a single type. Many features of Latin American society entered the main stream of modern life a long time ago. Many of the countries are better described as instances of arrested development rather than of underdevelopment. The very fact that they began to move forward, and then encountered various resistances which slowed down their progress, is the basis of much of the social and political tension that we read about in the daily newspapers.

The provincial towns in our samples were towns with primary, and in a few instances, low-level secondary schools. The capital cities, of course, had a full range of contemporary educational institutions. The significance of education as the sorting device leading to occupation can be simply demonstrated, and was about the same in metropolises and provinces. About 85 per cent of the men in our samples who had attended only primary school ended up in manual jobs. But about 75 per cent of those with secondary training obtained nonmanual jobs. Therefore, the most important career decision a man makes in his life is: How long to stay in school.

Many studies throughout the world have repeatedly shown that the most important single predictor of the education of a boy is the socio-economic status of his father. Generally speaking, fathers provide for their sons an education commensurate with parental status level. Nevertheless, the degree of predictability is less than often assumed. Only a third of the variation in education of sons can be accounted for by the status of fathers, a portion which is about the same for our samples in Brazil and Mexico as it is for the samples which have been studied in the United States. If one wishes to explain additional parts of the variation, he must introduce new variables.

The next most important variable has been shown in the United States to be the intelligence of the boy, as measured by standard IQ tests. Unfortunately we did not have information on this variable. Also, various studies have shown that the size of the town where a boy grows up is of significance, since small towns offer fewer educational opportunities than larger cities. Finally, many studies have shown that family structure and family values make a significant difference. That is, once we have defined the "objective" circumstances of a given family by locating it in socio-economic status and geographical space, there still is room for choice. The choice stems from the perceptions and goals of the family. Some are satisfied with their positions in life and put no pressures upon their sons to be different. On the other hand, many families are dissatisfied with the status the father has achieved, and shape the aspirations of their sons toward higher goals. Such families make special efforts to take advantage of whatever objective opportunities might be available, and they sacrifice other things to help their sons in school. Obviously the variables just mentioned are interrelated, so only methods which control some of them while contrasting others will allow us to disentangle their relative importance.

We were interested in the particular effect of family values upon the educational behavior of sons. The role of values is especially important in studying social mobility, for it is the family with values that are not typical of its own level that pushes its son toward higher levels. Thus our basic procedure was to hold geographic location and socio-economic status constant, and seek the special additional effect of values upon education. We studied it twice: once in terms of the effect of his father's values on the education of the respondent and once in terms of the effect of the respondent's values on the expected education of his sons.

We could not directly measure the values of the fathers of our respondents, but could estimate them indirectly by inquiring of the respondents their memory of the amount of education which their fathers urged them to obtain. Holding status level constant, we found that both the size of the town in which they grew up and the specific advice from their fathers influenced the amount of education actually achieved by the respondents.

Turning from the past to the future, we interrogated our respondents about the amount of education they expected for their sons. We then related this dependent variable to three separate independent variables: geographic location, socio-economic status, and modernism in values. Using partial correlation coefficients as the method of analysis, we found that in our sample, as in others which have been studied elsewhere, status was the most significant predictor—it explained about a third of the variation in educational expectations for sons. After that, modernism in values and metropolitan location had about equal weight—each accounted for about an eighth of the variation.

My explanation for this is as follows: Geographic location mainly is a measure of opportunities, the degree to which schools are readily available. Of course, it has some additional influence on goals, since small-town boys are less likely to learn of the importance of education and hence are less likely to value it. However, this latter influence is probably not very important, for the ideology about the utility of education has become quite widespread in both Brazil and Mexico. The construction of schools lags behind the desire for schooling.

Socio-economic status is a measure of both opportunity and desire. Obviously parents with means can more easily provide good educa-

NORTHWEST MISSOURI
STATE COLLEGE LIBRARY
MARYVILLE, MISSOURI

tions for their sons. But it is also true that these parents are more aware of the importance of education for modern life. It is likely, however, that opportunity is a more important factor than desire, since poor people are often well aware that they cannot climb out of poverty without more education. In a very general and vague way, they too desire education for their sons. But when it comes down to making the day-to-day decisions which might provide that education, the pressure of circumstance usually keeps them from fulfilling their abstract goal.

The goals of the parents are transmitted to their sons in two ways: first of all, through the transmission of the parents' general values about life, and second, through their specific insistence upon school attendance. There is no question that transmitting both general values and specific school attitudes is a central theme in family conversations. Our qualitative interviews have many instances of long and heated expression of the attempts of respondents to influence the thinking and behavior of their sons. Furthermore, many respondents remembered for years the instructions they had received from their fathers.

Since geographic location and socio-economic status are mainly measures of the availability of education, then values become mainly a measure of the degree to which people choose to take advantage of the opportunities open to them. They are the key to mobility, the explanation of why *some* sons of a given status level behave differently from the *average* for that level. If only a few sons are thus mobile, the system as a whole might retain its structure. But if enough sons begin to behave in new ways (usually at the urging of their parents), then we would witness the transformation of the structure itself.

The patterns influencing educational choice were identical in both countries. Once again we got confirmation not only of the validity of our instruments but also of the essential similarity of the social structures of Brazil and Mexico.

Values and Family Size

But when we turned to another dependent variable, we discovered important differences between the two countries.

We found that Brazilians preferred smaller families than do Mexicans, and this unexpected finding led us to explore its implications as far as the data would permit.

The social facts that set the framework within which individual married couples arrive at a decision about the "ideal" number of children to have are analogous to those that create the framework within which educational aspirations emerge. That is, there is an objective opportunity structure that is an important part of the picture. Children cost money to rear and educate. Families of high social status with more money can obviously afford more children. But here is an area of behavior where objective opportunities seem not to be the determining influence upon behavior itself. Generally speaking, throughout the world parents with means have fewer children than poor ones. Especially during the transition period from traditional to modern society, the usual experience is that parents of the urban middle classes are most likely to restrict the number of their offspring. The few very rich families at the top of the hierarchy may have somewhat larger families than the middle class, and the large mass of urban manual workers and of poor farmers are prone to many progeny. These generalizations are widely known, yet we know very little that would allow us to explain with precision why these trends take place.

Since middle-class people have more money than working-class people, we cannot use the explanation that because children are expensive the number of offspring is restricted by those too poor to afford large families. An alternative explanation is often given: urban middle-class people have high aspirations for their children, and particularly during the early stages of development they have limited resources to pay for them. That is, their aspirations rise faster than their incomes, and they attempt to close the gap by having fewer children. In that way they expect to provide full nurture and extensive education for the few children they do have, thus permitting them in the next generation to achieve the goals which the parents have not quite met. And it is assumed that urban working-class people and poor farmers have less of a gap between aspirations and resources; they can afford what little they want, and thus make no attempt (or less attempt) to restrict family size.

In recent years some more subtle interpretations have been added to those just given. It is suggested that although poor people may in a vague way prefer fewer children, their habits of self-discipline are less developed, their knowledge of scientific hygiene is weak, and their ability to buy contraceptives is restricted by their limited means. Some studies have suggested that the customary patterns of communication within the lower-class family make it difficult for husbands and wives to discuss sexual matters and arrive at common agreement, since male dominance and female modesty are inhibiting.

Our contribution to the dialogue is limited, since the study was not designed from the beginning as a research on fertility ideals. Nevertheless, the subject is so important for the future of Latin American development that I dare not ignore what data we do have. Our first conclusion, as already indicated, is that Brazilians prefer smaller families than do Mexicans. This is true even when the main variables that usually affect ideal family size are controlled, namely, geographic location and socio-economic status. The Brazilian men preferred a family size that averaged out to approximately two and a half children; the Mexicans by contrast preferred almost four children. There were differences by location and by status, but nevertheless once these differences were controlled, the Mexicans within each subgroup still preferred a larger family size by about one child than did the Brazilians.

Even more surprising was to discover that the differences by socioeconomic status were practically nonexistent in Brazil, but somewhat more important in Mexico. And we found that the differences by geographic location were small in Mexico but quite pronounced in Brazil. For some strange reason, metropolitans of *all* social classes in Brazil preferred small families, and middle-class people of *all* places of residence preferred small families in Mexico.

We then introduced the additional variable of measured values. In this case, instead of using a general scale of modernism, we used the scale of Low Integration with Relatives, which is a little closer to values about family life. (Actually, the statistical results would have been about the same if we had used the general scale of modernism.) We found that even with status and location controlled, values did make an additional difference. In both countries the importance of values was slightly more than the importance of status; however, in Brazil, metropolitan location outweighed the other two combined.

When studying educational aspirations, we found that our three variables of location, status, and values together accounted for more than half of the total variation in the dependent variable. In studying ideal family size, however, we were able to account for only a third of the variation with the three predictors combined.

Using "soft" data from the qualitative interviews and from my personal experience of having lived in both countries, and supported by a few scattered items from the questionnaire, I suggested the hypothesis that some very general values about the way people should deal with each other may be the clue that would lead to an explanation of the difference between the two countries. Brazilians appear to have a style of interpersonal relationships stemming from a long cultural tradition which is a little different from the Mexican style, despite the fact that both countries are strikingly similar regarding measures of their relative stage of economic and social development. Brazilians are somewhat more relaxed and trusting when they deal with each other; they make friends more easily; male dominance in family life is a bit less pronounced. The nuclear family seems less segregated from the rest of society. In Mexico, the nuclear family is tied strongly to extended kin but very weakly to other people. In Brazil the dependence upon kin is less and the trust in outsiders is greater. This style of interpersonal relationships seems to lead more easily toward adaptation to modern city life. It leads to greater communication between spouses, and to a stronger conviction that children should be educated to stand on their own feet and make progress through individual effort instead of nepotistic favor. Within this context, a smaller number of children given fuller educational experience would seem appropriate.

Extrapolation from our small samples to the national scene would suggest that as Brazil urbanizes, its birth rate will go down, but that the same will not be true in Mexico. Although crude national birth rates are about the same in both countries, there are some indications from census tabulations which do indeed suggest that the urban birth rate in Brazil has begun to decline, but in Mexico, which is slightly more urban than Brazil, this decline has not started. If this conclusion is supported by further evidence, many economists and government planners who have assumed that urbanization will automatically reduce the birth rate should become uneasy. Urbanization by itself is not enough. Life in the city affects the objective circumstances, the subjective perceptions, and the values and goals of its people. But apparently the impact of urban life is not always and everywhere the same. The specific decision to restrict the number of children is the outcome of a complicated process in which residence in the city is but the starting point, not the complete determinant. We must pursue in more detail the chain of influences and the intervening variables that occur between urban residence as initial cause and a low birth rate as final outcome.

Satisfaction and Politics

The analyses of education and fertility ideals just summarized used modernism as a key variable. They represented exercises which showed the utility of the scales of modernism in predicting attitudes and behavior of individuals, especially after geographic location and socio-economic status were held constant. The next subjects treated in our data analysis were somewhat tangential to the main argument: they dealt with various aspects of satisfaction with work, career, and life in general; the relation of satisfaction to political attitude; and the particular ways in which people evaluated their jobs. Since they are marginal to the main theme of the book, they will be treated very briefly here.[3]

Detailed comparison of different measures of satisfaction showed that there was a basic distinction between those which asked about contentment in general terms and those which specifically pointed toward a man's rewards in relation to the average for his society. When the first type of question was asked, a man tended to respond in terms of a vague sense of satisfaction about his job and life circumstances, and this in turn was clearly related not just to his objective rewards but to his initial aspirations. That is, when a man started out in life, he got from his parents and most particularly from his education an idea of the level in society he should achieve. He then compared his present situation with this initial aspiration and decided how well off he felt himself to be. Therefore men in the same objective position in the status hierarchy evaluated it differently, depending on their initial aspirations.

But when a man was asked to evaluate how well he was doing compared to the average in his society, he tended to suppress thoughts of his initial aspirations and make a factual judgment of just where he stood: equal to, above, or below the average. His answer was closer to objective reality.

Therefore measures based on a comparison of a man's position with the average in his society had a higher correlation with measures of

---

[3] And the analyses of indices of socio-economic status and the rates of intergenerational mobility, reported in Appendices A and B, will be ignored here.

socio-economic status. Measures based on more general questions about a man's personal satisfactions, which allowed him to evaluate them relative to his initial aspirations, had very low correlations with indices of socio-economic status. These correlations are improved somewhat when income is used as an independent variable and education as a control variable. In this way we approximated statistically the respondent's own psychological process of relating reward to initial aspiration.

One additional result is worth emphasis: in judging relative satisfaction, men used not only their initial aspirations but also their present group membership. Thus comparisons with other men tended to be made within either the white-collar or blue-collar strata, but not between them.

We gave attention to the measurement of satisfaction because of a theoretical bias which suggests that dissatisfaction is the cause of political radicalism. Our results showed that, generally speaking, and in terms of their initial aspirations, both Brazilians and Mexicans seemed rather content with life, and we could detect no major differences between metropolitans, provincials, and migrants, nor between high- and low-status levels. Nor could we detect any relation between satisfaction and radicalism, once status level was controlled.

Thus we redefined "radicalism" as a characteristic more of strata than of discontented individuals. Like general values, political ideology is part of the "collective conscience," the group culture. Working-class men, compared to middle-class men, are more traditional in values and more radical in politics. They learn their values and their ideology from their friends and workmates.

Of course, some men departed from the average of their group. Our earlier results enabled us to relate deviations in values within strata to specific ideas about education and about fertility, but we failed to relate deviations in personal satisfaction to variations in political attitude.

The material on political attitudes was richer among Mexicans than Brazilians, and it suggested that the radicals tended to come mostly from those who had begun to taste the benefits of modern life but were not receiving enough of them quickly enough. That is, those who had left rural zones, who held low-level industrial jobs, but who retained a traditional world-view, seemed most addicted to socialist ideas. Industrial workers who had been more successful turned toward middle-class leanings: individualistic competition instead of group benefit. They were more modern in values and more conservative in politics.

Work Attitudes

As I have stated, in family matters we found Brazilians more modern and Mexicans more traditional. In work attitudes, the opposite seemed the case: the Brazilians were more likely to stress traditional themes of loyalty to the boss and friendliness with workmates, and showed less interest in technical procedures leading to greater production and almost a disinterest in personal savings for capital formation.

This paradox should spur new researches in which the central theme is not, as in this book, the over-all contrast between traditional values and modern values, but rather the incongruities that are especially prevalent during times of rapid change, the ways in which modernism spreads in inconsistent and contradictory patterns. Men may learn one set of values at home, another in school, another on the job, and still another from radio and television. I believe there is a trend toward equilibrium, and indeed, that it is one of the pressures toward social change. But it takes time for the transition to occur, for men to readjust all their values to the new circumstances. Tensions within the personality, and tensions between groups of men, are most likely during the transitional phase.

Values: Means or Ends?

The more I study the role of values in social structure, the more I become convinced that their function is closer to means than to ends. I think we have in the past overstressed values as abstract goals which men seek, and we have understressed the way in which perceptions and values shape the selection of realistic alternatives. For example, Melvin Tumin has shown that in Puerto Rico, in a general way everybody thinks that education is a good thing for his children.[4] Yet some families are much more likely than others to feel that a high-school diploma is a practical goal, and much more likely to organize their day-to-day behavior in ways that help their children obtain the diploma. Indeed, although everybody thinks education is a good thing, some people in fact define "education" as attendance

---

[4] *Social Class and Social Change in Puerto Rico.*

at primary school, others think in terms of the high-school diploma, and still others in terms of a college degree.

Similarly, many recent studies have shown that poor people in Latin American cities wish they had fewer children. Indeed, they often attempt to carry out their wish by the most brutal method: the rate of abortion among the urban poor is extraordinarily high. Yet in terms of the way they organize their daily lives, poor people do not make much attempt to avoid conception. They recognize that a large family makes their poverty much harder to bear; they sometimes react by abortion; but they do not follow disciplined routines of birth control. Many researchers suggest that they are undisciplined, unlikely to plan carefully for the future in any aspect of life, unable to communicate between husband and wife with full frankness on sexual matters, and too fatalistic to really believe that they could do anything about it if they tried. Thus the way in which their perceptions and values shape their recognition of available means may be more important as a determinant of behavior than the desire to have fewer children.

This same theoretical conclusion has been reached by other researchers starting from other perspectives. For example, Gerhard Lenski writes as follows:

The data analyzed underline the crucial importance of the family as a source of those traits of personality which are so crucial for success in the job world. In much of the recent literature on the interrelations of personality and mobility, attention has centered chiefly on one such trait: ambition, or the desire to get ahead. Our data indicate, however, that motivation [ambition] is *only one of many* personality traits that influence the rise and fall of individuals and families. Furthermore, its importance may be greatly overrated, at least from the standpoint of explaining why some socio-religious groups are more successful than others. Our findings suggest that other personality characteristics such as *values, beliefs,* and *abilities* are of greater importance. Success may depend as much (or more) on the devaluation of kinship, the belief in the existence of opportunity, or the ability to think for one's self as on sheer ambition. In fact, those with only limited ambition may fare quite well in our society provided they possess these other important personality traits. A recognition of this fact is likely to increase our awareness of the influence of socio-religious groups on the mobility process, since, although their influence on ambition is negligible, their influence on other traits of personality is more substantial.[5]

[5] Gerhard Lenski, "The Religious Factor," in *Studies in American Society*, ed., D. L. Phillips, p. 50.

Lenski says that ambition as a goal (apparently, that which is measured by our own scale of Occupational Primacy) is less related to mobility than the devaluation of kinship (which we measured by the scale of Low Integration with Relatives), or the belief in the existence of opportunity (our Low Stratification of Life Chances). In the abstract, most people approve of ambition. What really counts is the way they go about achieving it: the means shape the end.

Indeed, means and ends form a single system: they are functionally interdependent. What used to be called "the strain toward consistency in the mores" results from the interplay between culture and personality, for men seek a pattern in their lives which minimizes strain. If their ambitions cannot be achieved, they lower their sights. If old norms no longer fit new circumstances, they try to effect a synthesis that is more consistent. If new opportunities appear, they permit themselves new ambitions.

Cultures need time and absence of outside pressures to produce a consistent pattern, to reach a state of equilibrium in which all (or most) aspects reinforce one another. Once it is reached, it is hard for individuals to change their behavior. A striking example can be found in the description given by Herbert Gans of working-class life among Italian-Americans in Boston. He writes that there are a few central themes that are the foci of their lives: emphasis on persons rather than objects, on the satisfactions stemming from interaction with peers and the family circle, on short-run pleasures rather than long-term careers, on distrust of outsiders. He shows that these patterns are produced by the socialization process that takes place, given the type of nuclear family structure that prevails. Once in existence, these patterns tend toward equilibrium in two ways: the values are mutually reinforcing and shape appropriate motivations, and the process of social control tends to pull individuals back to the center if they begin to deviate.

Gans contrasts the aspirations of typical working-class people with those of typical middle-class people, and shows that the gap is so wide as to make it difficult for one group to understand the other, let alone imitate its behavior:

To the object-oriented, person-oriented people seem to be without aspirations, to lack ambition, and to be unable to defer gratification. Conversely, to the person-oriented, those who strive for object goals seem cold and inhuman, pursuing selfish aims at the expense of others, and unable to enjoy life as a result.[6]

As a consequence of their integrated way of life, the people whom Gans studied made little effort to take advantage of the opportunities for upward mobility that existed in their environment. Other ethnic groups who shared their objective circumstances, such as the Jews, behaved differently and climbed into the middle class. The Italians also desired to live well, to spend money. But, unable or unwilling to organize their lives to achieve that end, they found alternative satisfactions.

Values and Economic Development

The general goals of economic development for one's nation and personal improvement in one's own material circumstances are now widespread throughout much of Brazil and Mexico. Only the most isolated rural regions, especially those which represent subcultural enclaves such as the Indian zones in Mexico, are exceptions. Progress has become a national slogan. President Kubitschek was—and is—a hero in Brazil because he led the march toward progress, despite casual neglect of its costs and problems. The annual increment in gross national product is a statistic almost as widely discussed in Mexico as are baseball scores in the United States.

Consequently, in seeking the connection between values and progress in countries that are already well into the development process, I do not think we should ask much about goals in general terms. Let us take the desire for progress as a given. But we should study the mechanisms people use to translate their desire for progress into specific acts which will lead them forward, for their ways of looking at the world around them vary, and these variations make a significant difference in their likelihood of success.

I think the initial spurt toward change comes from alterations in the opportunity structure; massive shifts in the political and economic situation open up vast new opportunities that shake people from their complacency. The ordinary citizen is unable to create such opportunities by any act of his own will. But once the new opportunities begin

[6] Herbert J. Gans, *The Urban Villagers*, p. 91. His ethnographic materials, congruent with our statistical results, vividly illustrate the theoretical insights of Florence R. Kluckhohn and Talcott Parsons which underlie our value scales (cited above in Chapter I).

to appear, there is differential response to them. The major differential response comes from those factors which are built into the stratification system. People with more education and more experience with the modern world are of course going to be able to take advantage of new opportunities more readily than those whose life experience has been more limited. Therefore, if one wants a crude predictor of what a man will do in the face of these new opportunities, he should use social-class background as the main index.

But if the investigator wishes to answer either of two additional questions, he must go beyond an index of socio-economic status: (1) Exactly how does status cause behavior? (2) How can we explain the considerable variation that remains after status has been controlled? Assigning a man an index score on socio-economic status is in fact a way of predicting that probably his perceptions and values will fit an expected or typical pattern, and that *if* they do, *then* he will behave in a certain way. Thus we are making both a probability statement and a causal statement at the same time. More detailed understanding of the way the causation works will obviously come if we can directly measure, instead of indirectly infer, those perceptions and values. Furthermore, when men are acting in ways that are not fully predicted from their status position, we usually assume that the explanation lies in the fact that they believe in values somewhat atypical for their status level. Thus direct measurement of values will aid us in studying deviations from the average, which in turn are the clue to an understanding of the mobility process.

I believe that the tools that have been developed in the present research are adequate to help us move a few steps forward. We can use these tools to aid in understanding and predicting behavior to a degree that will carry us beyond what we can do solely with measures of socio-economic status as the independent variable. The materials analyzed here on education and fertility ideals are examples.

However, if we wish to turn the question the other way around, and ask about the source of variations in values, then I suspect our research problem will be more difficult. Using values to predict behavior can be done in one moment of time: we compare men who behave differently, and explain the difference in terms of their values. But they reached their present values over a period of time; they had long life histories. How could we attempt to unravel the key factors in those biographies?

One procedure would be to use our value scales to identify different types of men. We could, for example, start by choosing any given status level, and then selecting samples of men who were modern on some values but traditional on others. In this way we would use value scales as a way of defining our sampling frame. But then we would have the complex task of detecting the variations in individual life histories which have caused variations in values. At the end of Chapter V some of those variations in personal background are suggested; they include past mobility experiences, differences in friendship contacts and influences, and peculiarities in individual personality characteristics. The number of variables that would have to be included in the research design would be quite large and would have to include subtle factors that are rather difficult to measure adequately. The idiosyncrasies of life histories are many and complex, and if one wished to handle them statistically he would need a large sample. Since the major gross influences on life history stem from socioeconomic background, and these we already understand rather well, new research to uncover the subtle influences that are left over, once status has been controlled, faces difficult tasks.

Consequently, I think the contribution of this research is in the other direction. I think that our value scales are more likely to be useful when seen as specifications of one aspect of what socio-economic status "really means" in terms of direct impact on the lives of individuals, and therefore as a way of predicting the attitudes and behavior of men beyond what we can do with an index of status by itself. And I think that the value scales can be useful in studies of the mobility process—particularly if we see that process in terms of choices that individuals make, both consciously and unconsciously, which allow them to take advantage of the new opportunities that open up during phases of rapid economic development.

Finally, I believe that the value scales can be useful in cross-cultural studies which are concerned not with predicting the differential behavior of individuals in a society, but rather with the convergence of cultures. If we wish to find out more about my initial question concerning the degree to which industrial societies are all tending to converge upon a common way of life, we must measure crucial aspects of that way of life. The value scales have proven to be reliable instruments in two different cultures, Brazil and Mexico, and we have some evidence that they also work in a third, namely, the United States. If they stand up in additional countries, we can use them in studies of the convergence process.

APPENDIX A

Socio-Economic Status

There is a strong relation between modernism and socio-economic status; indeed, the latter controls about one-third of the variance of the former. Having explained what I mean by "modernism," I must present a similarly explicit examination of the operations we used to measure status. And since relatively little comparative research of this type is available for Latin America, I will explore a variety of facets of the subject; it is interesting in its own right, as well as being important for the understanding of variations in values.

Social Stratification

Socio-economic status is a characteristic of an individual that reflects his position in the system of social stratification. It appears that the structure of stratification is markedly similar in all countries that are at least part way along the road to industrialization. Once a commercial economy has gained ascendance, there develops a set of social and economic characteristics that are mutually dependent. Some analysts choose to concentrate upon one or another of them and call it the "cause," and to deduce the others as "effects." I believe that a theoretically more satisfying and empirically more realistic approach is to recognize that the stratification system is in fact nothing more than the outcome of the mutual interrelationship among these characteristics.[1]

What are these characteristics? Listing them in the order by which they affect an individual in his life cycle, we can say that he begins by being taught a set of values about life and work by his parents. Those values, plus the economic resources of the parents, lead him to seek a certain level of formal education, which serves as preparation

[1] See Joseph A. Kahl, *The American Class Structure*, Chap. 1.

for a given type of occupation. Once at work, the success of the individual on the job (determined by the amount and quality of his education, by his native intelligence, by his values and ambitions, by his parents' friends, "connections," and wealth, and by "luck") leads to his income, which in turn shapes his style of life and influences his choice of wife and of friends. Through these friends he learns new values or reinforces old ones which he passes on to his children, and the cycle begins again.

Thus, education, occupation, income, interaction networks among friends who share consumption styles—all these are "objective" characteristics that impinge upon a man from the outside and shape his behavior. They combine to produce two crucial "subjective" characteristics: one is the rank put upon a man by his community, an evaluation of his worth, which we call his "social status," or the prestige he has in the eyes of his neighbors. The second is the mirror image of the first, namely, the sense of self-identification or class consciousness of the individual, his feeling of being a certain kind of person and his awareness of similarity to others who are the same kind of persons. Standing somewhat between the objective and the subjective characteristics are the values used by the community as abstract principles that guide and shape judgments about particular people.

Now, certain trends in the pattern of relations among these characteristics are concomitants of modernization. The role of capital wealth diminishes, as more and more men pursue careers for wages and salaries, and relatively fewer earn their living as proprietors, particularly landed proprietors. When the economy turns to modern technology, the complexity of production and the increasing scale of operations that expands the importance of bureaucratic forms of management (be they private or governmental) lead to a greater emphasis upon formal education as the basic preparation for career, and upon impersonal rules of promotion stressing efficiency as the guide to advancement. To the degree that the society democratizes, it makes education available through free public schools, colleges, and universities, and opens paths of upward mobility to large segments of the population. Finally, the pattern of the values which guide prestige judgments, and thus so strongly influence behavior, changes. Less emphasis is placed on the past, on family lineage, and more on current occupational accomplishment.

The net result of these changes is an altered stratification system. Instead of two relatively clear classes—landlords and peasants—with a few intersticial groups, the system becomes a complex one of many strata, and the divisions between them become blurred. There is more mobility, and there is a different distribution of the population among the strata, with the middle classes getting bigger and the lower classes getting smaller.

Let me quote from Charles Wagley, an observer of the changing Brazilian scene:

> . . . until very recently Brazil was a highly stable society and people were seldom able to change their circumstances. The son of a poor man was poor and the son of an illiterate remained illiterate; thus membership in a social class was, in a sense, hereditary. People were very conscious of family as a criterion for placing an individual in his proper class, and they tended to marry within their own class, thus perpetuating class solidarity.
>
> . . . Even today, in most Brazilian communities, the man with a clean suit, a white shirt, and a shine on his shoes is a man who has been to high school, has servants in his home, does not engage in manual labor, and comes from a family which has belonged to the upper or middle class for several generations. . . . This is particularly true of small communities. . . .

All observers of the Brazilian scene since World War II agree that the traditional Brazilian class structure is changing in a significant and fairly rapid fashion. To me, the direction of change is quite clear. New social sectors and even a new social class are appearing, and the quality of the relationships among all classes is being affected by the growth of impersonal, large-scale, industrial forms of wage employment, and the exigencies of a mass society. Brazil is no longer a stable society without social or economic mobility, but a highly dynamic society in a state of rapid flux. The traditional lower class is splitting into an agricultural peasantry, a new factory in the field proletariat, and a rapidly expanding metropolitan lower class which includes industrial workers. A new metropolitan upper class whose power stems from the ownership of industrial plants and commercial enterprises is taking the place of the traditional elite. A new middle class consisting of salaried professionals and white-collar workers is appearing.[2]

---

[2] Charles Wagley, *An Introduction to Brazil*, pp. 100-101. For analyses of the impact of the changing Brazilian class structure on politics, see Irving Louis Horowitz, *Revolution in Brazil*. For a penetrating study of changes in Brazilian stratification, see L. A. Costa Pinto, *Sociología e desenvolvimento*, Terceira Parte. For an ethnographic description of social classes in a small city in Mexico, with comparative data from a city in Colombia, see Andrew H. Whiteford, *Two Cities of Latin America*. For additional materials on the changing class structure in Latin America, see Gino Germani, *Política y sociedad en una época de transición*, Cap. VI; and Joseph A. Kahl (ed.), *La industrialización en América Latina*, Tercera Parte. See also a careful study of census data in Argentina and Chile that raises some impor-

The Respondents' Status Indices

Our data allow me to discuss some of the relations among the key characteristics of social stratification in precise statistical language. Wherever possible, I will make comparisons between the structures of the metropolitan cities and the provincial small towns which we studied in Brazil and Mexico, thereby drawing some indirect inferences about the direction of historical change. Once more, I remind the reader that our samples, though large, are not randomly representative, and thus our inferences must be considered tentative.[3]

We have data on all our respondents on four key variables: occupation, education, income, and self-identification; in Table 28 the correlation matrices of these four variables are shown for both Mexico and Brazil. The range of correlations—from .48 to .72— suggests that all four variables are intimately related.

The relations among the variables can be further summarized by a principal axis factor analysis, which indicates that all four reflect a single underlying dimension of socio-economic status. The loadings of each variable on that dimension are as follows:

	BRAZIL	MEXICO
Occupation	.87	.86
Education	.84	.84
Income	.77	.82
Identification	.77	.75

Since the loadings are correlations between the common factor and each variable within it, I conclude that these high loadings indicate that the underlying dimension is an excellent predictor of a man's score on any one of the component variables, and that the structure of socio-economic status is very similar in both countries.[4] Indeed, the

---

tant questions about the stereotype of a two-class system in traditional society: Torcuato S. Di Tella, *La teoría del primer impacto del crecimiento económico.*

[3] Only one study using a representative sample of a whole society in Latin America has been published: Melvin M. Tumin, *Social Class and Social Change in Puerto Rico.* For the city of São Paulo, see Bertram Hutchinson, *et al., Mobilidade e trabalho.* For preliminary reports on a comparative study of four capital cities, see various articles by Hutchinson, Germani, and others in *América Latina,* 1962, *et seq.*

[4] And similar to the United States; see, for example, Joseph A. Kahl and James A. Davis, "A Comparison of Indexes of Socio-Economic Status," *American Sociological Review,* 20 (June 1955), 317-325. In that study, income was somewhat less

Table 28

Correlations of Occupation, Education, Income, and Identification[1]

	BRAZIL EDUCATION	INCOME	IDENTIFICATION
Occupation	.72	.55	.52
Education	...	.48	.51
Income	...	...	.48
	MEXICO EDUCATION	INCOME	IDENTIFICATION
Occupation	.67	.60	.52
Education	...	.58	.48
Income	...	...	.50

[1] Classification of variables:

Occupation:	1.	Unskilled or semiskilled manual
	2.	Skilled manual
	3.	Foremen
	4.	Low white-collar
	5.	High white-collar
Education:	1.	Incomplete primary
	2.	Complete primary
	3.	Incomplete secondary
	4.	Complete secondary
	5.	Postsecondary
Income:	1.	Less than 7,200 cruzeiros (Brazil, 1960), or less than 800 pesos (Mexico, 1963)
	2.	7,201 to 12,000 cruzeiros, or 801 to 1,200 pesos
	3.	12,001 to 18,000 cruzeiros, or 1,201 to 1,600 pesos
	4.	18,001 to 36,000 cruzeiros, or 1,601 to 2,400 pesos
	5.	Over 36,000 cruzeiros, or over 2,400 pesos
Identification:	1.	Poor or operative class
	2.	Working class
	3.	Lower-middle class
	4.	Upper-middle or upper class

factor accounts for 66 per cent of the variance of the four indicators.

A rotation of axes designed to extract oblique subfactors shows that occupation and education are so intimately intertwined as to be inseparable, and that once they are "controlled," income and identification each appear as single-variable additional factors.

related to the other variables. See also Gino Germani on Buenos Aires, cited below, note 14.

To the degree that a stratification system is traditional, it should be "crystallized"—that is, the various status characteristics should be highly related, since change is slow and mobility uncommon. As Wagley wrote, all the characteristics are part of a single constellation, so prediction from one to another should be relatively safe. A man's position on any one status measure should be "congruent" with all the others. Therefore, we would predict *more* crystallization in small towns than in capital cities, even though the former do not reach all the way to the extreme pole of traditionalism.

A simple measure of such crystallization is the percentage of variance among the separate indices that is controlled by the common factor of socio-economic status.[5] To confirm the hypothesis, we should find a higher percentage in the provinces, yet the results do not fit the expectation:

Provincial Brazil:	67 per cent
Provincial Mexico:	62 per cent
Rio de Janeiro:[6]	63 per cent
Mexico City:[6]	67 per cent

Furthermore, examination of the factor loadings for each type of community discloses no consistent pattern distinguishing the towns from the metropolises. In both countries, income has a slightly higher weight in the provinces than the metropolises. However, in Mexico, identification has a higher weight in the provinces, whereas in Brazil the opposite is the case. In both countries, occupation is a little more important than education in the metropolises, but they are about equal in the provinces.

The most important result is not the small differences, but the uniformity. In all communities, education and occupation are the most significant indices, and whatever variations there are among the other indicators are all quite small. To judge from these materials, the provinces have stratification systems similar in structure to those of the capital cities.

I was surprised by the results, for I had expected several differences

---

[5] I believe this measure of crystallization of the *system* is novel; other authors have concentrated on measures for *individuals*, as, for instance, Gerhard E. Lenski, "Status Crystallization: A Non-Vertical Dimension of Social Status," *American Sociological Review*, 19 (August 1954), 405–413.

[6] I am using here only men reared in the big city; migrants to the city have been eliminated. The variance controlled for migrants in Brazil was 63 per cent, and for Mexico, 70 per cent.

between small towns and large cities. I had predicted that the provinces, in comparison to the metropolises, would show: (*a*) a higher correlation between education and occupation, reflecting a sharper split between working and middle classes; (*b*) a higher relation between education and identification, and a lower relation between income and identification, reflecting the influence of a man's self-image of family tradition and the cult of elitism through school diplomas; (*c*) less intergenerational mobility. None of these predictions was borne out by the data; some further details will be given below.

Index of SES

As an index of socio-economic status (SES) to relate to values and attitudes, we chose three variables in combination: occupation, education, and identification. The first two are the principal components of the common factor of socio-economic status, and the third has special theoretical interest (discussed below). This index usually correlates with class-related values and attitudes about five points higher than does either occupation or education by itself. Adding additional components would not increase the power of the index for the simple reason that the status components are so highly intercorrelated among themselves.[7]

Measures of Parental Status

When we inquired about the socio-economic status of a man's father, we found that many respondents lacked information. Eight per cent of the Brazilians and 29 per cent of the Mexicans were unable to supply data on both the occupation and education of their fathers. Eliminating those men from the samples, we then calculated correlations with the respondent's own occupation:

	BRAZIL	MEXICO
Father's occupation	.49	.50
Father's education	.44	.43

Similar coefficients with the respondent's own education were:

[7] In the index of SES, each component was weighted by its loading on the principal axis factor extracted from the three items. The weights were automatically applied by the computer program which extracted the factors and calculated index scores for each person. An unweighted index would produce almost identical results.

	Brazil	Mexico
Father's occupation	.52	.50
Father's education	.52	.55

Factor analysis showed that the status characteristics of the father fit into the principal axis factor of the son's socio-economic status, but that oblique rotations neatly separated out the scores of the father from those of the son. Thus the education and occupation of the father are more intimately related to each other than to the status indicators for his son. (Additional details on the relation between the status of fathers and sons are given in Appendix B.)

Social-Class Identification

Starting with the pioneering work of Centers, the empirical measurement of social-class identification has been of interest to many scholars; of course, its theoretical importance as an intervening variable between position in the social structure and attitudes and behavior has been recognized since Marx.[8]

We gave our respondents a number of labels and asked them to choose the one they considered best for themselves; not having much previous research of this nature in Latin America to draw on, we offered quite a few different terms, perhaps sacrificing some comparability between countries at the lower end of the hierarchy by so doing. The full list was as follows:

	Brazil	Mexico
Upper class	Classe alta	Clase alta
Upper-middle class	Classe média, parte de cima	Clase media alta
Lower-middle class	Classe média, parte de baixo	Clase media baja
Working class	Classe trabalhadora	Clase trabajadora
Operative class	Classe operária	Clase obrera
Poor class	Classe pobre	Clase pobre
Humble class	. . . .	Clase humilde

[8] Richard Centers, *The Psychology of Social Classes*. For Rio de Janeiro, see Gláucio Ary Dillon Soares, "Classes sociais, strata sociais e as eleições presidenciais de 1960," *Sociología* (September 1961). For the Brazilian provincial scene, see Celso Furtado, *Dialética do desenvolvimento*, Segunda Parte, Cap. III, and his *Pre-revolucão Brasileira*, both of which present penetrating theoretical analyses based on personal experiences and historical materials. A recent synthesis is helpful: Francisco C. Weffort, "Estado y masas en el Brasil," *Revista Latinoamericana de Sociología*, I (marzo 1965), 53-71.

| Lower class | . . . . | Clase baja |
| Country class | . . . . | Clase campesinada |

The last three categories were used in Mexico only. "Country class" was chosen by only seven men (though seventy-one used it to describe their fathers), and "lower class" was chosen by only eight men. "Humble class" was more popular (forty-five men), but seemed to be used by the same type of men as those who preferred to call themselves "poor class." In Table 29, these four categories are combined under the general heading of "poor." And since only six Brazilians and eight Mexicans chose to call themselves "upper class," they are combined with the upper-middle group.

Table 29 supports the idea that the basic split in a modern class hierarchy is between the white-collar workers, who tend to identify with the middle classes, and the manual workers, who tend to identify with the working or operative classes. Furthermore, the same basic line can be drawn between those who have attended secondary school and those who have not.

The term "working class" seems as ambiguous in Portuguese as it is in English. To some Brazilians, it means working for a living; thus a number of them with white-collar jobs and secondary educations choose that label. But for other men it means those who labor with their hands, especially in factories. Consequently, for the Brazilians it is not a very discriminating label, and among the Mexicans it has little popularity. By contrast, "operative" closely implies manual labor.[9]

The Mexicans at all levels identify upward considerably more than do the Brazilians.[10] Very few Mexicans with white-collar jobs or secondary education choose to call themselves "working" or "operative" class, whereas a substantial number of Brazilians do. Furthermore, 42 per cent of the Mexican manual workers—but only 23 per cent of the Brazilian manual workers—opt for the middle classes (this difference is partly, but not entirely, explainable by the fact that a

[9] Gláucio Soares, in his article cited in Note 8 and in "Economic Development and Political Radicalism" (unpublished doctoral dissertation, Washington University, St. Louis, 1965) has shown that among manual workers in Brazil and Mexico the label "operative" is preferred to "working" by those men who are more active in unions and more radical in politics; it carries Marxist connotations.

[10] And more than do North Americans, whose pattern is similar to that of the Brazilians. See Centers, *The Psychology of Social Classes*, p. 86.

higher percentage of the Mexican manual workers had attended secondary school).

But it is not just that Mexicans identify upward more than Brazilians: metropolitans in both countries identify upward more than provincials. We prepared tables similar in format to Table 29 for men in the small towns separate from men in the capital cities. In all the comparisons possible, the metropolitans always, with one exception, were more likely to call themselves "middle class" than were the provincials, usually to the extent of about ten percentage points. Only one comparison was opposite to the trend: Mexican provincials who had completed primary school identified with the middle class 61 per cent of the time, whereas metropolitans did so only 38 per cent of the time.

A combination of occupation and education improves the predic-

TABLE 29

Social-Class Identification, by Occupation and by Education

	BRAZIL						
	SOCIAL-CLASS IDENTIFICATION IN PERCENTAGE						
	POOR	OPERATIVE (OPERÁRIA)	WORKING (TRABALHADORA)	LOWER-MIDDLE	UPPER-MIDDLE	TOTAL %	N
Occupation							
Executive	0	04	08	33	55	100	72
Supervisor	0	11	29	35	25	100	28
Clerk or salesman	05	05	25	36	29	100	174
Foreman	05	24	38	19	14	100	37
Skilled manual	10	38	24	20	08	100	152
Unskilled or semi-skilled manual	10	37	37	11	05	100	164
All occupations	07	22	27	24	20	100	627
Education							
Postsecondary	00	04	10	40	46	100	50
Complete secondary	02	05	15	36	42	100	105
Incomplete secondary	04	10	28	34	24	100	108
Complete primary	08	30	33	17	12	100	168
Incomplete primary	11	37	33	14	05	100	196
All educations	07	22	27	24	20	100	627

MEXICO
SOCIAL-CLASS IDENTIFICATION IN PERCENTAGE

	POOR	OPERATIVE (OBRERA)	WORKING (TRABAJADORA)	LOWER-MIDDLE	UPPER-MIDDLE	TOTAL %	N
Occupation							
Executive	00	00	01	20	79	100	100
Supervisor	03	03	06	41	47	100	80
Clerk or salesman	10	10	05	31	44	100	108
Foreman	05	17	13	42	23	100	60
Skilled manual	12	29	14	27	18	100	238
Unskilled or semi-							
skilled manual	19	38	15	18	10	100	154
All occupations	11	21	09	27	32	100	740
Education							
Postsecondary	01	01	03	21	74	100	108
Complete secondary	06	06	08	41	39	100	64
Incomplete secondary	04	14	06	40	36	100	160
Complete primary	07	29	14	30	20	100	159
Incomplete primary	20	31	15	17	17	100	249
All educations	11	21	09	27	32	100	740

tion of identification, as shown in Table 30. Men with white-collar jobs (clerks and higher, Table 29) *and* at least some secondary education have better than 77 per cent probability of choosing the middle classes in Brazil, and 90 per cent in Mexico. Men with the same level of job, but only primary education, choose the middle classes 41 per cent of the time in Brazil, and 77 per cent in Mexico.

Similarly, manual workers with only primary education are highly likely to choose a label connecting them with the working classes, but those with some secondary education (especially in Mexico) are less likely to do so.

Deviant Cases

At this point, the analysis of deviant cases becomes challenging. For instance, who are the unusual men who identify with the working classes despite the fact that they hold white-collar jobs and have been to secondary school? As might be expected, they tend to be those who have some status characteristics lower in the scale than have the men who call themselves "middle class." That is, their jobs are routine, not supervisory; they did not finish secondary school; their incomes are lower; and in Mexico, their fathers' status is lower and they come from smaller towns of origin.[11]

TABLE 30
Social-Class Identification, by Occupation and Education Combined

	BRAZIL			
	SOCIAL-CLASS IDENTIFICATION IN PERCENTAGE			
	MIDDLE OR	WORKING OR		TOTAL
EDUCATION	UPPER	BELOW	%	N
All white-collar workers				
Some secondary or more	77	23	100	225
Primary or less	41	59	100	49
All manual workers				
Some secondary or more	37	63	100	38
Primary or less	21	79	100	315
All men	44	56	100	627

	MEXICO			
	SOCIAL-CLASS IDENTIFICATION IN PERCENTAGE			
	MIDDLE OR	WORKING OR		TOTAL
OCCUPATION	UPPER	BELOW	%	N
All white-collar workers				
Some secondary or more	90	10	100	224
Primary or less	77	23	100	64
All manual workers				
Some secondary or more	69	31	100	108
Primary or less	33	67	100	344
All men	59	41	100	740

Switching to manual workers with primary education who are deviant enough to identify up to the middle classes, we find that by comparison with similar men who identify with the working classes, they have higher levels of income and occupation, and have fathers of higher status. In Brazil, they come from larger towns of origin.

Other comparisons indicate the same pattern: all the "objective"

[11] All the comparisons given in the text are significant at .05 level or better.

status characteristics have some influence on identification. Therefore, although the dichotomies of occupation and education shown in Table 30 go a long way in predicting identification, some variance is left over that can be controlled further through finer categorization of occupation and education, and through additional objective status variables such as income, family background, and even the size of the town of origin.

Deviant identifications have interesting correlates with other subjective attitudes. For example, the men who had secondary education and hold white-collar jobs should normally call themselves "middle class." The small minority who call themselves "working class" can be thought of as unfortunate exceptions: their careers seem to them not quite so good as they "should" be. As a result, one might predict that in comparison with the majority, those men would have lower job satisfaction, feel less recent improvement in their standard of living, be more pessimistic, and expect less education for their sons. Those predictions are correct for both countries.[12]

Similarly, men with primary education who hold manual jobs should normally call themselves "working class." The small minority who call themselves "middle class" should be lucky exceptions, men whose careers seem a little better than they "should" be. Consequently, such men should sense more improvement in their standard of living, be less pessimistic, aim higher for their sons, and show more job satisfaction—as in fact, they do.[13]

Time Sequence

The time sequence of status events in the life cycle of a man could be posited to have an increasing effect upon his identification. That is, a status characteristic that is a symbol of his current adult status, that sums up all previous status events, should have more influence on his thinking than some earlier characteristic. The natural time sequence should be: father's education, father's occupation, respondent's education, respondent's occupation, respondent's income, respondent's identification. We tested this hypothesis through correla-

[12] And in Mexico, which was the only country in which this scale was used, they indicated less Life Satisfaction (see Chapter V for definition). The differences on Pessimism failed to reach the .05 level of significance in Brazil.

[13] The differences on Job Satisfaction in Brazil failed to reach the .05 level of significance.

tion coefficients, and found that the facts of life only partially match the neatness of the theory.

The zero-order coefficients connecting the father's status characteristics to the respondent's identification range from .35 to .42, whereas the coefficients connecting the respondent's own objective status characteristics to his identification are all close to .50. The latter predict identification better than the former, as theory would suggest. But, among the respondent's objective characteristics, there is no rank order of sufficient power to predict identification; they are all about equal.

Multivariate Analysis of Identification

It is useful to analyze all the indicators simultaneously for both the respondent and his father by means of multiple and partial correlations, in order to discover the *relative* influence of each objective status characteristic upon identification, holding the others constant.

The multiple correlation between identification and all five background characteristics (respondent's occupation, education, and income and his father's occupation and income) is .59 in both countries. The relative strength of each of the five background characteristics as a predictor of identification is shown by the Beta Weights:

	BRAZIL	MEXICO
Occupation	.17	.24
Education	.17	.14
Income	.22	.21
Father's occupation	.14	.11
Father's education	.06	.02

In both countries, the indicators for the respondent's current position are more influential than the indicators for the father's status, yet the latter are not negligible. In Brazil, income is the most important indicator; in Mexico, occupation is in first place.[14]

---

[14] For a similar operation in Buenos Aires, see Gino Germani, "Clase social subjectiva e indicadores objectivos de estratificación," Colección Datos No. 3 (Instituto de Sociología, Universidad de Buenos Aires, 1963). He got a multiple correlation of .58 and Beta coefficients as follows:

Occupation	.23
House type	.22
Education	.11
Income	.09

A comparison of metropolitan with provincial men discloses one interesting fact: when other status characteristics are held constant, the identification of provincials is more influenced by income than is the identification of metropolitans. This implies that the provincial man, contrary to most theorizing, is not rigidly tied to a self-image reflecting family lineage or even schooling. When he makes more money, he changes his mental picture of himself. Therefore he may act more like the stereotype of the "economic man" than does his metropolitan cousin.

Identification as an Intervening Variable

If identification were a clear-cut intervening variable between objective social position and subjective attitudes about life and politics, as the theory of Marx would predict, then identification should have a higher relation to such attitudes than do objective status indicators. That is, a person who identifies with the middle class, even if he is a manual worker (which Marx would call "false consciousness"), should think like a middle-class person. But whether we use as our dependent variable such attitudes and values as modernism, or expected education of sons, or opinion as to whether the government should be active in economic life, in all instances the objective status indicators predict opinions somewhat better than does identification (usually with correlation coefficients about ten points higher).[15] However, when the objective indicators are held constant, identification does add a little to the prediction of attitudes.

We must conclude, therefore, that identification is but one of several indicators of socio-economic status, rather than an intervening variable of particular power to predict opinions.

Clerks versus Skilled Workers

The literature on social stratification has paid much attention to the line separating white-collar workers from manual workers. I

Father's occupation	.07
Father's education	.07

Germani found an additional fact of importance: When given the choice of the framework within which to indicate their level of identification, persons of higher status preferred a scheme of "prestige classes" (upper, middle, or popular), whereas persons of lower status preferred a scheme of "economic classes" (well-off, modest, or humble).

[15] Centers' data for the United States show the same thing, although he does not point it out in his *The Psychology of Social Classes*.

showed above that this occupational division is in fact rather clearly reflected in the subjective identifications of the men involved: above the line, most men called themselves "middle class," whereas below the line most men called themselves "working class."

But some authors have suggested that in modern society this distinction decreases in importance through time. It is said that as high schools become more widespread, upper-level manual workers as well as lower-level white-collar men receive secondary education. It is posited that differences in income, and thus variations in style of life, have become less marked than formerly. However, it has also been pointed out that national income statistics often exaggerate the blurring of the line in recent years, for women are now common in clerical positions but not in skilled manual positions, and they receive less money than men even when the work is equivalent. And it has been shown that age differences are important, for a higher proportion of clerical than skilled workers are young men starting their careers who will eventually climb up to supervisory positions.[16]

We took the two occupational categories closest to the "frontier" (excluding foremen, since their position is ambiguous and their number small): office workers and salesclerks on the one hand, and skilled manual workers on the other. There were 174 clerks in Brazil, and 108 in Mexico. There were 152 skilled workers in Brazil, and 238 in Mexico. We tested a series of contrasts between the two occupational groups, predicting that the clerks would score significantly "higher" than the skilled workers. Using the .01 level of significance as a guide, we found that clerks were definitely higher with respect to:

1. Their background (father's education and occupation).
2. Their education (most clerks had attended secondary school, whereas most skilled workers had not).
3. Their income in provincial zones (in the provinces, clerks earned about 50 per cent more than skilled workers; in the metropolitan zones, there were no differences).
4. Their identification (the clerks mostly calling themselves "middle class," the skilled men "operative class"; the difference was greater in Brazil).

[16] For a summary of the theoretical arguments, plus some data on the United States, see Richard Hamilton, "The Income Difference Between Skilled and White Collar Workers," *British Journal of Sociology*, XIV (December 1963), 363-373; see also his "Income, Class and Reference Groups," *American Sociological Review*, 29 (August 1964), 576-579.

5. Their modernism (as measured by Modernism I, Activism, or Trust. Interestingly enough, Pro Manual Work, which has a very low relation to the general syndrome of modernism, took on special meaning at this point of the stratification hierarchy: in both countries, the skilled workers were more in favor of it than the clerks, although the difference was not significant in Mexico).
6. Their belief in the importance of education (most of the clerks, but not the skilled workers, said that some education beyond secondary school was necessary nowadays; the difference was greater in Mexico).
7. The amount of education they expected for their sons (more of the clerks expected postsecondary for their sons. Interestingly enough, there was no difference between countries, despite the difference on the preceding item).

I had expected that clerks would prefer smaller families than would the skilled workers. Here the results were surprising, for in contrast to all the items listed above, the difference between countries turned out to be more important than the difference between occupational levels. In Mexico, the clerks, as predicted, preferred smaller families to a significant degree: an average of 3.5 instead of 4.2 children was considered as "ideal." In Brazil, there was almost no distinction between occupational groups, but the ideal family size was much smaller than in Mexico: the average came out to 2.6 children for clerks, and 2.5 for skilled workers.[17]

The final variables tested were job satisfaction and career satisfaction. There are two alternative hypotheses, both with considerable support in the literature: (1) Satisfaction is directly related to accomplishment, thus there is a linear positive correlation between occupational level and satisfaction. (2) Satisfaction is a relative matter, and depends as much upon aspiration as upon accomplishment—and since clerks aspire to higher levels than do skilled workers, they will be less satisfied despite more pay. In Brazil, the second hypothesis was significantly supported; in Mexico, the direction of the differences supported the first hypothesis, but the size of the differences hovered on the line of significance.[18]

I think the most interesting result of this exploration of the distinction between clerks and skilled workers is the finding that there

[17] See Chapter V for more details.
[18] See Chapter VI for more details.

is a major difference in educational background, but a very small difference in pay, especially in the metropolis. This contradicts the common assumption that only in advanced industrial countries do blue-collar workers approach a standard of living similar to that of white-collar workers. Persons who make the assumption probably underestimate the scarcity of trained factory workers in underdeveloped countries, and overestimate the scarcity of clerks. After all, clerks have a long history in traditional society, and the very prestige of white-collar work leads many young men to prepare for it. But the level of skilled factory workers is a newer category, and factory managers are always complaining of the difficulty of finding enough good men for the available jobs. Scarcity pushes up their pay. All the data I am acquainted with do support the notion that for less developed economies the range of pay from unskilled workers at the bottom to technicians and managers at the top is greater than it is in advanced economies (true for socialist as well as capitalist societies). However, our sample suggests that the difference in pay at the particular line separating skilled workers from clerks is not necessarily very great, at least in the big cities.

Conclusions

The data presented in this appendix support the idea that socioeconomic status is a multivariate phenomenon—there are several important "objective" characteristics that in combination shape "subjective" identifications and attitudes. Occupation and education are the most important among the former, but income, family background, and the size of the place of origin all have some additional effect. Furthermore, occupation and education are continua rather than discrete attributes: although it is sometimes helpful to simplify by contrasting such groups as "manual workers" with "white-collar workers," as soon as we make finer categorizations of occupational level we control additional variance in identification and in attitude.

Thus, those who begin with an analytic model (be it based on Marx or on Weber) that creates "ideal types" using dichotomous attributes must beware of reifying their categories. It may be theoretically legitimate to hypothesize from such a model that over a period of time factory workers will be more likely to identify with the working class and consequently to behave in a politically "appropriate" manner, but such a theoretical hypothesis should not be confused with a description of reality at any one moment, nor should it be accepted as "true" without some historical trend data to support it. Our data, which lack historical trends, nevertheless suggest that the model seriously oversimplifies reality. Not all factory workers identify alike; those in large cities, which presumably are further along the road to modernization, are more likely to identify with the middle classes than those in small towns, although Marxist theory would predict the opposite. Furthermore, the "objective" indicators of status predict many attitudes better than does self-identification.

So from many points of view it seems that a multivariate approach emphasizing several continua instead of one or two dichotomous attributes is the most powerful approach to an understanding of social stratification.

APPENDIX B

Fathers and Sons: Intergenerational Mobility

A society changes over a period of time from traditional to modern, but the capacity of an individual to make such a transition is often limited; once trained as a traditionalist, it may be hard for him to become a modernist. Consequently, the change of society often takes place through the alternation of generations; the son accomplishes what the father cannot. For example, the man who moves from the farm to the city is usually a very young man just starting his career; less hampered by the deeply ingrained habits of his father, he is more readily adaptable to a new milieu. Indeed, the father who may himself desire to make such a change, but recognizes his lack of the necessary skills, may deliberately inculcate in his son the desire to move, and may show him how to learn the needed skills, most particularly through staying in school longer than did the father.

Not only change, but also stability may be studied through the sequence of generations. A man who has achieved something he values will teach his son how to continue in the same path.

Our data permit analysis of this social process through three succeeding generations, for we have some information about the fathers of our respondents, and also some about the plans the respondents have for their sons. Here I shall attempt to measure the rates of succession and mobility. In Chapter IV I examined the role of values in the mobility process, and in Chapter VI assessed some consequences of mobility as subjectively experienced by our respondents.

Let it be stated once more: because our samples are not representative of total communities, I cannot legitimately compare one community as a whole with another. But since we are interested in social process, I can and must manipulate the data in ways which illuminate that process, generate ideas, and challenge myths. In this appendix, much of the material is designed to explore, not to demonstrate.

Rates of Mobility: Correlation Coefficients

The measurement of succession and mobility has become a favorite concern of sociologists. In recent years, this interest has narrowed to a study of the rates of mobility as defined by the relative rank of fathers and sons in the occupational hierarchy, both because occupation is the best single clue to over-all social status, and because data on occupations are readily obtainable. It is easy to ask a man about his own occupation, that of his father, and also about the occupational ambitions he has for his son. The answers to these questions can be used as indicators of more complex statuses. And the information taken from respondents in a survey can be related to information about the changing distribution of the labor force taken from census materials.

The intricacies of measurement are, however, more complex than they appear at first glance, and recent discussions of statistical problems have disclosed serious oversimplifications in earlier work. Furthermore, they have indicated a number of alternative methods, and the researcher thus must choose those which are most suited to his purposes and to his data.

Let us start with a simple measure of the over-all relation between the occupations of the respondents and the occupations of their fathers: the correlation is .49 in Brazil and .50 in Mexico.[1]

These coefficients are based, however, on a debatable assumption: that a simple classification of occupations into a series of crude categories that approximate a ranked hierarchy of status comes close enough to the requirements of an interval scale to justify the use of regression analysis. My position is that we can follow this procedure to make comparisons between different samples so long as we use the same procedure for the different samples, and that we can arrive at useful ideas of "more" or "less" mobility from one sample to another. But I do not think we are justified in applying the full logic of regres-

[1] These coefficients are based on a grouping of occupations into four ranks, as shown in a note to Table 32 and explained in the text commentary related to Table 32, below ("Matrices for Brazil and Mexico"). The highest rank was assigned a score of 4; the lowest, a score of 1. We have experimented with alternative groupings, including the five ranks shown in Appendix A, Table 28; despite the "hourglass" shape of the latter distribution, caused by the small number of foremen, the results are almost the same. So are results from a more detailed grouping into nine levels. Changing the number of levels rarely changes the coefficients more than .02 points.

sion analysis to data that depart so far from the assumptions underlying that technique; thus I do not recommend that one seek precise conclusions about percentage of variance explained, or degree of statistical significance.

Are the correlations for Brazil and Mexico "high" or "low"? Only by comparisons of various groups can we arrive at some standard of judgment. We can compare various subgroups within our samples, or we can compare our samples to the results of other researches. But here we run into the difficulty that our samples were not drawn as representative of the communities studied. However, their bias is known: they deliberately omit the extremes of university-trained professionals at the top, and underemployed workers at the bottom. Since all communities show more succession (less mobility) at the extremes than in the middle of the hierarchy, we can suspect that our samples underestimate the correlations between fathers and sons, and therefore overestimate the amount of mobility.[2]

Computing correlation coefficients from the grouped data shown in the occupational mobility matrices of various researches, we arrive at the series of correlation coefficients in Table 31. Commentary on Table 31 will follow after a short digression.

The basic assumption underlying an occupational classification is that it reflects a scalable hierarchy of socio-economic status, such that an occupation placed in a high category usually is one providing a high income, demanding a high education, granting high prestige, and leading to high self-identification. One of the difficulties of the occupational classification we have used above (which is similar to that used by most other researchers) is that the categories are not sufficiently homogeneous; for example, the level of "low nonmanual" includes people with a rather wide range of education, income, and prestige. The classification is somewhat improved for the present purpose of father-son comparison by using an index of socio-economic status instead of a mere classification of occupations. In Appendix A, I described the computation of such an index for the respondents, based upon occupation, education, and self-identification. We lacked data on the identification of fathers, but were able to compute for them an index that combines information about occupation and education (weighted equally). These indices for each generation were

---

[2] The reader must remember that the correlation coefficients measure the closeness of relation between fathers and sons; thus, the higher the coefficient, the *more* succession and the *less* mobility.

TABLE 31

Occupations of Fathers and Sons: A Comparison
of Correlation Coefficients

	CORRELATION
Brazil	
Total sample	.49
Metropolitans	.44
Migrants	.39
Provincials	.46
Mexico	
Total sample	.49
Metropolitans	.48
Migrants	.46
Provincials	.47
São Paulo[1]	.61
Indianapolis[2]	.32
United States[3]	.52
Puerto Rico[4]	.21

[1] From Bertram Hutchinson, as reported in S. M. Miller, "Comparative Social Mobility," *Current Sociology*, Vol. IX, No. 1 (1960), p. 68.
[2] From Natalie Rogoff, *Recent Trends in Occupational Mobility*, p. 45.
[3] From Survey Research Center, University of Michigan, as reported in S. M. Miller, *loc. cit.*, p. 78.
[4] From Melvin Tumin, as reported in S. M. Miller, *ibid.*, p. 76.
N.b.: For purposes of comparison, the data from the original sources have been reorganized into four categories: Upper nonmanual, Lower nonmanual, Upper manual, and Lower manual. In all instances, respondents who are farmers have been eliminated. See text commentary ("Matrices for Brazil and Mexico") for Table 32, below, for precise definitions of the categories.

standardized for each country (with the samples divided into six equal-sized categories). We then computed the correlation between the SES of fathers and sons; it is .60 in both Brazil and Mexico, an increase of ten points over the coefficients for the occupations of fathers and sons.[3]

[3] For a careful examination of the logic of such a procedure, see Otis Dudley Duncan and Robert W. Hodge, "Education and Occupational Mobility: A Regression Analysis," *American Journal of Sociology*, LXVIII (May 1963), 629-644. Using a technique analogous, but not identical, to our own, Duncan and Hodge arrived at a father-son correlation of .30 for a representative sample of Chicago males (omitting sons of farmers) between the ages of twenty-five and sixty-four years in the labor force in 1951. They report that Kaare Svalastoga found a coefficient of .49 for older men and .41 for younger men in a national sample of Danes.

What conclusions can we draw from correlational analysis? Even though our samples contain a bias which underestimates the true correlation coefficients of succession, they still come out rather high by comparison with other countries. Using the occupational ranks, we got coefficients similar to that for the United States, but much higher than those for the city of Indianapolis or the island of Puerto Rico. Only the city of São Paulo showed a coefficient higher than any in our data. Using indices of SES, we got coefficients that are much higher than those for the United States as a whole, or France, or Denmark, or the cities of Indianapolis and Chicago. Thus our data suggest relatively high rates of succession in Brazil and Mexico.

I was surprised that the rates of succession in our data were about the same for the provincial towns as for the capital cities. Indeed, the only subgroup with a somewhat lower rate than the others was the category of migrants in Brazil. Ordinarily, the theory of succession and mobility expects less succession in big and rapidly growing industrial centers than in small and supposedly stable provincial towns. Let us then explore alternative explanations for our unexpected results.

Are our rates of succession too high for the capital cities, thus obscuring the expected regional difference? The data from Hutchinson for São Paulo (based on a random sample of the city) tend to support our results from Rio de Janeiro: compared to cities in other countries, there is much succession and little mobility in *both* of the big and growing cities of Brazil.

Are our rates of succession too low for the provincial towns? This in fact may be the case. I was reminded by Professor Raúl Benítez Zenteno that we went to some small towns that had experienced a recent intrusion of new industry and commerce. Therefore, by choosing in those towns men who held positions paying wages and salaries we were selecting men whose jobs often did not exist a generation ago, so of course the respondents had to be mobile with respect to their fathers, who were often farmers. If the occupational structure

---

In an article (written in 1964) titled "Methodological Issues in the Analysis of Social Mobility" (in *Social Structure and Mobility in Economic Development*, ed. Neil J. Smelser and Seymour Martin Lipset), Duncan applied his method to the data of Natalie Rogoff on Indianapolis for 1940 and got a coefficient of .37. For a national sample of the United States, he got a coefficient of .42. And for a national sample of France, which used a somewhat different method of scaling occupations, Duncan recalculated data of Marcel Bresard (1948) and got a coefficient of .45.

remains roughly constant for another generation, then the supposed traditionalism of provincial culture may reassert itself, and the sons of the present incumbents of the jobs may have a high probability of succeeding their fathers. In other words, for certain types of occupational structure (in small towns more than big cities), changes may come in spurts rather than through continuous steps. We chose towns which had recently undergone a spurt of change, and thus may well have picked towns with higher than ordinary mobility.

In summary: If one is willing to accept the results of our inadequate sampling procedure, he would conclude that Brazil and Mexico have high rates of succession (low mobility) compared to other countries, and that metropolitan-provincial differences in rates have not been proved.

But contrastingly, analysis by a different statistical procedure—inflow percentages, instead of correlation coefficients (presented below)—suggests no major differences between Brazil and Mexico and other countries.

Father's SES, Son's Education, Son's SES

The preceding analysis showed that the status position of a son is strongly influenced by that of his father. But nevertheless, there is still considerable room for maneuver that permits a son to find a level that differs from that of his father. The chief way of finding such a different level is through obtaining an increased amount of education. Yet our analysis is complicated by the fact that the status of the father influences the amount of education gained by most sons.

In other words, the status of a father has a direct influence on the status of his son, and also an indirect influence via the son's education.

Combining the direct and indirect influences gives us a high level of prediction: the multiple correlation of father's SES, plus son's education, with the dependent variable of son's SES, produces a coefficient of .85 in both countries. Holding the son's education constant produces a partial correlation between the SES of father and son of approximately .25. Holding the father's SES constant, on the other hand, produces a partial coefficient between the son's education and his SES of about .75—a much smaller change. (The Beta Weights are .17 for the father's SES, and .74 for the son's education, which explain 11 per cent and 50 per cent, respectively, of the variance in the son's SES.)

We see, therefore, that the paramount way in which the father influences the status of his son is through the education he helps the son obtain.[4] Nevertheless, there is some additional influence from the father's status that continues to be felt *after* the son has left school, be it through monetary aid, through the help of relatives and friends in high places, or perhaps through the continuing effect upon behavior of the values that the father taught the son.

Problems of Matrix Analysis of Occupational Mobility

For the comparisons of the average mobility in different samples, the correlation coefficient appears to be the most useful measure. It does not depend so directly upon the size and number of categories used as does an index that is based on a count of the proportion of men who have moved out of one category into any unspecified other category (such as the Index of Association, described below, or any of its variants), since correlational analysis is sensitive to the *distance* moved as well as to the *fact of movement*. Thus, dividing the samples into three, four, ten, or a hundred levels should produce roughly equivalent estimates of the coefficients of correlation.[5]

For many purposes, however, we are less interested in the average rate of mobility over an entire sample than we are in the rates of movement out of, or into, certain specific categories. We may wish to ask such questions as: Is the professional elite relatively "open" to new members? Is the son of an unskilled laborer "stuck" at the bottom of the system? Notice that these two questions are posed in an opposite direction: the first asks, What proportion of the present members of the elite have moved into that level from some lower rank? This is called *inflow* analysis. The second asks, What proportion of the sons of some group of unskilled workers have succeeded in climbing to a higher rank? This is known as *outflow* analysis.

[4] The zero-order relation between the father's SES and the son's education is .58 in both countries. Since the son's SES includes his education, some readers may prefer an analysis based on his occupational rank alone. The multiple correlation between the father's SES plus the son's education with the son's occupation is about .70 in both countries. Holding the son's education constant reduces it to about .21; holding the father's SES constant reduces it to about .54. The Beta Weights are about .20 for the father's SES and about .57 for the son's education, which explain 14 per cent and 40 per cent, respectively, of the variance in the son's occupation. See Duncan and Hodge, "Education and Occupational Mobility: A Regression Analysis," for similar data on Chicago.

[5] By contrast, any measurement that merely counts movement across the boundaries between categories will automatically increase the movement every time the number of boundaries is increased.

The data come from the same source: a matrix cross-classifying the occupations of a set of respondents with the occupations of their fathers. But outflow analysis computes percentages for the table so that fathers in each category add up to 100 per cent, whereas inflow analysis computes percentages for the table so that sons in each category add up to 100 per cent. The conclusions we reach may be diametrically opposite. For example, in most tables there will be a small professional elite and a large group of unskilled workers. Thus a small outflow from the latter (say, 5 per cent) may produce a large inflow (say, 60 per cent) into the former. Concentration on the first percentage leads one to talk of low mobility, and concentration on the second percentage leads one to exclaim over high mobility!

In S. M. Miller's[6] careful work on international comparisons of mobility data, he lists some advantages and some disadvantages of each perspective; I shall follow him, and add some additional aspects.

Inflow analysis is in many respects the most meaningful technique for the sociological issues that lead us to study mobility rates. What we are usually trying to do is discover the background of a given stratum as a clue to its *current* ideology and behavior. If, for example, the lower-middle class is mainly composed of people who have moved up from manual-worker backgrounds, we expect that their ascent will lead them to be contented with their current positions, and mildly conservative in their political outlook, for they should want to preserve their gains. On the other hand, if the lower-middle class consists mainly of men who have been forced down from higher levels (perhaps from independent entrepreneurs to clerks and salesmen, reflecting the growth of large-scale enterprises), we suspect that their outlook may be one of bitterness and discontent, and that they will join the "radical right" or fascist types of social movements.

Furthermore, inflow analysis to a large degree abstracts us from the necessity of a random sample of the population involved. So long as we have quite a large number of men in the lower-middle class (enough to assume that our sample may be representative of that class itself), we need not have in our sample a number of lower-middle class men that is proportionate to the percentage of that stratum in the community.

---

[6] S. M. Miller, "Comparative Social Mobility," *Current Sociology*, Vol. IX, No. 1 (1960). The other basic source of comparative data is S. M. Lipset and R. Bendix, *Social Mobility in Industrial Society*. Lipset and Bendix use outflow analysis to study the mobility in both directions across the line separating manual from non-manual workers, and inflow analysis in their discussion of elites.

The drawback in inflow analysis is that many conclusions reached about a given cell in a matrix are so closely dependent on the occupational distribution of the generation of fathers. Thus if we note that 50 per cent of the professionals in the sample come from professional backgrounds, we cannot assess the full significance of that percentage until we know how many fathers in general were professionals. If we find that only 4 per cent of all fathers were professionals, then we conclude that 50 per cent is a high figure, one that goes well beyond "chance" expectation (which assumes no determinant relation between the positions of fathers and their sons). But if 50 per cent of all the fathers were professionals, then we would conclude that there is no special advantage in being the son of a professional.[7]

The occupational distribution of fathers will vary from one society to another. Thus if our purpose is to compare two systems in terms of sheer amounts of mobility, inflow analysis is defective; but if our purpose is to concentrate on the *present* composition of a given stratum in terms of its background, and compare it to another stratum in the same sample, or to a similar stratum from a different sample, then inflow analysis is appropriate.

For comparing different samples in order to judge the relative amounts of mobility, outflow analysis has certain advantages. Here the occupational distribution of the generation of fathers is unimportant; we can estimate from a survey, for example, that a given percentage of the sons of manual workers climb into white-collar ranks, regardless of the proportion of manual-worker fathers in the system. This takes us out of the difficulty of estimating the distribution of fathers from sample data based on responses of sons.

However, the opportunity for the son of a manual worker to climb into white-collar ranks does depend upon the proportion of white-collar jobs that currently exists in the system. Therefore, comparisons between two systems that do not control for the current occupational distribution may lead to misleading conclusions.

---

[7] There is an additional problem: it seems to be impossible to estimate properly the occupational distribution of the generation of fathers. The fathers in the sample are not representative of the generation of fathers, since not every father has only one son, and the sampling frame is based on sons. And the census distribution for an earlier year does not properly portray the generation of the fathers of the men in the sample, since varying ages (and differential reproduction) mean that the fathers were in the labor force at varying points in time. See Duncan, "Methodological Issues." His critique invalidates some conclusions I reached in *The American Class Structure*, Chap. IX.

The effect of the distribution of occupations is particularly important when it is changing during the period under study. If there is a growth in the proportion of white-collar workers over time (as is true during industrialization), then sons have more abstract opportunity to be white-collar workers than did their fathers. Now, an individual who has climbed either does not know or does not care whether he has climbed into a newly created position; thus the problem is unimportant if we are interested in the ideology of the present strata. But if we are concerned with the measurement of an abstract concept such as "openness," or lack of rigidity in a system, then we may want to concentrate on movement that is pure exchange of persons: some move up because others move down. For this purpose, we have to control for changes in the distribution of occupations from fathers to sons, as estimated by the differences between the marginal distributions of the matrix table.[8]

Matrices for Brazil and Mexico

The most complete description of the succession and mobility that is shown by our data would be a set of six father-son matrices: one for each country for each of three subsamples—metropolitans, migrants, and provincials. But it is difficult to absorb such a mass of numbers. Since the samples are not representative of their particular communities, and since we are primarily interested in the effects of mobility upon attitudes, the most appropriate summary statistics are the percentages of inflow of men into key strata from above and below, plus the percentage of those who have remained stable.

Our data are shown in Table 32. I have decided to use four strata: first is the division into nonmanual and manual workers, since so much cross-national research has been done using that dichotomy. Then each category is subdivided into two parts in order to get a more refined picture of the situation. And to give some comparative facts, similar data for a few other samples are given in Table 33. The categories are defined as follows:[9]

---

[8] This has usually been done through the Index of Association, worked out by Glass in England and Natalie Rogoff in the United States; see D. V. Glass *et al.,* *Social Mobility in Britain;* and Rogoff, cited above in Table 31, note 2. See also the critique of this index by Sabura Yasuda, "A Methodological Inquiry into Social Mobility," *American Sociological Review,* 29 (February 1964), 16-23.

[9] It must always be remembered that for matrix analysis the number and definition of strata are crucial, and must be the same for all samples that are compared: the more strata, the more mobility.

High nonmanual: professionals or semiprofessionals; employers or managers with five or more subordinates.

Low nonmanual: nonmanual supervisors or employers with fewer than five subordinates; clerks or salesmen; farmers with subordinates.

All nonmanual: both High and Low nonmanual.

High manual: foremen and skilled workers.

Low manual: semiskilled and unskilled workers; farmers without subordinates.

All manual: both High and Low manual.

TABLE 32

Inflow Mobility Percentages for Brazil and Mexico

PERCENTAGE AND NUMBER	BRAZIL				MEXICO			
	TOTAL	MET.	MIG.	PROV.	TOTAL	MET.	MIG.	PROV.
High nonmanual								
Upward	69	59	100	80	64	60	64	85
Stable	31	41	000	20	36	40	36	15
Downward	00	00	000	00	00	00	00	00
N	(72)	(49)	(8)	(15)	(100)	(73)	(14)	(13)
Low nonmanual								
Upward	33	31	56	30	32	39	21	28
Stable	48	43	33	62	57	47	68	66
Downward	19	26	11	8	11	14	11	6
N	(199)	(120)	(18)	(61)	(185)	(90)	(28)	(67)
All nonmanual								
Upward	30	28	42	29	28	29	24	26
Stable	70	72	58	71	72	71	76	74
Downward	00	00	00	00	00	00	00	00
N	(271)	(169)	(26)	(76)	(285)	(163)	(42)	(80)
High manual								
Upward	29	18	48	31	27	18	25	36
Stable	39	43	18	48	46	46	39	50
Downward	32	39	35	21	26	37	37	14
N	(183)	(82)	(40)	(61)	(296)	(112)	(52)	(132)
Low manual								
Upward	00	00	00	00	00	00	00	00
Stable	55	35	69	58	44	39	68	35
Downward	45	65	31	42	56	61	32	65
N	(160)	(51)	(64)	(45)	(149)	(66)	(31)	(52)

All manual

Upward	00	00	00	00	00	00	00	00
Stable	72	65	76	76	75	67	69	86
Downward	28	35	24	24	25	33	31	14
N	(343)	(133)	(104)	(106)	(445)	(178)	(83)	(184)

TABLE 33

Inflow Mobility Percentages for Other Researches[1]

PERCENTAGE AND NUMBER	SÃO PAULO	INDIANAPOLIS	PUERTO RICO	U.S.A.
High nonmanual				
Upward	53	61	70	71
Stable	47	39	30	29
Downward	00	00	00	00
N	(180)	(1,511)	(417)	(102)
Low nonmanual				
Upward	38	55	33	35
Stable	54	21	52	58
Downward	9	24	15	7
N	(375)	(2,188)	(522)	(215)
All nonmanual				
Upward	31	52	32	33
Stable	69	49	69	68
Downward	00	00	00	00
N	(555)	(3,699)	(939)	(317)
High manual				
Upward	40	39	43	30
Stable	37	41	19	50
Downward	22	20	39	20
N	(353)	(2,163)	(314)	(118)
Low manual				
Upward	00	00	00	00
Stable	78	57	42	54
Downward	22	43	58	47
N	(148)	(3,925)	(974)	(170)
All manual				
Upward	00	00	00	00
Stable	83	82	52	82
Downward	17	18	48	18
N	(501)	(6,088)	(1,288)	(288)

[1] See Table 31 for sources of data.

Let us start our comparisons by looking at the percentage of non-manual workers who have arrived at that position by climbing up from manual backgrounds: it is approximately 30 per cent for our total samples in Brazil and Mexico, as well as for São Paulo, for Puerto Rico, and for the United States. Only the city of Indianapolis shows a higher figure—just over 50 per cent. Comparing our sub-samples, only the migrants in Brazil show a higher figure than the other groups; in contrast to our expectations, the provincial towns are not much different from the capital cities.[10]

If we confine our attention to just the upper part of the nonmanual group, men in supervisory or technical positions, we note that about two-thirds of them in Brazil and Mexico have climbed from some-what lower origins (not necessarily manual-worker backgrounds, but also from low nonmanual). Interestingly enough, the figure is higher for provincial towns than for metropolitan areas. (The exclusion of men with university degrees from our samples makes it inadvisable to compare our upper nonmanual group with those from other re-searches.)

We seem justified in suspecting that the present upper-status men in the provincial towns in Brazil and Mexico may not be what the stereotype of a rigid, traditional stratification order would suggest, namely, sons of elite men. The stereotype grows out of the notion of large landowners; it may be true of them, but is probably not true of the small-town businessmen and clerks. At any rate, our results, which contradict the stereotype, suggest that a more systematic study with larger and better samples would be worth while.

What about downward mobility? About 25 per cent of the manual workers in our total samples for Brazil and Mexico have descended from nonmanual backgrounds. The figure is just under 20 per cent for São Paulo, Indianapolis, and the United States as a whole. Only Puerto Rico diverges sharply from this pattern, with the higher figure of 48 per cent, which may reflect the decline of independent artisans.

Interestingly enough, the manual workers of the big cities have experienced more downward movement than those from the smaller towns—and the same is true if we look at the more refined figures separating high from low manual workers (with the one exception of low manual workers in Mexico). One explanation for this might be

[10] The correlation coefficients in Table 31 lead to the same conclusions about our subsamples, but not about international comparisons.

that a generation ago there were not many nonmanual fathers in small towns, hence not many sons who could slip into manual jobs.

Thus, international comparisons of mobility based on inflow percentages suggest that Brazil and Mexico are similar to the United States, whereas comparisons based on correlation coefficients suggested that Brazil and Mexico had less mobility. Since correlations are sensitive to the distance moved, perhaps the mobility in Brazil and Mexico occurs in very small steps.

Education and Mobility

Given a modern social structure, in which a son does not directly inherit his father's job, the son must obtain an "appropriate" education just to maintain his status at the same level as his father's, and must get even more training if he wishes to climb above his father. If the father is a bookkeeper, for example, it is likely that the son needs some secondary education before he can get a job similar to that of his father.

This process can be generalized in answer to the question: How much education is necessary at each level of status for a son to equal his father? There is a certain cutting point of years in school; above it, at least half of the sons will be equal to, or above, their fathers in status; below it, more than half the sons will fall in status relative to their fathers.

From the details shown in Table 34, I can indicate the approximate cutting point of the education that a son must have in order to avoid falling below his father in occupational status:

	BRAZIL	MEXICO
High nonmanual fathers:	Complete secondary	Complete secondary
Low nonmanual fathers:	Incomplete secondary	Complete primary
High manual fathers:	Incomplete primary	Incomplete primary

Note that a Mexican son of a low nonmanual father can maintain his position with less education than a similarly placed Brazilian son. And note, too, that only partial primary schooling is sufficient for skilled manual work. This finding suggests that the problem of "dropouts" from school which so perturbs educators may not be crucial at this level.

Let us change slightly the question to this form: How much education does a son need to *exceed* the level of his father? Again using the data from Table 34, we can construct a graphic picture as shown in Figure 2. The horizontal line which indicates the point at which 50 per cent or more of the sons exceed their fathers intersects with the curve of the son's education to give us the answer to the question. (Obviously, the sons of high nonmanual men cannot climb higher than their fathers, according to our definitions, so they are omitted.) The graphs indicate that for both categories of manual respondents

TABLE 34

Occupational Mobility of Respondents, by Father's Occupation and Respondent's Education

	Occupational Status of Son Relative to Father, in Percentage[1]						
	Brazil				Mexico		
	N	Higher	Same	Lower	N	Higher	Same	Lower
Father's occupation: High nonmanual Respondent's education:							
Postsecondary	(18)	0	56	44	(30)	0	77	23
Complete secondary	(24)	0	46	54	(9)	0	56	44
Incomplete secondary	(19)	0	11	89	(22)	0	36	64
Father's occupation: Low nonmanual Respondent's education:							
Postsecondary	(22)	23	64	14	(51)	51	35	14
Complete secondary	(49)	33	65	2	(29)	28	48	24
Incomplete secondary	(50)	16	60	24	(69)	10	54	36
Complete primary	(54)	7	28	65	(65)	6	51	43
Incomplete primary	(42)	00	12	88	(38)	00	8	92
Father's occupation: High manual Respondent's education:							
Postsecondary	(8)	75	25	00	(18)	78	17	6
Complete secondary	(23)	87	9	4	(19)	58	32	11
Incomplete secondary	(31)	65	29	6	(52)	31	58	12
Complete primary	(54)	11	65	24	(59)	19	56	25
Incomplete primary	(43)	2	53	44	(96)	3	68	29
Father's occupation: Low manual Respondent's education:							
Incomplete secondary	(7)	86	14	0	(17)	71	29	0
Complete primary	(47)	64	36	0	(31)	52	48	0
Incomplete primary	(106)	34	66	0	(108)	58	42	0

[1] Read percentages *across* rows only.

Figure 2

Education Required to Climb in Occupational Status Relative to Father

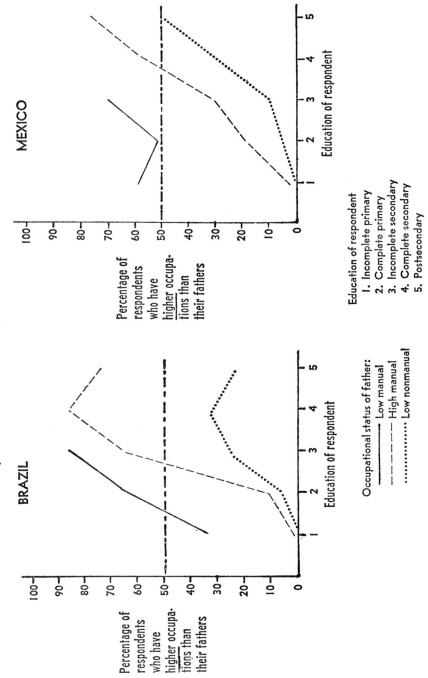

BRAZIL

MEXICO

Percentage of respondents who have higher occupations than their fathers

Education of respondent

Occupational status of father:
——— Low manual
– – – High manual
·········· Low nonmanual

Education of respondent
1. Incomplete primary
2. Complete primary
3. Incomplete secondary
4. Complete secondary
5. Postsecondary

it takes a little more education to get ahead of their fathers in Mexico than in Brazil. They also show that for sons of low manual fathers a little education goes a long way, but that for sons of low nonmanual fathers, even some postsecondary education is usually not enough for mobility—it takes a university degree, and our samples do not include such men.

Conclusions

This analysis began with a discussion of intergenerational mobility: the similarities and differences in the occupational and general socio-economic status of fathers and sons. Strengths and weaknesses of various measures of mobility were examined, and the limitations of our samples for certain of them were acknowledged. Correlational analysis suggested that Brazil and Mexico had rates of mobility that were rather low compared to some other countries, whereas inflow percentages indicated that they were similar to those countries. No firm decision can be reached as to which conclusion is "correct." It does seem reasonable to conclude, however, that regardless of which measure is used, the differences between Brazil and Mexico are slight, and that the differences between our particular towns and the metropolitan districts are also slight.

Then the steps through which a son achieves adult status were examined, and the importance of his education was high-lighted. The influence of the father's status upon the son's education was demonstrated. The amount of education the son needs to maintain status equal to that of his father was shown, as well as the amount necessary to provide upward mobility. These data should be interpreted in relation to the discussion of education given in Chapter IV.

APPENDIX C

Portuguese Translation of Value Scales

(See Chapter II, Table 1)

	Saturação fatorial, Brasil
I. Ativismo	
1) Fazer planos sòmente traz infelicidade, porque os planos dificilmente se realizam.	—.74
2) Não faz muita diferença se a gente elege um ou outro candidato porque nada vai mudar.	—.65
3) Hoje em dia, como as coisas andam, a pessoa inteligente deve se preocupar com o presente, sem se incomodar com o que pode acontecer amanhã.	—.63
4) Nós brasileiros sonhamos com grandes coisas, mas na realidade somos ineficientes com a indústria moderna.	—.57
5) O segrêdo da felicidade é não esperar demais da vida, e se conformar com aquilo que acontece.	—.47
6) (Não foi utilizado no Brasil)	
7) (Não foi utilizado no Brasil)	
II. Baixa estratificação das oportunidades profissionais	
8) A gente precisa ter boas relações com pessoas influentes para progedir na profissão.	—.71
9) O filho de um trabalhador não tem muita chance de chegar até as profissões liberais.	—.70
10) O homem de negócios tem amigos influentes que garantem o êxito de seus filhos.	—.70
III. Baixa estratificação da comunidade	
11) O contrôle desta cidade está nas maos de um pequeno grupo de pessoas, e um cidadão comum não tem muita influência.	—.84
12) A gente não gosta de admitir, mas esta cidade é realmente formada de grupos ou "panelinhas" bastante fechadas.	—.73
13) Esta cidade não é um lugar muito simpatico; a gente só pode fazer amizades com pessoas do mesmo tipo que o nosso.	—.67

IV. Baixa ênfase na ocupação

14) O emprêgo deve vir antes de tudo, mesmo acarretando prejuizo no tempo para diversão. —.68

15) O melhor meio de julgar um homem é pelo seu sucesso na profissão. —.61

16) A qualidade mais importante par um homem é sua fôrça de vontade e sua ambição acentuada. —.64

17) A coisa mais importante para um pai, é auxiliar seus filhos para conseguir na vida uma posição mais elevada do que a dêle. —.45

V. Baixa integração com parentes

18) Quando se está procurando um emprêgo, a gente deve arranjar um lugar perto dos pais, mesmo que isto signifique perder uma boa oportunidade. —.76

19) Quando uma pessoa está numa fase má da vida, sòmente pode contar com a ajuda dos parentes. —.75

20) Se houver oportunidade de contratar um ajudante no trabalho, sempre é melhor contratar um parente do que um estranho. —.64

VI. Individualismo

21) Para ser feliz, a gente deve se comportar como os outros desejam, mesmo que seja preciso não manifestar suas próprias idéias. —.75

22) Eu prefiro o emprêgo onde a gente trabalha dentro de um grupo, e onde todos participam igualmente do reconhecimento pelo trabalho bem feito. —.62

23) (Não foi utilizado no Brasil)

VII. Confiança nas pessoas

24) Não é bom deixar seus parentes saberem tudo a respeito de sua vida, pois êles podem tirar proveito de você. —.78

25) Não é bom deixar seus amigos saberem tudo a respeito de sua vida, pois êles podem tirar proveito de você. —.74

26) A maior parte das pessoas retribuirá sua amizade com ingratidão. —.55

27) A maior parte das pessoas é decente, e não se aproveita de você. (+.32)

28) (Não foi utilizado no Brasil)

29) (Não foi utilizado no Brasil)

Saturação fatorial,
Brasil

VIII. Participação em meios de divulgação de massa
30) O Sr. se interessa por notícias nacionais nos jornais e no rádio? (muito)   +.85
31) O Sr. se interessa por notícias internacionais nos jornais e no rádio? (muito)   +.79
32) O Sr. se interessa por notícias locais nos jornais e no rádio? (muito)   +.76
33) Pode dizer-me o nome do Presidente dos Estados Unidos? (resposta correta)   +.41
34) O Sr. discute muitas vêzes assuntos políticos com seus amigos? (sempre)   +.48
35) Pode dizer-me o nome do Presidente do México? (resposta correta)   +.36

IX. Desconfiança nas grandes empresas
36) Em geral, as grandes companhias são mais honestas e mais eficientes do que as pequenas companhias.   −.77
37) As grandes companhias são geralmente justas com seus empregados, a dão igual chance para todos subir.   −.74
38) As pessoas jovens têm melhor chance de progredir numa grande firma do que trabalhando por conta própria.   −.73

X. Preferência pelo trabalho manual
39) Trabalhar com ferramentas não é tão bom como lidar com papéis.   −.78
40) O emprêgo que faz uma pessoa sujar as mãos, não é bom emprêgo.   −.67
41) O Sr. preferiria ter um emprêgo num escritório, com salário menor, ou um emprêgo numa fábrica, com salário maior? (fábrica)   +.57

XI. Preferência pela vida urbana
42) Em geral, a vida é melhor nas cidades pequenas, porque todos se conhecem.   −.85
43) As pessoas nas cidades grandes são frias e fechadas; é difícil fazer novos amigos.   −.85

XII. Modernismo familiar
(Não foi utilizado no Brasil)

XIII. Baixa religiosidade
(Não foi utilizado no Brasil)

Saturação fatorial,
Brasil

XIV.   Assumir riscos
       (Não foi utilizado no Brasil)
       A maior parte das perguntas têm as seguintes respostas alternativas:
            Eu Concordo   Eu Discordo
            ———— Bastante   ———— Bastante
            ———— Um pouco   ———— Um pouco

APPENDIX D

Spanish Translation of Value Scales

(See Chapter II, Table 1)

	Peso factorial, México
I. Activismo	
1) Hacer planes solamente trea infelicidad, porque los planes siempre son difíciles de realizar.	—.63
2) No tiene mucha importancia si la gente elije uno u otro candidato pues nada va a cambiar.	—.58
3) Hoy en día, como andan las cosas, la persona inteligente debe pensar en el presente, sin preocuparse con lo que puede pasar mañana.	—.67
4) Nosotros lo mexicanos tenemos muchos sueños, pero en realidad somos ineficazes con la industria moderna.	—.54
5) El secreto de la felicidad es no esperar demasiado de la vida, y aceptar lo que pasa.	—.61
6) Es importante hacer planes para la vida y no solamente aceptar lo que venga.	+.46
7) ¿Qué importancia tiene para usted conocer anticipadamente y con toda claridad sus planes para el futuro? (muy importante)	+.41
II. Baja estratificación de oportunidades profesionales	
8) Uno necesita de buenas conecciones para poder adelantar en el mundo del trabajo.	—.75
9) El hijo de un obrero no tiene muchas probabilidades de llegar a ser profesionista.	—.54
10) Los hombres de negocios tienen amigos importantes que ayudan a sus hijos a tener éxito.	—.71
III. Baja estratificación de la comunidad	
11) El control de esta ciudad está en manos de un pequeño grupo de personas y el ciudadano común y corriente no tiene participación en lo que pasa.	—.74
12) A la gente no le gusta reconocerlo, pero esta ciudad está formada por pequeños grupos cerrados.	—.69

	Peso factorial, México

13) Esta ciudad no es un lugar muy agradable, uno solo puede tener amigos entre las personas que se asemejan mucho a uno. — −.77

IV. Bajo énfasis en la ocupación

14) El empleo debe ser considerado en primer lugar, aún cuando signifique sacrificar tiempo para divertirse. — −.58

15) La mejor manera de juzgar a un hombre es por su éxito en su ocupación. — −.67

16) Las cualidades más importantes de un hombre son la determinación y la ambición impulsora. — −.80

17) (No fue utilizado en México)

V. Baja integración con parientes

18) En busca de empleo, uno debería encontrar ocupación en un lugar cerca de sus padres, aunque esto implique perder una buena oportunidad en otra parte. — −.73

19) Cuando está uno en dificultades, solamente puede depender de la ayuda de los parientes. — −.78

20) Si uno tiene la oportunidad de dar un empleo a alguien, siempre es mejor darselo a un pariente que a un extraño. — −.65

VI. Individualismo

21) Para ser feliz, uno debe comportarse como les gusta a las demás personas, aún cuando uno tenga que reprimir sus propias ideas. — −.73

22) (No fue utilizado en México)

23) Cuando usted está en grupo, ¿prefiere tomar las decisiones usted mismo, o prefiere que otros las tomen? (usted mismo) — +.73

VII. Confianza en la gente

24) No es bueno dejar los parientes sepan todo de su vida, pues pueden aprovecharse de usted. — −.66

25) No es bueno dejar que los amigos sepan todo de su vida, pues pueden aprovecharse de usted. — −.71

26) La mayor parte de la gente paga la bondad con la ingratitud. — −.67

27) La mayoría de la gente es honrada y no se aprovecha de usted. — +.38

28) La gente se ayuda mutuamente no tanto por espíritu de justicia, sino por esperanza de ventaja. — −.62

	Peso factorial, México

29) Uno solo puede tener confianza en aquellos a quien conoce bien. — .40

VIII. Participación en medios de comunicación masiva

30) ¿Tiene interés en seguir las noticias nacionales en los periódicos, en el radio o en la televisión? (mucho) +.78

31) ¿Tiene interés en seguir las noticias internacionales en los periódicos, el radio o la televisión? (mucho) +.75

32) ¿Tiene interés en seguir las noticias de la comunidad local en los periódicos o en el radio o la T.V.? (mucho) +.65

33) ¿Como se llama el Presidente de los Estados Unidos? (respuesta correcta) +.49

34) ¿Discute frecuentemente problemas politicos con sus amigos? (siempre) +.52

35) ¿Podría usted decirme el nombre del Presidente del Brasil? (respuesta correcta) +.49

IX. Desconfianza en grandes empresas

36) En general las empresas grandes son más honestas y eficientes que las chicas. — .71

37) Las empresas grandes, por lo regular, son justas con sus empleados, y dan a cada hombre igual oportunidad de salir adelante. — .75

38) Los jóvenes tienen mejor oportunidad de salir adelante en una empresa grande que trabajando por cuenta propia. — .66

X. Preferencia por trabajo manual

39) Trabajar con instrumentos no es tan deseable como trabajar con papeles. — .72

40) Empleos en los que uno se ensucia las manos no son buenos empleos. — .79

41) Qué prefiere: ¿un trabajo de oficina con menos salario, o un trabajo en una fábrica, con mayor salario? (fábrica con mayor salario) +.40

XI. Preferencia por la vida urbana

42) En general, la vida es mucho mejor en ciudades pequeñas en donde se conoce a todo el mundo. — .85

43) La gente de la ciudad grande es fría e impersonal, y es difícil hacer nuevos amigos. — .85

XII. Modernismo familiar

  44) ¿Qué opinión prefiere usted?

      Si el esposo y su mujer son infelices, deberían
poder obtener el divorcio, o

        (El matrimonio es sagrado, y nunca debería ser terminado por el divorcio.)   +.52

  45) Que cuando las familias son grandes, los esposos limiten el número de hijos, o

      (Que no debe limitarse en ninguna forma el número de hijos.)   +.36

  46) Una esposa debe en el matrimonio hacer sus propias decisiones, aún en el caso en que no esté de acuerdo su marido, o

      (Una buena esposa es aquella que siempre obedece en todo a su marido.)   +.69

  47) A los niños, en ocasiones se les debe permitir estar en desacuerdo con sus padres, o

      (La obediencia y el respeto por la autoridad son las cosas más importantes que deben aprender los niños.)   +.64

  48) No hay porque las mujeres casadas no puedan trabajar si así lo desean, o

      (Las mujeres casadas deberían quedarse en casa y no trabajar para ganar dinero.)   +.62

XIII. Baja religiosidad

  49) ¿Qué es más importante para el futuro de México?

      El trabajo duro de la gente misma, o

      (la ayuda de Dios.)   +.54

  50) ¿Se considera usted más religioso o menos religioso que su padre? (Menos religioso)   +.64

  51) ¿Usted se considera estar religioso? (Muy religioso)   −.75

  52) ¿Cuantas veces estuvo usted en la Iglesia en los últimos dos meses? (ninguna o raremente)   +.75

XIV. Exposición a riesgos

  53) La clase de trabajo que usted preferiría sería:

      Un trabajo en donde casi siempre se dependa de uno mismo, o

        (Un trabajo en el que casi siempre haya una persona destinada a ayudar en los problemas que se presenten.)   +.48

Peso factorial,
México

54) Un trabajo en el que se tomen numerosas decisiones, o
(Un trabajo en el que se tomen pocas decisiones.)   +.58
55) Un trabajo en el cual lo que se haga está sometido al propio criterio como autoridad final, o
(Un trabajo en el que haya casi siempre una persona o procedimiento que corrija los errores.)   +.52
56) Un trabajo en el cual se pueda obtener un gran éxito o un completo fracaso, o
(Un trabajo en el cual jamás se obtendría un gran éxito pero tampoco un completo fracaso.)   +.65
57) Un trabajo sujeto a continuos cambios, o
(Un trabajo sujeto a poco cambios.)   +.47
58) Un trabajo excitante pero que podría ser de corta duración, o
(Un trabajo menos excitante pero indudablemente de larga duración.)   +.41

La mayoría de las preguntas hasta número 43 tiene las siguentas respuestas alternativas:

De Acuerdo	En Desacuerdo
——— mucho	——— mucho
——— un poco	——— un poco

BIBLIOGRAPHY

Almond, Gabriel A., and Sidney Verba. *The Civic Culture.* Princeton, N.J.: Princeton University Press, 1963.

Bennett, John W., and Iwao Ishino. *Paternalism in the Japanese Economy.* Minneapolis: University of Minnesota Press, 1963.

Blake, Judith, and Kingsley Davis. "Norms, Values and Sanctions," in *Handbook of Modern Sociology,* ed. Robert E. L. Faris. Chicago: Rand McNally, 1964.

Blalock, Hubert M., Jr. *Social Statistics.* New York: McGraw-Hill, 1960.

Blauner, Robert. "Work Satisfaction and Industrial Trends in Modern Society," *Labor and Trade Unionism,* ed. W. Galenson and S. M. Lipset. New York: Wiley, 1960.

Bori, Carolina Martuscelli. *Mobilidade e trabalho,* ed. B. Hutchinson. Rio de Janeiro: Centro Brasileiro de Pesquisas Educacionais, 1960.

Centers, Richard. *The Psychology of Social Classes.* Princeton, N.J.; Princeton University Press, 1949.

Collver, Andrew A. *Birth Rates in Latin America.* Berkeley: University of California, Institute of International Studies, Research Series No. 7, 1965.

Corwin, A. F. "Contemporary Mexican Attitudes toward Population, Poverty and Public Opinion," *Latin American Monographs,* No. 25, University of Florida, September 1963.

Costa Pinto, L. A. *Sociologia e desenvolvimento.* Rio de Janeiro: Editôra Civilização Brasileira, 1963.

————— (ed.). *Resistências a mudança.* Rio de Janeiro: Centro Latino-Americano de Pesquisas em Ciências Sociais, 1960.

Couch, Arthur, and Kenneth Kenniston. "Yeasayers and Naysayers," *Journal of Abnormal and Social Psychology,* 60 (March 1960), 151–174.

Duesenberry, James S. *Income, Saving and the Theory of Consumer Behavior.* Cambridge, Mass.: Harvard University Press, 1949.

Duncan, Otis Dudley. "Methodological Issues in the Analysis of Social Mobility," in *Social Structure and Mobility in Economic Development,* ed. N. J. Smelser and S. M. Lipset. Chicago: Aldine, 1966.

—————, and Robert W. Hodge. "Education and Occupational Mobility: A Regression Analysis," *American Journal of Sociology,* LXVIII (May 1963), 629–644.

Durkheim, Emile. "A Durkheim Fragment," *American Journal of Sociology*, LXX (March 1965), 527–536.

————. *The Division of Labor in Society*. Glencoe, Ill.: The Free Press, 1947. First published in Paris in 1893.

Elder, Glen H., Jr. "Family Structure and Educational Attainment," *American Sociological Review*, 30 (February 1965), 81–96.

Erasmus, Charles. *Man Takes Control*. Minneapolis: University of Minnesota Press, 1961.

Form, William H., and James A. Geschwender. "Social Reference Basis of Job Satisfaction," *American Sociological Review*, 27 (April 1962), 228–230.

Foster, George M. "Peasant Society and the Image of Limited Good," *American Anthropologist*, 67 (April 1965), 293–315.

————. *Traditional Cultures: The Impact of Technological Change*. New York: Harper, 1962.

Furtado, Celso. *Pre-revolução brasileira*. Rio de Janeiro: Fondo de Cultura, 1962.

————. *Dialética do desenvolvimento*. Rio de Janeiro: Fondo de Cultura, 1964.

Gans, Herbert J. *The Urban Villagers*. New York: Free Press, 1962.

Germani, Gino. "Clase social subjectiva e indicadores objectivos de estratificación," Colección Datos No. 3, Instituto de Sociología, Universidad de Buenos Aires, 1963.

————. *Política y sociedad en una época de transición: de la sociedad tradicional a la sociedad de masas*. Buenos Aires: Editorial Paidos, 1963.

Glass, D. V., *et al. Social Mobility in Britain*. London: Routledge & Kegan Paul, 1954.

Gonzáles, Casanova, Pablo. *La democracia en México*. México, D. F.: Era, 1965.

Goode, William J. *World Revolution and Family Patterns*. New York: Free Press of Glencoe, 1963.

Greeley, Andrew M. *Religion and Career: A Study of College Graduates*. New York: Sheed and Ward, 1963.

Hagen, Everett E. *On the Theory of Social Change*. Homewood, Ill.: Dorsey Press, 1962.

Hamilton, Richard. "The Income Difference Between Skilled and White Collar Workers," *British Journal of Sociology*, XIV (December 1963), 363–373.

————. "Income, Class and Reference Groups," *American Sociological Review*, 29 (August 1964), 576–579.

Harmon, Harry H. *Modern Factor Analysis*. Chicago: University of Chicago Press, 1960.

Harris, Marvin. *Town and Country in Brazil*. New York: Columbia University Press, 1956.

Homans, George Casper. *The Human Group*. New York: Harcourt Brace, 1950.

Horowitz, Irving Louis. *Revolution in Brazil*. New York: Dutton, 1964.

Hoselitz, Bert F., and Wilbert E. Moore (eds.). *Industrialization and Society.* Paris: UNESCO, 1963.

Hutchinson, Bertram, *et al. Mobilidade e trabalho.* Rio de Janeiro: Centro Brasileiro de Pesquisas Educacionais, 1960.

Inkeles, Alex. "Industrial Man," *American Journal of Sociology,* LXVI (July 1960), 1–31.

Jackson, Elton F. "Status Consistency and Symptoms of Stress," *American Sociological Review,* 27 (August 1962), 469–480.

Jaffe, A. J. *People, Jobs and Economic Development.* New York: Free Press of Glencoe, 1959.

Kahl, Joseph A. "Educational & Occupational Aspirations of 'Common Man' Boys," *Harvard Educational Review,* XXIII (Summer, 1953), 186–203.

———. "Some Social Concomitants of Industrialization and Urbanization," *Human Organization,* XVIII (Summer, 1959), 53-74.

———. "Some Measurements of Achievement Orientation," *American Journal of Sociology,* LXX (May 1965), 669–681.

———. *The American Class Structure.* New York: Holt, Rinehart and Winston, 1957.

——— (ed.). *La industrialización en América Latina,* Segunda Parte, "La fuerza de trabajo." México, D.F.: Fondo de Cultura Económica, 1965.

———, and James A. Davis. "A Comparison of Indexes of Socio-Economic Status," *American Sociological Review,* 20 (June 1955), 317–325.

Kiser, Clyde V., and P. K. Whelpton. "Summary of Chief Findings and Implications for Future Studies," *Milbank Memorial Fund Quarterly,* 36 (July 1958), 282–329.

Kluckhohn, Clyde. "Values and Value-Orientations in the Theory of Action," in *Toward a General Theory of Action,* ed. Talcott Parsons and Edward A. Shils. Cambridge, Mass.: Harvard University Press, 1951.

Kluckhohn, Florence Rockwood, and Fred L. Strodtbeck. *Variations in Value Orientations.* Evanston, Ill.: Row Peterson, 1961.

Lambert, Jacques. *Os dois Brasis.* Rio de Janeiro: Centro Brasileiro de Pesquisas Educacionais, 1959.

Lenski, Gerhard E. "Status Crystallization: a Non-Vertical Dimension of Social Status," *American Sociological Review,* 19 (August 1954), 405–413.

———. *The Religious Factor.* New York: Doubleday, 1961.

———. "The Religious Factor," in *Studies in American Society,* ed. D. L. Phillips. New York: Crowell, 1965.

Lerner, Daniel. *The Passing of Traditional Society.* New York: Free Press, 1958.

Lewis, Oscar. *The Children of Sánchez.* New York: Random House, 1961.

Lipset, S. M., and F. T. Malm. "First Jobs and Career Patterns," *American Journal of Economics and Sociology,* XIV (1955), 247–261.

Lipset, S. M., and R. Bendix. *Social Mobility in Industrial Society*. Berkeley: University of California Press, 1959.

Lockwood, David. *The Black-Coated Worker: A Study in Class Consciousness*. London: Allen and Unwin, 1958.

Mack, Raymond, *et al.* "The Protestant Ethic, Level of Aspiration, and Social Mobility," *American Sociological Review*, 21 (June 1956), 295–300.

McClelland, David C. *The Achieving Society*. New York: Van Nostrand, 1961.

Miller, S. M. "Comparative Social Mobility," *Current Sociology*, Vol. IX, No. 1 (1960).

Miró, Carmen A. "The Population of Latin America," *Demography*, Vol. I, No. 1 (1964), pp. 34–38.

Moore, Wilbert E. *Industrialization and Labor*. Ithaca, N.Y.: Cornell University Press, 1951.

Moore, W. E., and A. S. Feldman (eds.). *Labor Commitment and Social Change in Developing Areas*. New York: Social Science Research Council, 1960.

Parsons, Talcott. *The Social System*. New York: Free Press of Glencoe, 1951.

———. *Structure and Process in Modern Societies*. New York: Free Press of Glencoe, 1960.

Paz, Octavio. *The Labyrinth of Solitude*. New York: Grove, 1961.

Rainwater, Lee. *Family Design*. Chicago: Aldine, 1965.

Ramos, Samuel, *Profile of Man and Culture in Mexico*. Austin: University of Texas Press, 1962.

Redfield, Robert. *The Folk Culture of Yucatán*. Chicago: University of Chicago Press, 1941.

Rogoff, Natalie. *Recent Trends in Occupational Mobility*. New York: Free Press of Glencoe, 1953.

Rosen, Bernard C. "The Achievement Syndrome: A Psychocultural Dimension of Social Stratification," *American Sociological Review*, 21 (April 1956), 203–211.

———. "Socialization and Achievement Motivation in Brazil," *American Sociological Review*, 21 (December 1956), 690–695.

Rosenberg, Morris. "Misanthropy and Political Ideology," *American Sociological Review*, 21 (December 1956), 690–695.

———. *Occupations and Values*. New York: Free Press of Glencoe, 1957.

Scott, Robert E. "Mexico: The Established Revolution," in *Political Culture and Political Development*, ed. Lucian W. Pye and Sidney Verba. Princeton, N.J.: Princeton University Press, 1965.

Simpson, Richard L. "Parental Influence, Anticipatory Socialization, and Social Mobility," *American Sociological Review*, 27 (August 1962), 517–522.

Smith, David Horton, and Alex Inkeles. "The OM Scale: A Comparative Socio-Psychological Measure of Individual Modernity," *Sociometry*, 29 (December 1966), 353–377.

Smith, M. Brewster. "Personal Values in the Study of Lives," in *The Study of Lives*, ed. Robert W. White. New York: Atherton, 1963.

Soares, Gláucio Ary Dillon. "Classes sociais, strata sociais e as eleições presidenciais de 1960," *Sociologia* (September 1961).

————. "Economic Development and Political Radicalism" (unpublished doctoral dissertation, St. Louis; Washington University, 1965).

Stouffer, Samuel A. *Social Research to Test Ideas.* New York: Free Press of Glencoe, 1962. Published originally in *The American Soldier* (Princeton, N.J.: Princeton University Press, 1949).

Strodtbeck, Fred L. "Family Interaction, Values and Achievement," in *Talent and Society*, ed. D. C. McClelland. New York: Van Nostrand, 1958.

Stycos, J. Mayone. "Social Class and Preferred Family Size in Peru," *American Journal of Sociology*, LXX (May 1965), 651–658.

Di Tella, Torcuato S. *La teoría del primer impacto del crecimiento económico.* Buenos Aires, 1964.

Tumin, Melvin M. *Social Class and Social Change in Puerto Rico.* Princeton, N.J.: Princeton University Press, 1961.

de Vries, E., and J. M. Echavarría (eds.). *Social Aspects of Economic Development in Latin America.* Paris: UNESCO, 1963.

Wagley, Charles. *An Introduction to Brazil.* New York: Columbia University Press, 1964.

Weffort, Francisco C. "Estado y masas en el Brasil," *Revista Latinoamericana de Sociología*, I (marzo 1965), 53–71.

Whiteford, Andrew H. *Two Cities of Latin America.* Garden City, N.Y.: Doubleday "Anchor Books," 1964.

Williams, Lawrence K. "The Measurement of Risk-Taking Propensity in an Industrial Setting" (unpublished doctoral dissertation, Ann Arbor, University of Michigan, 1960).

Yasuda, Sabura. "A Methodological Inquiry into Social Mobility," *American Sociological Review*, 29 (February 1964), 16–23.

INDEX

Date Due

JUN 25 '74			
MAR 9 '79			
OCT 23 '84			
MAR 22 '84			

Demco 38-297